THE LAW AND CUSTOM OF SLAVERY IN BRITISH INDIA

THE LAW AND CUSTOM OF SLAVERY IN BRITISH INDIA

WILLIAM ADAM

GYAN

Published by

GYAN

Gyan Publishing House
5, Ansari Road
Daryaganj, New Delhi-110002
Phone: 011-47034999, 9811692060
E-mail: books@gyanbooks.com

Distribution Network
gyanbooks.com
India, USA, Canada, UK, Australia

ISBN: 978-93-7169-219-9 (PB)

First Published, 1840

2nd Impression 2025

Printed at: Gyan Press, Delhi.

THE LAW AND CUSTOM OF SLAVERY IN BRITISH INDIA
Author: WILLIAM ADAM

THE

LAW AND CUSTOM

OF

SLAVERY IN BRITISH INDIA,

IN A SERIES OF LETTERS TO

THOMAS FOWELL BUXTON, ESQ.

BY WILLIAM ADAM.

"A *vis inertiæ*, hostile to all change, seems inherent in the local governments of India."—"Responsibility is avoided by following the beaten track, and silence is the safest reply to those who propose a deviation from it, even for the sake of humanity. The outcry raised in India against the suttee was long powerless, until it returned reverberated from the British shore; and that against slavery will continue disregarded, unless it receives support from all the energy of the home government."—*A. D. Campbell, Esq., late Member of the Board of Revenue at Madras.*

BOSTON:
WEEKS, JORDAN, & COMPANY,
NO. 121 WASHINGTON STREET.
1840.

NOTICE.

THE Introduction to the first of the following Letters will show that it was originally intended to publish them in the first instance where they were written, in the United States of America; but circumstances having brought the Author temporarily to England, they now first appear in this country.

W. A.

London,
June 8th, 1840.

CONTENTS.

APPENDIX.

LETTER I.

TO THOMAS FOWELL BUXTON, ESQ.

Introduction—Hindu Law of Slavery—Muhammadan Law of Slavery —British Law of Slavery.

SIR,—Having been requested by a benevolent institution in Boston to deliver a public lecture on some subject connected with India, I thought of presenting a view of the state of slavery in that country, a subject to which I had paid some attention while resident there; but on preparing a memorandum of the materials I possessed for such a purpose, I found that they far exceeded the limits of a single discourse. I therefore selected another topic, and resolved, as my leisure might permit, to bring under full review the whole subject of slavery in British India, and to take some other mode or occasion of drawing public attention to its details. I now propose to submit to you the results of my inquiries, observations, and reflections.

My primary design is to co-operate with a society which has lately been established in England, called the British India Society, the objects of which are to collect and communicate information respecting India, to excite an interest in the welfare of its people, and to promote measures for their protection and improvement. By the force of circumstances I have been separated both from India and England, but my thoughts are constantly reverting to both countries, and I shall be in some measure satisfying equally the affec-

1*

tions of my heart and my convictions of duty in contributing my aid to give a right direction to the efforts of that association.

There are various reasons which encourage me to prosecute the consideration of this subject. Slavery is indeed only one of many evils under which India suffers, and I will even admit that its operation is less extensive and its effects less injurious than some other evils that I could mention. But it is of such a nature that, while it exists and wherever it exists, it checks the improvement of human character and the development of human society; aids all other bad influences and impedes all good influences; and its removal, therefore, will not only remove a large amount of positive injustice, degradation, and suffering, but is essential to the free and salutary working of every other measure that may or can be devised for the advancement of mankind in the country where it prevails. This is the inherent and radical attraction of the subject; but there are also collateral and subordinate inducements to bring it before the public.

Slavery in India has not received, and, as far as I am aware, is not likely to receive, the attention of the benevolent society to which I have referred, unless by some such means as that which I am employing. Even in India it has excited so little active discussion, that I have known its very existence denied by generally well-informed persons, although in certain parts of the country it is found in its most aggravated forms. In England, the subject is not known or publicly recognised as one affecting the welfare of India or the honor of Great Britain; and it even seems to be generally assumed, since the abolition of slavery in the British West Indies, that it has ceased to exist throughout the British dominions, although it may be shown that the number of slaves in the East Indies, under the authority of the British government, is probably as great as the number of those who have been emancipated in the West Indies. I say that the number is probably as great, because, since there has been no complete census of the population in India, much less a registry of slaves, it is impossible to speak of their number with certainty or precision. But if there is even only half or quarter so many, it is proper that the facts of the case should be known, that all undue exultation and vaunting may be repressed, and that the necessary impulse may be given to the friends of humanity in England to complete the work which they have only begun. Slavery may not be the greatest—I will admit, if required, that it is the least—of the evils tolerated or inflicted by the British government of India; but if the pre-occupation of the public mind with this subject in relation to other countries has qualified the Christian world to judge of the facts belonging to it in relation to India, it is justifiable, it is obligatory on the well-wishers of that country to avail themselves of this advantage in the existing state of the public sentiment, in order to fix attention on the condition, the wants, and the interests of a people whose numbers alone constitute them an important division of the population of the world; and whose distance, whose isolation, whose ignorance, and superstition and degradation, whose uncomplaining helplessness, shut them out from the ordinary sympathies of mankind. There will be this advantage also in taking what may be called low ground, that if slavery in India, such as on indubitable authority I shall depict it to you, is the least of the evils under which that country groans, you will be the better able by this standard to judge of the greater evils under which it suffers.

There is another point of view in which the exposition of this subject may be attended with advantage. Great Britain, by an extraordinary combination of circumstances, has established her dominion over a hundred millions of people in India, and her influence over at least fifty millions more, and the civilized world is entitled to know for what purposes of good or of evil such an unexampled power is exercised. The British Crown and Parliament, by an act passed in 1833, have delegated the sovereignty of India, for a period of twenty years, to a corporation of private citizens, exercising their authority through a board of directors and the people of England are specially bound to inquire and to judge how this grave trust is fulfilled. England, in establishing the existing system of government for India, may be discharging her duty to the world, or she may not; and the East India Company, in the administration of that system, may be discharging her duty to England, or she may not. But neither the negative nor the affirmative can be determined by indiscriminate censure or praise; it can be ascertained only by a dispassionate examination of details, and by an impartial estimate of the spirit and character of the British Indian government and administration, and every honest and well-meant contribution to such an object may aid in arriving at a right conclusion. The question of slavery in India certainly covers only a very small portion of the whole ground, but it does cover a portion in itself not insignificant, and when the judgment of the world is pronounced on England, or that of England on the East India Company, it will not be difficult to show that it is no unimportant item in the account.

It may perhaps be deemed that here the agitation of the subject of slavery in India is inappropriate, and that it will do no good, and may do some harm. I certainly feel that what I have to say will establish a charge of inconsistency against England, tending to lessen the force of her example in the West Indies, and to furnish a temporary triumph to the friends of slavery in this country. This triumph, however, will only be temporary, for the agitation of the subject cannot fail to lead to the removal of the evil; and whatever the delay may be, the cause of truth, of justice, and of humanity, cannot be promoted by the concealment of facts. But it may be said the subject of domestic slavery presents in itself questions sufficiently grave and difficult, and that by introducing the question of slavery in India, I shall be embroiling myself with the interests, and passions, and prejudices that divide and afflict society here on this ominous question. On this question I have not the information that would enable me with intelligence and undoubting conviction to advocate the views of any of the parties that represent the subdivisions of public opinion; but because I feel that I am powerless at present to promote the good of the slave in this country, I should be exceedingly sorry to have it supposed that I am indifferent to his welfare, a neutral or uninterested spectator of the exertions made for his benefit, and without sympathy with those who devote their days and their nights, their time and strength, the best energies of their bodies and minds, to his cause. Although not a citizen of the United States, yet as a citizen of the world—a far higher and nobler title—I look upon every slave, in every country, as an injured and oppressed fellow-man; and from the bottom of my soul I wish God speed to every attempt based on Christian principles, and executed in the spirit of Christian charity, to strike off the fetters of the slave and to let the oppressed go free. It will thus be perceived that I do not abstain from the question of slavery in this country from indifference; and that I limit myself to the question of slavery in India, simply because I know that I possess information on that subject, the publication of which may tend to promote the cause of humanity. If it should be further suggested that this cause would be best promoted by the publication of that information in England, the answer is, that for the present Providence has here cast my lot, and that effectual means will be taken, through the British India Society, of calling public attention in that country also to this important subject. It will be no disgrace to America—it will be one more honor to the city of Boston, already distinguished for its enlightened and philanthropic character—that the first appeal to the public opinion of the civilized world against slavery in India was made in this country, and favorably received in this city.

Grievous and deplorable as is the inconsistency of America on the subject of slavery, yet a sound public opinion is daily gaining ground, and with the growth and triumph of that opinion the influence of America on all great social questions will be increasingly felt abroad. It is, however, to the people of England that I chiefly appeal, and I appeal to them, Sir, through you, because your name has been associated in my mind for many years with efforts for the emancipation of the slave, because your recent publication, exposing the increased extent and horrors of the slave-trade, proves that your zeal is unabated, and because I hope to convince you that, without abandoning the peculiar province that you have nobly and humanely selected for yourself, British India should be included within the range of your philanthropic exertions. If the respect and confidence with which your persevering and disinterested labors have inspired the Christian philanthropists of Great Britain and the members of Her Majesty's government, shall enable you to speak with useful effect a word in favor of the slave in India, I feel confident that word will not be withheld.

And is not the subject one that may well awaken the attention both of the government and of the people of England? The people of England have just paid twenty millions sterling to emancipate eight hundred thousand slaves in the British West Indies; and while they are congratulating themselves that now at length every British subject is a freeman, and insultingly reproaching republican America with her slavery, they are to be told that their congratulations are premature; that their reproaches may be retorted; that their work is only half done; that there are probably 800,000 slaves more, British subjects, in the East Indies; that this slavery has been perpetuated and sometimes aggravated by the East India Company's government; and that there is no prospect of its ceasing, unless their powerful voice shall be put forth to demand its extinction. The government of England have been engaged for years in a hard-fought battle with slave-holders in the West Indies, and with the slave-holding interest in England, and they have just succeeded, at the expense of the people of England, in the great work of emancipation. They have been for years engaged in a diplomatic war, too unsuccessfully waged, with foreign powers against the slave-trade, and with praiseworthy energy and perseverance they are still adopting measures against this hydra-headed monster. Her Majesty's ministers are now to be told—(are they *now* to be told, or have they long known and neglected their duty in this matter?)—that one of the heads of this monster is in British India; that even the slave-trade has not wholly ceased there; that the laws enacted by the Parliament of Great Britain against the slave-trade are in part, either expressly set aside, or are acknowledged to be wholly a dead letter; that slavery itself exists in British India; that it exists probably as extensively, and to a great extent in as aggravated a form, as it did lately in the West Indies; that it has been and is legalized, and nourished, and supported by the East India Company, a creature of their own forming; and that notwithstanding the express requisition of Parliament to that effect, no movement has been made by the East India Company's government towards its extinction. This is the bearing of the subject to which I am desirous of soliciting your attention; and will you, will the government and people of England, listen to the proofs of all this with patient acquiescence? Must it not be perceived that this is a state of things compromising the honor and consistency of the government, and the humanity and justice of the people of England, and invoking the prompt and indignant interference of every honest statesman and every good man?

The whole subject of slavery in India will be embraced by considering, first, the law of slavery; second, the custom or practice of slavery; and, third, the means that have been or may be employed for the mitigation of the evil or for its entire abolition.

Slavery exists legally under the British government in India as an effect of the legal existence which it possessed under the former Hindu and Muhammadan governments. The British government affirms, administers, and enforces, with exceptions to be hereafter mentioned, the Hindu and Muhammadan laws of slavery; and hence, in order to acquire a just view of the subject, it is necessary to consider, first, the Hindu law; second, the Muhammadan law; and third, the British law of slavery in India. In explaining the Hindu and Muhammadan laws of slavery, I shall present only those general views that are necessary to understand the force and effect of the law of slavery as administered by British authorities, without going into the numerous and minute details which the two former systems of law embrace.

The provisions of Hindu law limiting the *liability* to slavery are first to be noticed. Hindu institutions recognise four classes or orders of men subject to them, the sacerdotal, military, commercial, and servile classes, and all who do not belong to those four are outcastes, foreigners, barbarians, and impure. With reference to this division of the Hindu race, the law of slavery expressly provides that a member of the first or sacerdotal class never can become legally a slave, and this limitation is extended to females of that class, whose enslavement is declared null and void and punishable by amercement, as is that of a man of the sacerdotal class by the highest amercement which the law imposes. A further limitation is, that members of the military, commercial, or servile class can, under certain circumstances, become slaves only in the direct, not in the inverse, order of the classes, and that under certain other circumstances they may be made slaves to persons of an equal class, and even in the inverse order of the classes. Thus the customs of Hindu society suppose that a man, from various considerations—for the payment of debt, for instance—may vol untarily make himself the slave of another, but this can be done only in the direct order of the classes; that is, a member of the second class can make himself a slave only to a member of the first class; a member of the third class only to one of the first or second; and a member of the fourth only to one of the first, second, or third class. On some accounts also the law permits the servitude of men of the military, commercial, and servile classes to one of an equal class. Once however that a man has ceased to be his own master, he may be subjected to slavery in the inverse order of the classes, that is, a man of inferior caste may hold in slavery a man of superior caste. Thus a man of the military class holding a slave of the commercial class may deliver him to be the mancipated servant of a freeman of the servile class. According to the spirit of Hindu institutions, and the spirit as well as the letter of Hindu law, a state of servitude is natural to men of the servile class * without exception or limitation; but then no individual of that class can be a slave to an individual of any of the other classes without special legal grounds, independent of the general liability. The numerous aboriginal tribes of India are regarded as members originally of the military class, who, by their omission of holy rites and neglect of Hindu institutions, have gradually sunk to the lowest of the four

* Institutes of Menu, Chap. VIII. v. 414.

2

classes; and they are practically held to be liable to slavery to the Hindu race. There are, further, certain outcastes so degraded that they are considered wholly unworthy to perform even the most menial offices of slavery, and they are in consequence practically exempted from liability to that state, just as much as a member of the sacerdotal class, although from a directly opposite cause.*

The *modes* in which those who are liable to slavery may become actually and legally slaves, are various. With reference to the legal modes of creating the actual state of slavery, one Hindu legislator, followed by various other authorities, has enumerated fifteen different sorts of slaves, and another has reduced them to seven. Keeping in view the former division, I shall, for the sake of brevity and perspicuity, follow the latter. None of the different sorts of slaves about to be enumerated are to be confounded with any description of servants. Hindu legislators carefully distinguish on the one hand between the service which a pupil of sacred knowledge owes to his spiritual teacher, which an apprentice in any art or trade owes to his instructor, which a hired servant owes to his master, and which a commissioned servant owes to his employer, and on the other hand the service which a slave must give to his owner. The servant, of whatever description, can be legally required to perform only work which is religiously and ceremonially pure, involving no loss or degradation of caste: the slave may be required to perform all work, whether pure or impure, however offensive or degrading.

The *first* sort of slave is one who has been made captive under a standard or in battle; not every person conquered in battle, whether he take quarter or not, but one who claims quarter on the condition of becoming a slave. Under this

* Colebrooke's Digest of Hindu Law, Vol. II. p. 370—375; p. 349; Institutes of Menu, x. 43, 44, 50—56.

head also is classed one who in gaming has staked his own personal freedom, declaring that if vanquished in the contest he shall become the slave of his opponent; or he may stake not his own freedom, but his property in a slave, and the winner becomes the owner of the slave so staked. The *second* sort of slave is one maintained in consideration of service; that is, one who has agreed to slavery in consideration of maintenance, whether in a season of scarcity or abundance; but in every such case consent is a requisite condition, since dominion cannot be acquired by maintenance alone. The *third* sort of slave is one born in the house, that is, one born of a female slave in the house of her master. By this rule the progeny of female slaves take the condition of their mothers. The *fourth* sort of slave is one bought for a price, sold by his father and mother, or by either of them, or by himself. Children thus sold, by either or both parents, may become slaves, although they did not consent to it at the time; and a person self-sold may either offer his services as a slave for a fixed term, or may leave the time indefinite and stipulate for a fixed remuneration, or may sell himself absolutely and without limitation or restriction. To this sort also belongs the case of a slave pledged by his master to a creditor for a loan received, to be his slave during the period of the loan, which pledge is considered ultimately to become of the nature of a sale. The principal sum being considered as the price, there is in fact the complete act of relinquishment at a subsequent time after a prior receipt of the price. The *fifth* sort of slave is one given by his father and mother, or by either of them, or by himself, and acquired by the acceptance of such donation. He who agrees to slavery in consideration of relief from distress, is sèlf-given; for he gives himself on account of the favor conferred in delivering him from distress. Under this head also is included the case of a freeman, who, from attachment to the female slave of another, acquiesces in slavery for her sake; that is, the marriage of a freeman with a female slave imposes the condition of slavery on the husband; and in like manner a free woman, or one who is not a slave of the same master, becoming the bride or wife of a slave, also becomes a slave to her husband's owner. To the fourth and fifth classes belong also the case of boys bought for a price or given in donation, for the purpose of being adopted as the sons of him who has purchased or received them, but who, in consequence of some failure in the form of adoption prescribed by the law, cannot carry his original intention into effect. They have ceased to belong to those who sold or gave them away: in consequence of a failure in the form of adoption, they cannot become sons; and the law in that case directs that they shall become slaves. The *sixth* sort of slave is one inherited from ancestors, that is, a slave of the father or other ancestor passing in succession to the son or other heir. The *seventh* sort of slave is one enslaved by way of punishment, that is, one who has agreed to become a slave to acquit a fine or discharge the debt by his labor. This may be deemed to include the case of one who has been relieved from great debt, that is, redeemed from his creditor's custody on account of a great debt, and therefore becoming a slave to the person who has satisfied the creditor. It also includes the case of a man who, after having consecrated himself to a life of religious asceticism and mendicity, forsakes that mode of life, for instance, by taking a wife and living as a householder. If a member of the sacerdotal class thus violates a sacred vow, he is to be lacerated by the feet of dogs and banished from the kingdom, but if a member of the military or commercial tribe, he is to be condemned to slavery.*

* Colebrooke's Digest of Hindu Law, Vol. II. p. 340—346; p. 368; Menu's Institutes of Hindu Law, Chap. VIII. v. 415.

The *powers* possessed by masters or owners over their slaves are absolute. Hindu law "treats the slave as the property of his master, familiarly speaking of this species of property in association with cattle, under the contemptuous designation of *bipeds and quadrupeds.* It makes no provision for the protection of the slave from the cruelty and ill-treatment of an unfeeling master, nor defines the master's power over the person of his slave; neither prescribing distinct limits to that power, nor declaring it to extend to life or limb. It allows to the slave no right of property even in his own acquisitions, except by the indulgence of his master."* "Those slaves who correspond to the designation of *adscripti glebæ*, or hereditary serfs," "are subject to the laws of ancestral real property, and cannot be transferred except under similar restrictions."—"All other descriptions of slaves would appear to class with personal property;"† and, as has been shown, may be sold for a price, pledged for a debt, or staked at play. There is no bar to the institution of a judicial proceeding by a slave against his master, relative to his own peculiar interests; and although, in defining competent and incompetent witnesses, the law does not expressly declare a slave to be either the one or the other, yet in the opinion of living expounders of the law, and in the practice of the courts, his evidence is held to be good and legal against, but not for, his master.‡

The modes of *enfranchisement* from slavery provided by the law are various, and with reference to them, all slaves

* Colebrooke, cited in Harington's Analysis, Vol. III. p. 743; Colebrooke's Digest of Hindu Law, Vol. II. pp. 365—368; Macnaghten's Translation of the Mitacshara in Hindu Law, Vol. I. pp. 227, 229.

† Macnaghten's Hindu Law, Vol. I. p. 115.

‡ Macnaghten's Translation of the Mitacshara in Hindu Law, Vol. I. pp. 227, 242—245; Vol. II. pp. 317, 318.

are divided into two classes, those whose slavery is permanent and hereditary, and those whose slavery is temporary and personal. To the former or permanent class, belong those who have been born of female slaves in the houses of their masters; those who have been bought for a price; those who have been received in donation; those who have been inherited from ancestors; and those who for a pecuniary consideration have bartered their personal freedom. These five sorts may be legally held in perpetual slavery; but various circumstances may lead even to their enfranchisement. *First*, none of them can claim release from slavery as of right, but they may any or all of them be at any time enfranchised by the sole favor and act of their master, who in performing the ceremony of manumission is pronounced a benevolent man. "Let the benevolent man who desires to emancipate his own slave, take a vessel of water from his shoulder," (the usual way in which water is carried by a slave,) "and instantly break it" (denoting the discontinuance of servile duties). "Sprinkling his head with water containing rice and flowers, and thrice calling him free," (thus confirming his emancipation,) "let the master dismiss him with his face towards the east. Thenceforward let him be called 'one cherished by his master's favor:' his food may be eaten and his favors accepted; and he is respected by worthy men." This simple and graphic ceremony, performed for so important a purpose, is finely illustrative of ancient Hindu manners. Manumission at the pleasure of the master may, of course, be extended to temporary as well as hereditary slaves. The *second* ground of enfranchisement does not leave it optional to the master, but makes it obligatory on him, and a right on the part of his slave. This right is conferred if the slave should, at the risk of his own life, save the life of his master from some impending danger. It is necessary to the effect, that the life of the slave should be endangered in the attempt to save that of his master, and in that case he is not only entitled to release from slavery, but shall also receive the share of a son in his master's wealth. If the master should refuse him emancipation and a share of the inheritance, the slave may institute a judicial proceeding against his master, and the law would recognise his claim. Under the supposed circumstances, these rights are possessed by the temporary as well as by the hereditary slave. The *third* ground of enfranchisement makes it equally obligatory on the master, and equally the legal right of the slave. If a female slave bears a son to her master, and if he has no legitimate or adopted son, under those circumstances the son of the female slave is free from his birth, and the mother, in consideration of her progeny, is enfranchised. In this case, also, there is a remedy at law against the master refusing emancipation. On these three grounds alone, the indulgence of the master, the saving of his life, or the bearing to him of a son, can any one of the five descriptions of permanent and hereditary slaves receive manumission.

The modes in which temporary or personal slaves may be enfranchised, are also various. *First*, one maintained in a famine, that is, saved from death by food supplied during a scarcity of provisions, and thereby subjected to slavery, is liberated by the gift of a pair of oxen. *Second*, one maintained in consideration of service, that is, a person consenting to perform the work of a slave for the sake of subsistence, is released on relinquishing his subsistence. This case is distinguishable from that of a hired servant only by the nature of the work performed. *Third*, a slave for a fixed period is emancipated by fulfilling the stipulated term. *Fourth*, a slave-debtor is released from servitude by paying the debt with interest. *Fifth*, a slave for the sake of his bride is emancipated by divorcing his wife or separating himself from her; and, by analogy, a free woman who has become a slave for the sake of her slave-husband is liberated by divorce or separation, but there is no express authority to that effect. And *sixth*, one who has voluntarily subjected himself to slavery for any other than a pecuniary consideration, for instance, for a religious purpose, one who has been made captive in war and a slave who has been won in a stake, are emancipated on giving a substitute, that is, another slave equally capable of labor.*

Such is a summary of the leading provisions of Hindu law on the subject of slavery.

The leading provisions of Muhammadan law on the same subject will now engage our attention, differing both in principles and details from those of the Hindu law.

† There are only two descriptions of persons recognised as slaves under the Muhammadan law: first, infidels made captive during war; and secondly, their descendants. These persons are subjects of inheritance and of all kinds of contracts, in the same manner as other property. The general state of bondage is subdivided into two classes, and slavery may be either entire or qualified, according to circumstances.

Qualified slaves are of three descriptions. The *first* is he between whom and his master there may have been an agreement for his ransom, on the condition of his paying a certain sum of money, either immediately, or at some future period, or by instalments. If he fulfil the condition, he will become free, otherwise he will revert to his former unqualified state

* Digest, Vol. II. pp. 347—369.

† The following summary of Muhammadan slave-law is derived, with slight modifications, from Mr. Macnaghten's Principles and Precedents of Muhammadan Law, the only authority on Muhammadan law relating to this subject within my reach. See Book I. Chap. IX. pp. 65—68.

of bondage. In the mean time, his master parts with the possession of, but not with the property in him. He is not however in the interval a fit subject of sale, gift, pledge, or hire. The *second* description of slave is he to whom his master has promised *post-obit* emancipation. Such promise, however, may be made absolutely, or with limitation; in other words, the freedom of the slave may be made to depend generally on the death of his master, or it may be made conditionally to depend on the occurrence of the event within a specified period. This description of slave is not a fit subject of sale or gift, but labor may be exacted from him, and he may be let out to hire, and in the case of a female, she may be given in marriage. Where the promise was made absolutely, the slave becomes free on the death of the master, whenever that event may happen; and when made conditionally, if his death occurred within the period specified. The general law of legacies and debts is applicable to this description of slaves, they being considered as much the right of the heirs as any other description of property. Now, the law of legacies is, that they cannot be made to a larger amount than one-third of the testator's estate without the consent of the heirs; and of debts, that all debts due by the testator must be liquidated before the legacies can be claimed. It follows that those slaves to whom their master has promised *post-obit* emancipation, can only be emancipated to the extent of one-third of the value of their persons when the master leaves no other property, and they must perform emancipatory labor for the benefit of the heirs, to the extent of the other two-thirds; and when the master dies insolvent, they do not become free until, for the benefit of the deceased's creditors, they have earned by their labor property to the full amount of their value. The *third* description of slave is a female slave who has borne a child or children to her master. The law is the same regarding this description of slave as regarding the second, with this difference in her favor, that she is emancipated unconditionally on the death of her master; whether he may or may not have left other assets, or whether he may have died in a state of insolvency or otherwise. But the parentage of the children of such slave is not established in her master unless he acknowledge the first-born.

Entire or unqualified slaves are infidels who have been made captive in war, and their descendants, and who have no claim to emancipation on any of the grounds just mentioned. They are absolutely and perpetually, without qualification or limitation, slaves; and besides those who answer to this description, Muhammadan law recognises no others as such.

According to Muhammadan law, slaves labor under almost every species of legal incapacity. They cannot marry without the consent of their masters. Their evidence is not admissible, nor their acknowledgment, (unless they are licensed,) in matters relating to property. They are not generally eligible to fill any civil office in the state; nor can they be executors, sureties, or guardians, (unless to the minor children of their master, by special appointment;) nor are they competent to make a gift or sale, nor to inherit or bequeath property. But as some counterpoise to these disqualifications, they are exempted from many of the obligations of freedom. They are not liable to be sued except in the presence of their masters; they are not subject to the payment of taxes; and they cannot be imprisoned for debt.* Any description of slave, however, may be licensed either for

* Mr. Macnaghten here adds—"In criminal matters, the indulgences extended to them are more numerous;" but he has not stated what those indulgences are, and I have no means of ascertaining. By Muhammadan law, a master who has killed his slave is exempt from *kisas*, or retaliation, to which he would be subject if he had killed any other person but his slave, a provision which does not indicate a spirit very indulgent to the slave in criminal matters.

a particular purpose, or generally for commercial transactions; in which case they are allowed to act to the extent of their license. Masters may compel their slaves to marry. Unqualified slaves may be sold to make good their wives' dower and maintenance, and qualified slaves may be compelled to labor for the same purposes. A man cannot marry a female slave so long as he has a free wife; nor can he under any circumstances marry his own slave girl; nor can a slave marry his mistress. Persons who stand reciprocally related within the prohibited degrees* cannot be the slaves of each other. When issue has been begotten between the male slave of one person and the female slave of another, the maxim of *partus sequitur ventrem* applies, and the former has no legal title to the children so begotten.

It is a question how far the sale of a man's own person is lawful when reduced to extreme necessity. It is declared justifiable in the *Moheet-oo-Surukhsee*, a work of unexceptionable authority. But while deference is paid to that authority by admitting the validity of the sale, it is nevertheless universally contended that the contract should be cancelled on the application of the slave, and that he should be compelled by his labor to refund the value of what he had received from his purchaser. It is admitted, however, by all authorities, that a person may hire himself for any time, even though it amount to servitude for life; but minors so hired may annul the contract on attaining majority.

* "A man may not marry his mother, nor his grandmother, nor his mother-in-law, nor his step-mother, nor his step-grandmother, nor his daughter, nor his granddaughter, nor his daughter-in-law, nor his granddaughter-in-law, nor his step-daughter, nor his sister, nor his foster-sister, nor his niece, nor his aunt, nor his nurse. Nor is it lawful for a man to be married at the same time to any two women who stand in such a degree of relation to each other, as that, if one of them had been a male, they could not have intermarried."—Macnaghten's Muhammadan Law, p. 57.

Such is a summary of the leading provisions of Muhammadan law on the subject of slavery.

It now remains to show what is the British law of slavery in India; and this might be stated in a single sentence, viz., that it is a confirmation, with modifications, of the Hindu and Muhammadan laws of slavery; but in order to do justice to the British government of India, and to furnish a clear conception of the whole case, it is necessary to explain the principle on which that confirmation professes to be based.

An extensive territory by cession or conquest had, through the agency of the East India Company, become subject to the crown and sovereignty of Great Britain. A primary and essential duty of every just government towards its subjects is that of publishing and enforcing an equitable system of law, adapted to their actual condition and circumstances, and calculated to protect them in the secure enjoyment of their rights, natural and acquired. In the view of this obligation, by various statutes in the reign of George III., a supreme court of judicature, consisting of a chief justice and three other judges, was established at Calcutta, and the benefit of the laws of England, as far as applicable to India, was extended by the legislature to all persons residing within the town of Calcutta, and subsequently to all British subjects, natives of Great Britain, or their descendants, resident in India or elsewhere within the limits of the East India Company's exclusive trade. But the laws of England were justly deemed inapplicable to the native population, who, whether Muhammadans or Hindus, were previously in possession of their respective written laws, under which they had acquired property by descent, purchase, gift, and other modes, and which they had been educated and habituated to regard and venerate as sacred. There was accordingly, in the statutes above mentioned, a reservation of the laws and usages of the native inhabitants of Calcutta in cases of "inheritance and succession to lands, rents, and goods, and all matters of contract and dealing between party and party, as well as the rights and authorities of fathers and masters of families;" that is, in all such cases, native laws and usages were to be recognised and maintained. In 1772, the laws and usages of the native inhabitants of the provinces were as distinctly recognised. In that year, a plan for the administration of justice in the provinces was adopted, and it was provided "that in all suits regarding inheritance, marriage, caste, and other religious usages or institutions, the laws of the Koran with respect to Muhammadans, and those of the Shaster with respect to Gentoos, shall be invariably adhered to. On all such occasions the Moulavies" (interpreters of Muhammadan law) "or Brahmins" (interpreters of Hindu law) "shall respectively attend to expound the law, and they shall sign the report, and assist in passing the decree." Instead of the judicial plan of 1772, a more comprehensive system of law and regulation was established by the Marquis Cornwallis in 1793, and in that system also the following rule was laid down for preserving to the natives their own laws and usages: "In suits regarding succession, inheritance, marriage, and caste, and all religious usages and institutions, the Muhammadan laws with respect to Muhammadans, and the Hindu laws with regard to Hindus, are to be considered the general rules by which the judges are to form their decision." This, then, was an original, and has always continued to be a primary, rule of British law in India; and if the fundamental principle of all civil laws is, that they ought to be "suitable to the genius of the people" subject to their authority and operation, the wisdom, the justice, and the humanity of adopting and adhering to it, must be pronounced equally honorable to the British nation and government, and conducive to the protection and contentment of the natives of India.

Under this rule, however,—this wise, just, and humane rule—for giving the natives the benefit of their own civil laws regarding succession, inheritance, marriage, caste, and all religious usages and institutions, the question early arose whether it was applicable to cases of slavery. In 1798, this question was referred to the Sudder Dewany Adawlut, the supreme court of civil judicature on all questions of native law, and it was explicitly admitted by that court that slavery was not included in the letter of the rule. Slavery, as we have seen, both in the Hindu and Muhammadan systems, has provisions of law proper to that subject, and distinct from those which regulate succession, inheritance, marriage, and caste. Nor can slavery be deemed one of the religious usages or institutions either of the Hindus or Muhammadans. The rule is not, at least directly and strictly, applicable to questions of personal freedom and bondage, and the Sudder Dewany Adawlut had the strongest ground for denying that slavery was included in the letter of the rule. And yet, in the face of this admission or denial voluntarily made by the court, that body, as if straining a point,—not to protect the interests of the community,—not to extend the shield of justice over those whom the mere letter of the law would have left unguarded,—but to inflict a lasting curse on society, and to rivet the fetters of the slave, whom, by their own acknowledgment, the plain and direct letter of the law would have liberated from his bonds—that body, as if straining a point for such a purpose, delivered the opinion that the *spirit* of the rule for observing the Muhammadan and Hindu laws was applicable to cases of slavery, and this construction was confirmed by the governor-general in council, under date the 12th April, 1798. This construction has never been reversed, and it is the foundation on which slavery in British India legally rests at the present day.*

* Harington's Analysis of the Laws and Regulations, Vol. I. p. 1, 5, 6, 20, 67, 68; Macnaghten's Hindu Law, Vol. I. p. 113.

There are many views connected with the law and practice of slavery in British India that remain yet to be presented. All that I have now attempted has been to give a general outline of the original native systems of slavery, and of the legal grounds on which those systems have been perpetuated by the British government; and thereby to establish the fact of the existence of slavery in British India, the groundlessness of the claim put forth that slavery has ceased throughout the British dominions, and the obligation on the British people to renew their efforts in order to remove this taint which still clings to the national character—the obligation on all good men of every nation to shame the British government to act up in India to the professions in connection with this subject of which they are so profuse elsewhere. Slavery not only exists in India, but it has been unnecessarily and wantonly perpetuated by a decision of the judges and resolution of the government, in avowed disregard of the plain letter of the law. The sanction of the British name, and of the power and authority of the British government, professing to be a Christian government, has thus been unworthily given to the antiquated systems of slavery originating in the barbarous and intolerant policy of the Hindu and Muhammadan govern ments; and this has been done in alleged conformity wit the spirit of the rule which secures to the natives of Indi the enjoyment of their own civil laws and usages, but in real opposition, not only to the letter, but even to the spirit of that wise, just, and humane principle. For what is the spirit of that law, apart from its mere letter, but to protect, not any one class, but all classes, in the rights which legitimately belong to them? And to place any one class, however poor, however ignorant, however degraded, at the absolute and irresponsible disposal of another class, is alike inconsistent with wisdom, with justice, and with humanity

—inconsistent with the fundamental principle of all civil law and the primary object of all civil society, the equal protection of all, and therefore inconsistent with the constitution of a government which, like that of British India, professes to recognise that principle and to aim at that object in its actual administration.

LETTER II.

TO THOMAS FOWELL BUXTON, ESQ.

Examination of the Legality of Hindu and Muhammadan Slavery under the British Government in India.

Sir,—The purport of what has been advanced on the subject of slavery, is, that slavery exists in British India, under the forms of law, and with the knowledge, authority, and sanction of the British government. I propose now to consider the grounds on which this legal sanction has been given to slavery in British India.

At the bar of public reason and justice, are the grounds sufficient on which the British government has given its sanction to Hindu and Muhammadan slavery in India? I do not appeal here to any abstract principle of natural justice or equality between man and man, which would put an end to all slavery, but I ask whether the legal grounds on which this sanction has been given, are adequate? I think it may be shown that there are reasons for questioning the validity of the decision on which the legality of the whole system of Indian slavery now rests.

It has already been seen that the principle of the British government is to give the natives of India the benefit of their own laws regarding succession, inheritance, marriage, caste, and all religious usages and institutions; the Muhammadan laws with regard to Muhammadans, and the

Hindu laws with regard to Hindus, being considered the general rules by which the judges are to form their decisions. A second principle is, that while the civil law of both classes is thus specifically recognised, both Hindus and Muhammadans are subjected to the Muhammadan criminal law, on the ground that the administration of criminal justice would not admit of two systems essentially differing from each other in the definition of crimes and punishments; and the Muhammadan criminal law was adopted as the basis of a future uniform system, not so much from any consideration of its specific provisions, as from its having been long in force under the Musalman government, and from its being therefore generally known to the inhabitants of the country. A third principle is, that the British government, while it recognises Hindu and Muhammadan civil law and enforces Muhammadan criminal law, reserves to itself the right, by its own laws and regulations, of modifying all these systems of law, and of prescribing forms of procedure, as wisdom and experience may suggest.

In endeavoring to form a sound and accurate judgment of the legal effect on slavery of this complicated state of Hindu, Muhammadan, and British law, the first fact important to be borne in mind is, that until the recognition of Hindu civil law by the British government in 1772, that law had no legal force or obligation wherever the authority of the Muhammadan government extended, during a preceding period of from 700 to 750 years. By this it is not meant to be affirmed that Hindus, during that period, under the Muhammadan government, did not practically observe their own laws of succession and inheritance, marriage and caste, and even of slavery; but that those laws were not recognised and enforced by the Muhammadan government, and that the only law recognised and enforced by that government, was the law of Islam. This is a necessary consequence of the spirit and principle of the

Muhammadan religion, and of all Muhammadan governments. By the Muhammadan law a foreign province or country becomes annexed to the Muhammadan dominions by the mere act of conquest and the exercise of even a part of the law of Islam in it; and to establish the law of Islam within the Muhammadan dominions is mandatory on Muhammadan rulers, and not optional to them. Even questions of inheritance among non-Moslem subjects are not left to the decision of any other than a Moslem tribunal, but must be decided according to the Muhammadan law, and by Moslem judges, for every judge must be a Moslem. During the whole period of the Muhammadan history in India, though Hindus were employed in the highest offices of trust and emolument, yet a Hindu judge was never heard of, and assuredly no Muhammadan Kazi could ever have been found to administer the civil laws of the Hindus.* It follows that the Hindu law, including the law of slavery, however it may have been reverenced and observed by the Hindus themselves, or tolerated by the more enlightened Muhammadan princes, had no force or obligation during the whole period of the Muhammadan rule, and that it was in every legal sense a dead letter until it was re-enacted by the British government in 1772, and confirmed by the system of law and regulation promulgated in 1793. Up to the former of these periods, the Hindu law had no vitality. It could not be pleaded in any court of justice. It could not form the ground of any judicial decision. It was legally as if it had never been.

This was the state of the law in 1765, when the British acquired the government of Bengal, Behar, and part of Orissa; and Muhammadan law alone continued to be administered under their authority, by native officers under

* See Observations on the Law and Constitution of India, Chapter I. p. 10—25.

European supervisors, till 1772. This enables us to perceive what was the precise effect of the plan for the administration of justice adopted in the last-mentioned year. Previous to that period, Hindu slavery may have existed, and no doubt did exist practically; that is, by the force of immemorial custom and usage, persons of the Hindu race and religion no doubt held slaves, and by the force of the same ties persons were no doubt found willing to submit to that condition of life under Hindu masters. There was a Hindu institution of slavery just as property descended, marriage was contracted, caste was observed, and religion practised according to Hindu law, and no otherwise. All these institutions existed, slavery as well as every other, but they existed only as customs, not laws. They were not recognised under the Muhammadan law, the only law administered by the rulers of the land, and they had only the force which the opinion, the practice, and the mutual consent of the parties concerned gave them. Under these circumstances the British law of 1772 was promulgated, providing "that in all suits regarding inheritance, marriage, caste, and other religious usages or institutions, the laws of the Koran with respect to Muhammadans, and those of the Shaster with respect to Hindus, shall be invariably adhered to." This was confirmed in the code of 1793, and extended, from time to time, to the provinces acquired by arms or by treaty. The effect of this was to secure to Muhammadans living under the British government the continued enjoyment of their own laws; to free Hindus from subjection to Muhammadan laws; and further, to give legal force and obligation in favor of Hindus to their own laws and institutions. This was not done in general and unexceptional terms, but it was definitely and specifically provided that each class of the population should have the benefit of its own laws only in suits regarding inheritance, marriage, caste, and religion.

If the terms employed had been absolute and indefinite, this would have amounted to an adoption by the British government of all Hindu and Muhammadan laws, without exception; but it was expressly stated that it was only in certain descriptions of suits that each class was to enjoy its own laws. If in this specification suits of slave against master, or master against slave, had been mentioned, then the institution of slavery would have been legalized; but there was no mention of slavery, and thus Hindu slavery, at least, still remained as it had been for hundreds of years, beyond the pale of the law; illegal, existing by custom alone, unauthorized by any known or acknowledged government.

It thus appears that the Sudder Dewany Adawlut, the supreme court of native judicature in Bengal, when the subject was referred to it in 1798, had ample ground for affirming that the law of 1793, which is the same in substance and almost in terms with that of 1772, did not in its letter include slavery; and we are now also prepared to consider how far that body was justified in pronouncing that the spirit of that law did include slavery. On this very extraordinary assumption, let it in the first place be remarked, that the spirit of all law, except that which is the mere expression of brute-force, consists in doing justice between man and man. There is probably not an instance of a law enacted by any nation or government except for the purpose of enforcing some real or supposed obligation, or protecting some real or supposed right. In this general view of the spirit and end of all law, there cannot be any doubt that the person called a slave has a better right to his freedom and the fruit of his own labor, than another person called a master has to deprive him of them. But waving this general view, and looking only at the particular law under consideration, it may be further affirmed that the only legitimate way of ascertaining the spirit of this or of any law, is by attending to its letter; and that to attempt, as in the present instance, to divorce the letter from the spirit, and to find in the spirit that which is confessedly not contained in the letter, is inconsistent with the plainest dictates of reason and common sense. By seeking for the spirit of a law elsewhere than in its letter, where is the limit that can be put to conjectural or interested interpretations, emendations, and additions? If then, adhering to this rule, we seek the spirit of the law in its letter, what does the letter teach us? What spirit does it breathe? It breathes a spirit eminently friendly to civil and religious liberty, and in the same degree honorable to the British nation and government from which it emanated. If the British government of India had imitated the Muhammadan government which it displaced, whatever it might have connived at, it would have refused all legal toleration both of the Hindu and Muhammadan religions, and would have subjected both classes of the native population to one unvarying system of English law, thus subverting all native institutions, and introducing endless confusion into native society. Instead of pursuing such a course, the very first law which the English government in India promulgates on its own authority, is one which grants both to Hindus and Musalmans full legal protection in the free profession and exercise of their respective religions, and at the same time assures to them the enjoyment of their own laws and usages regarding the descent of property, marriage, and caste, which include those relations and transactions of life, the legal regulation of which according to established custom is essential to the peace and good order, the happiness and contentment of society. There can be no doubt that policy as well as wisdom, a sense of the weakness and instability of incipient power as well as the liberality of their own dispositions and principles, dictated these provisions to the English; but while this is admitted, let it not at the same time be forgotten that at the very height of the paramount authority which they now possess in India, the same wise, and just, and enlightened principles of civil and religious liberty are publicly recognised and faithfully maintained. The errors and crimes of the English in India have been neither few nor small; but the principle of their government contained in this law breathes a spirit equally wise and just, honorable and humane. By what perversion of mental vision is it that, while the letter of this law makes no mention of slavery, the spirit of it has been misunderstood and misrepresented so as to call into legal existence a system of slavery, that of the Hindus, which probably for a period of 700 years had possessed only an illegal existence? By what obliquity of judgment, by what torturing interpretation is it, that while the spirit of this law breathes only toleration, protection, and kindness to every other class and individual in the native society of British India, the man who is illegally held in bondage by a Hindu master has his fetters rivetted by it, and the unjust power of his master over him confirmed and perpetuated? By what fatal blindness, by what perverted ingenuity, by what criminal inattention is it, that while the British government of India was raising a monument to its own glory, in the establishment of a law at once just and generous, such a false gloss was put upon its spirit by the judges, and adopted by the government, as turns that glory into shame, by giving its sanction to Hindu slavery, and legalizing the bondage of hundreds of thousands of oppressed and injured men and women? Such are the deplorable effects flowing from the construction put upon the spirit as contra-distinguished from the letter of this law by British judges, legislators, and statesmen in India.

Such a distinction, however untenable, as I conceive, on sound legal principle, may yet be defended and justified on the ground of the practical good which it would secure. It is possible to conceive that the letter of a law rigidly interpreted would inflict palpable injustice in the way either of inclusion or exclusion, either by including a case plainly not contemplated by the legislator, or by excluding a case which the legislator as plainly designed to embrace in its provisions. Under such circumstances, pending a remedy by a fresh act of legislation, the interpreter of the law would be justified in correcting its spirit to the disregard of its letter; and accordingly, under every government there is a discretionary and corrective authority lodged somewhere, to temper the strict and indiscriminating operation of the letter of the law, and to bring it into a conformity with its real spirit. But who ever heard, except under the most flagrant tyrannies, of the spirit of a law being invoked against its letter, not to guard against a possible injustice, but to inflict a certain, a wide-spreading, a cankering, withering, destructive national injustice? Not to guard personal freedom, but to outrage it? Not to protect the rights of industry, but to trample upon them? Not to protect the poor against the rich, the few against the many, the weak against the powerful, but to overwhelm the illegally oppressed with legal bonds, and to tighten, not to loose, the bonds of the oppressor?

The preceding remarks refer exclusively to the legalization given to Hindu slavery by the interpretation put on the judicial regulations of 1772 and 1793; but the case is very different with regard to Muhammadan slavery. Slavery is a recognised institution of Muhammadan law, and Muhammadan law, as we have seen, was in full force under the Muhammadan government, and continued to be enforced under the British government by the agency of Muhammadan judges at least till 1772. It may be made a question what was the precise effect on Muhammadan slavery of the law passed in that year, providing that in all suits regarding inheritance, marriage, caste, and religious usages and institutions, the laws of the Koran should be invariably adhered to with respect to Muhammadans. There can be no doubt that the fact that Muhammadan law had continued to be enforced and administered up to that date, renders it probable that the Muhammadan law of slavery would not be abrogated without an express declaration to that effect; and it may even be contended with some plausibility that as the law of slavery is merely one of the forms of the law of property in as far as the master is concerned, the recognition of the Muhammadan law for Muhammadans, in suits regarding succession and inheritance to property, is a virtual and *de facto* recognition of the Muhammadan law of slavery. On the other hand, it may be alleged that slavery is not expressly mentioned, and that it is too important not to have been mentioned if it had been intended to include and legalize it as one of the civil institutions of the country; and it may be further urged in favor of a tacit disallowance of the Muhammadan law of slavery in the law of 1772, that in the same law there is an analogous tacit disallowance of the Muhammadan laws of inheritance and marriage, for instance, with regard to Hindus, by expressly allowing the latter the free enjoyment of their own laws and usages in such matters. The Hindu laws of inheritance and marriage are expressly re-enacted, which amounts to a tacit or implied abrogation of Muhammadan law in as far as it had been previously applied to such subjects; and in like manner it might not unreasonably be deemed that the silence of the law of 1772, regarding Muhammadan slavery, was a virtual abrogation of it. On the principle that, in doubtful questions of law, that interpretation should be maintained which is most conformable to natural right and liberty, it would be justest and safest to hold that the Muhammadan law of slavery was not recognised as a civil institution under the British government by the law of 1772, and by the confirmatory code of 1793.

However this question may be regarded, there cannot be

any doubt that the Muhammadan law of slavery has been formally recognised by the British government as a portion of the Muhammadan criminal law. For, in the first place, the law of 1772 expressly recognises slavery as a mode of punishment. As this is the first legal recognition of slavery by the British government in India, and as it contains provisions which every Englishman must read with a salutary shame, and every friend of his fellow-man with a just indignation, the clause in question shall be quoted here entire:—

"That whereas the peace of this country hath for some years past been greatly disturbed by bands of Decoits, who not only infest the high roads, but often plunder whole villages, burning the houses and murdering the inhabitants; and whereas these abandoned outlaws have hitherto found means to elude every attempt which the vigilance of government hath put in force, for detecting and bringing such atrocious criminals to justice, by the secrecy of their haunts, and the wild state of the districts which are most subject to their incursions; it becomes the indispensable duty of government to try the most rigorous means, since experience has proved every lenient and ordinary remedy to be ineffectual: That it be therefore resolved, that every such criminal, on conviction, shall be carried to the village to which he belongs, and be there executed for a terror and example to others; and for the further prevention of such abominable practices, that the village of which he is an inhabitant shall be fined according to the enormity of the crime, and each inhabitant according to his substance; *and that the family of the criminal shall become the slaves of the state, and be disposed of for the general benefit and convenience of the people, according to the discretion of the government.*"*

This clause of the law of 1772 has been quoted solely in

* See Colebrooke's Digest of the Regulations, Supplement, p. 7.

proof of the fact that slavery was thus early recognised by the British government of India. But who can fail to perceive that it proves more than this? It proves that some at least of the Englishmen of those days were heartless monsters, unworthy to be called men, not only fining every inhabitant of an entire village, without discrimination, for the crime of one of their number which the criminal himself had been made to expiate by his death, but in the calm deliberation of a legislative act ruthlessly condemning the innocent and helpless children of the criminal to perpetual slavery for the crime of their parent. I do not recollect to have met with any example of legislation in modern times to be compared with this for inhuman, cold-blooded, atrocious cruelty. It must be added, that this was an addition* by British rulers to Muhammadan law, and an addition so grossly unjust that the Muhammadan judges who, under their control and authority, administered the law, refused, for this and other reasons, to conform the sentences which they pronounced to the law which had been prescribed to them. In consequence of this opposition, it is doubtful whether it was ever enforced,† but if it was not, its inoperation was not for want of strenuous efforts on the part of its principal author, the notorious Warren Hastings, to enforce it. Finding the native judges too just, humane, and independent for his purposes, he wrote an official letter or minute ‡ with express reference to the article that has just been quoted of the Judicial Regulations, which declares that Decoits or gang-robbers shall suffer death, and their families be condemned to perpetual slavery, and proposed that these punishments should be "literally enforced," and that where they are not included in the sentences of the native court, they should be

* See Harington's Analysis, Vol. I. p. 308.

† See Harington's Analysis, Vol. I. pp. 300, 301.

‡ See Colebrooke's Digest of the Regulations, Supplement, p. 114.

superadded to those sentences by an immediate act of government The natural abhorrence of men at unnecessary cruelty seems to have prevented the success of his truculent efforts, and this stain upon the British name and British legislation was wiped away by the Judicial Regulations of 1793, which provided other punishments for gang-robbery.

Another recommendation which Warren Hastings offered was carried into effect, and it still further proves the recognition of slavery by the British Indian government even in those early days of its power. He proposed that every convicted felon and murderer not condemned to death by the sentence of the court, and every criminal who had been already sentenced either to work during life upon the roads, or to suffer perpetual imprisonment, should "be sold for slaves, or transported as such to the Company's establishment at Fort Marlborough," that is, at Bencoolen, in the island of Sumatra. "By this means," he coolly argued, "the government will be released from a heavy expense in erecting prisons, keeping guards in monthly pay, and in the maintenance of accumulating crowds of prisoners. The sale of the convicts will raise a considerable fund if these disorders continue; if not, the effect will be yet more beneficial."* Such were the crude notions and the barbarous forms of penal legislation among civilized Englishmen in 1772 and 1773; and their influence was felt to a very late period. At Bencoolen, the best and most extensive plantations of the nutmeg and clove are worked by slaves. There the East India Company had a body of negro slaves, held in contempt and detestation by the natives, who considered them as a species of incarnate devils, and lost no opportunity of doing them an injury.† It was to add to this slave population, that the East India Company continued to transport convicted felons

* Colebrooke's Digest of the Regulations, Supplement, p. 115.

† Hamilton's Gazetteer, Vol. I. p. 172; Vol. II. p. 597.

from the continent of India to Bencoolen, until that place, with all their other settlements on the island of Sumatra, was delivered up to the Dutch in 1825.

It is essential to our present purpose to notice the legal forms in which Muhammadan slavery continues to be recognised by the British Indian government of the present day; and this is done by the adoption of the Muhammadan as the British Indian criminal code, and by the amendment relating to slavery which has been introduced into it. The entire body of Muhammadan criminal law, with exceptions, has been adopted by the British Indian government. Instead of abrogating the Muhammadan criminal law, which, however defective, had been long in force, and was therefore well known to the people, the courts of judicature established on the part of the East India Company throughout their territorial possessions, are required, in the administration of criminal justice, to be guided by the Muhammadan law, excepting cases wherein a deviation from it may have been expressly authorized by the regulations of the British government. Now, according to Muhammadan law, if a man kill the slave of another, capital punishment, or, in the language of that law, retaliation of death, is incurred; but retaliation of death in cases of murder, being considered with respect to slaves the right of their masters, they are at liberty to remit the claim and forgive the offender, or to compound with the consent of the murderer for a compensation. Still further, if a master murder his own slave he is not liable to retaliation of death. The demand of retaliation is further barred if the person murdered be the joint slave of the murderer and others; the right failing in proportion to the murderer's share, and retaliation of death not admitting of being inflicted in part only. The same principle is applicable if the person killed be a slave appropriated by the owner to the public service, that is, capital punishment is not incurred.* It must be evident that this makes the life of the slave the sport of caprice and passion, without any protection from the law; and accordingly the Regulations of the East India Company have enacted that in those cases in which a convicted murderer would not be liable under the Muhammadan law to suffer death by retaliation, solely on the ground of the murdered person having been the slave of the murderer, or of any other person, or a slave appropriated for the service of the public, the murderer shall be sentenced to suffer death. This amendment of the Muhammadan criminal law affords only just and equal protection to the slave, and its enactment was equally wise and humane; but it will be observed, that it contains a distinct legal recognition of slavery, and of slavery as founded on and authorized by Muhammadan law. It corrects certain grossly partial and unjust provisions of the Muhammadan law of slavery, and *ipso facto* it recognises all the remaining provisions of that law. The Muhammadan law of slavery then is undoubtedly the law of British India. It is recognised as such in those legislative acts called the Rules and Regulations of the East India Company, passed by the local government, confirmed by the Court of Directors, approved by the Parliament of Great Britain, and thus having all the force and effect of law in British India.

The conclusions at which we have arrived regard, first, Hindu, and second, Muhammadan slavery. It has been shown that Hindu slavery is not legal under the British government, but that the force of a practical legality has been given to it by the mistaken application to this subject of the law which secures to Hindus the benefit of their own laws in suits regarding inheritance and succession, marriage, caste, and religion. The effect of the unfortunate interpretation given to this law, is unnecessarily to legalize Hindu slavery. It is not by a positive, direct, and unequivocal law

* Harington's Analysis, Vol. I. pp. 261, 262, 264, 314.

of the British government that Hindu slavery has been legalized, but by a doubtful interpretation of a law, the letter of which is silent on the subject, but the spirit of which is conceived to include slavery. A different, and as I believe a more correct, interpretation would make Hindu slavery illegal, and would at once entitle to their liberty thousands of slaves now held in bondage by Hindu masters. I know that much may be said about the generally mild character of Hindu domestic slavery, of which I shall hereafter treat, and which, to whatever extent it really may exist, I am not disposed either to deny or to conceal; but the question here is not whether slaves held by Hindu masters are well or ill treated, but whether they are entitled to the use of their own limbs and the fruits of their own industry. Much also may be said about the danger of disturbing property by a mere interpretation of law; but it is by a mere interpretation of law that thousands of persons held as slaves by Hindu masters have been for two generations, and are to this day, deprived of their liberty, and it is to remedy this state of the law that a more thorough investigation of the case is now urged. The subject, which is merely one of oppressed humanity, is so remote from the usual fiscal objects which almost absorb the attention of the British Indian government, that the required investigation is not likely to be made, unless demanded by public opinion, the public opinion of India, of England, and of the friends of human liberty in every part of the civilized world. The investigation, if made, may result differently from what I anticipate, by establishing the correctness of the interpretation which I call in question; but believing, as I firmly do, in the incorrectness of that interpretation, knowing that it is the sole legal ground on which Hindu slavery rests, and that the disallowance of it would be the simplest, the safest, and the least offensive mode of abolishing the whole system of Hindu slavery, I have deemed it my duty to bring forward the subject as I have now done, that the necessary stimulus may be applied to those who wield the powers of the Indian government, whether in England or in the East.

The conclusion at which we have arrived regarding Muhammadan slavery, however apparently different, is in fact equally friendly to the early termination of that system of slavery. It has been shown that the only legal slavery existing under the authority of the British government in India, is Muhammadan slavery, that is, slavery as recognised and sanctioned by Muhammadan law. But under the Muhammadan law there are only two descriptions of persons recognised as slaves: first, infidels made captive during war; and secondly, their descendants. All other descriptions of slavery, such as that created by the mere force of immemorial custom or usage, by bond-debts, by purchase of free children, by kidnapping, by importation, all are illegal; and all that is required to liberate such slaves, is, that they should understand their legal condition, should have the courage to claim and exercise the freedom that belongs to them, and that in claiming and exercising it they should be supported and countenanced by the authorities constituted to administer justice. With regard to the two descriptions of slavery recognised by the Muhammadan law, it cannot be affirmed that such slaves are to be found throughout India at the present day. The first description is that of infidels made captive in war; but the Muhammadan power has ceased to exist in India for three quarters of a century, except in the case of four tributary and dependent princes, who have never carried on any religious war, nor made slaves of their captives. Previous to that period, the Muhammadan power was either in name or in reality supreme and paramount, and the wars that were waged for centuries were, almost without exception, between Muhammadan princes, the rival pretenders to supreme authority, and not directed against infidels. From the accession of the house of Timur in 1525, there was no religious war carried on by Muhammadans against Hindus, except during the period intervening between 1678 and 1681, by Aurungzeb, against the Rajputs, a Hindu race of Central India. In the first campaign, conducted by the emperor in person, he was signally unsuccessful; in the second, his arms were more prosperous; and after the third, he was necessitated to grant them a peace; nor, as far as I have been able to discover, is there any proof in history that he made any of his captives slaves. The most recent example of a proselytizing Muhammadan sovereign was Tippoo Sahib, the ruler of Mysore, who employed coercion to make both Hindus and native Christians Musalmans; but it does not appear that he made any of them slaves, and after his death there were found in the Mysore territories only about 17,000 Muhammadan families in a total number of 482,612 families, and of 2,171,754 inhabitants. It is thus physically impossible that there should exist at the present day any slaves who have become such by being captured by Muhammadans in war. The second description of slaves is that of persons descended from those who had been made slaves by such means. It is not to be denied that by a mere possibility such persons may exist as slaves at the present day; but how is their descent, the proof of which is necessary to the legality of their slavery, to be established? It is in the highest degree improbable that such proof should exist, and as it belongs to the master to establish by proof the legality of the grounds on which he holds another in unwilling servitude, this description of slavery also, if not absolutely non-existent, which is probable, is yet untenable by legal proof. Thus, under the Muhammadan law, the only legal kinds of slavery are either non-existent or unprovable, and the only actual kinds of slavery are illegal—a state of things which a wise and humane government would promptly turn to account to put an end to slavery altogether, in name and fact as well as in law; and which a government neither wise nor humane, or one inattentive to the rights of humanity and to the dictates of a wise policy, must be taught to employ for that purpose.

It is fit that I should state that the views I have presented both of the Hindu and Muhammadan laws of slavery are not new, although the practical inferences deducible from them have been wholly neglected. In 1808 and 1809, Mr. Richardson, then judge and magistrate of the district of Bundlecund, proposed for the adoption of the Bengal government a "Regulation for checking and reforming the abuses that have crept into practice and at present exist with respect to slavery within the British dominions subordinate to the presidency and government of Fort William;" and in the correspondence which ensued on this subject he took the ground that the Hindu law of slavery should be set aside as having been long dormant under the Musalman government, and that operation should be given only to the strict provisions of the Muhammadan law as the established system enforced by the British criminal courts, not only in cases affecting personal freedom, but even in such as extend to life and death. Mr. Harington, the author of a valuable analysis of the Laws and Regulations of the British Indian government, controverted this doctrine, resting his judgment on the opinion pronounced by the supreme court of native judicature, "that the spirit of the rule for observing the Muhammadan and Hindu laws was applicable to cases of slavery, though not included in the letter of it," without perceiving that that opinion itself had no tenable foundation to rest upon. Thus he argues that "*if* the spirit of the rule for observing the Muhammadan and Hindu laws which has guided the East India Company's courts of judicature, since their first establishment in these provinces, be applicable to cases of slavery, the fair and impartial application of it will require, as heretofore, the same regard to the Hindu law as to the Muhammadan, when the claimants may be of either persuasion;" the very point thus assumed being the very point to be proved in order to the validity of the argument. "The actual existence," Mr. Harington goes on to argue, "of numerous slaves in the possession of Hindu landholders, contradicts the supposition that the Hindu law of slavery had remained dormant under the Musalman government;" whereas this is only one of several illegal forms of slavery which then existed, and which even still continue to exist. The possession of stolen property does not establish the honesty of the holder. The readiness to inflict and even to submit to injustice does not convert wrong into right. "I am not aware," he adds, "of any preference given by the judicial regulations now in force to the Muhammadan law where the parties are Hindus, except in the administration of criminal justice." Now this exception is the precise exception which applies to the case under discussion, even according to his own showing, for he had expressly admitted in a preceding paragraph "that all claims and disputes respecting slavery," "as involving the right of personal freedom, may be considered in that respect within the proper jurisdiction of the criminal courts," and consequently as falling under the exception which establishes a preference in favor of Muhammadan law, and gives it a force which is not conceded to Hindu law.*

With respect to Muhammadan law, which he had more thoroughly studied, Mr. Harington's views are clearer and more explicit, and they fully and strongly confirm all the statements I have advanced. "With respect to slaves," he says, "it must be remembered that those referred to in the Muhammadan law, and in a strict view of it alone to be considered legal slaves, are infidels conquered and made

* Harington's Analysis, Vol. I. pp. 68—73.

captive in war. They are held to be the property of the captors by right of conquest."—"Nor can any other title legalize the slavery of a freeman, whether Musalman or infidel, so as to bring it within the provisions of the Muhammadan criminal law."* Mr. Macnaghten, another high authority on native law, employs still more decided language. "The question of Muhammadan slavery seems to be but little understood. According to strict law, the state of bondage, as far as Musalmans are concerned, may be said to be almost extinct in this country, (India.) They only are slaves who are captured in an infidel territory in time of war, or who are the descendants of such captives. Perhaps there is no point of law which has been more deliberately and formally determined than this."—"Of those who can legally be called slaves but few at present exist. In the ordinary acceptation of the term, all persons are counted slaves who may have been sold by their parents in a time of scarcity, and this class is very numerous. Thousands are at this moment living in a state of hopeless and contented, though unauthorized, bondage. That the illegality of this state of things should be known is certainly desirable."†

I have thus, as I proposed, examined the grounds on which a legal sanction has been given to slavery in British India, and have shown that those grounds demand reconsideration. That reconsideration will not be given with the requisite earnestness, promptitude, and friendly regard for the rights of personal freedom, unless the stimulus of public opinion shall be applied. "A *vis inertiæ*," says Mr. A. D. Campbell, speaking from an experience of twenty-two years in the exercise of numerous and grave

* Harington's Analysis, Vol. I. p. 262, note.

† Macnaghten's Principles and Precedents of Muhammadan Law, Preliminary Remarks, pp. xxx—xxxix.

functions under the Indian government—"a *vis inertiæ* hostile to all change seems inherent in the local governments of India, imbibed perhaps from the people subject to their rule, whose characteristic peculiarity is a tenacity of long-established customs. Even when improvements are suggested by the constituted authorities, the voice of their servants has little weight in favor of new measures. Responsibility is avoided by following the beaten track, and silence is the safest reply to those who propose a deviation from it, even for the sake of humanity. The outcry raised in India against the Suttee was long powerless, until it returned reverberated from the British shore; and that against slavery will continue disregarded, unless it receives support from all the energy of the home government."* The fact of this deplorable apathy is undoubted, and is attested by all experience; the explanation of it, as arising from the contagious example of the natives, is more than questionable. It is to be traced to the radical vice of the British government of India, which is, that that government has been exercised, sometimes avowedly, always in fact, for the profit of English rulers, not for the benefit of the Indian people. The proof of this is found in the fact that "long-established customs" have never been permitted to stand in the way of any plan or project promising an increase of revenue; while an objection of this nature, nay, even the semblance of such an objection, when the objection is wholly without foundation, is deemed all but insuperable, and sometimes wholly so, in opposition to any design proposing the amelioration of the condition of the people. What have rulers with the increase of revenue uppermost in their thoughts and most prominent in their objects and calculations,—what have rulers acting on such a principle to do with a question of humanity, which has no direct or

* Report from Select Committee on Affairs of the East India Company, Appendix, Public, pp. 576, 577.

apparent connection with their primary and ultimate purpose, which merely proposes to strike off the shackles from some hundreds of thousands of their subjects, and to raise them from the degradation of slaves to the dignity of men and members of civil society? This is a vice which pervades equally the home and the local governments of India, perhaps the former in a higher degree, because those who conduct the home government have seldom that vivid perception of the evil which local residence and observation alone can bestow. Its strength has been shown by the neglect with which a recommendation of the Imperial Parliament on the subject of slavery has been treated. In the original draft of the bill for renewing the East India Company's charter in 1833, there was a clause providing for the total abolition of slavery throughout British India. In the progress of the measure through the House of Lords, that clause was struck out and another substituted, which appears as the 88th clause of the present charter act, enacting that "The governor-general in council shall, and he is hereby required forthwith to take into consideration the means of mitigating the state of slavery, and of ameliorating the condition of slaves, and of extinguishing slavery throughout the said territories so soon as such extinction shall be practicable and safe; and from time to time to prepare and transmit to the said Court of Directors drafts of laws and regulations for the purposes aforesaid," &c. &c. Such was one of the conditions on which the charter was granted in 1833, and up to the present time nothing has been suggested by the home government or done by the local government to mitigate the state of slavery, to ameliorate the condition of slaves, or to extinguish slavery. The recommendation has been practically inoperative upon slaves and slavery in India from 1833 to 1840. Nothing has been done, and nothing will be done effectually, until public opinion be aroused to demand justice for India and attention to the wants and the wrongs of her people.

LETTER III.

TO THOMAS FOWELL BUXTON, ESQ.

Administration of Hindu and Muhammadan Slave-Law under the British Government in India.

Sir,—We have hitherto considered Indian slavery as it is presented in the letter of Hindu, Muhammadan, and British law. I propose now to exhibit that law as interpreted and administered in British Indian courts of justice. As a necessary preliminary to this view, I shall mention the source from which I draw my materials, and thus enable you to judge of the degree of confidence to which my statements may be entitled.

The general regulations for the administration of justice made and ordained by the president and council in Bengal on the 21st August, 1772, provided that, in all suits in which the Muhammadans and Hindus were to have the benefit of their own laws, "the Moulavies or Brahmins," (that is, the learned Muhammadan or Hindu law-officers attached to the courts,) "shall respectively attend to expound the law; and they shall sign the report and assist in passing the decree."* This provision was embodied in the code of 1793. "The Muhammadan and Hindu law-officers, attached to the several civil courts, are required to expound the law of their respective persuasions; and the judges are

* Colebrooke's Digest of Regulations and Laws, Supplement, p. 5.

directed to be guided by their exposition, in all cases wherein they have no reason to doubt the accuracy of it. But if in any case they entertain such doubt, either from objections of the parties, founded on other law opinions exhibited by them; or from a reference to the known books of Muhammadan and Hindu law; or from whatever cause, if the court trying the suit consider the exposition given by its immediate law-officer insufficient; it is declared at liberty to obtain a further exposition from the law-officers of the superior courts, by a reference of the case to them through the judges of those courts. But no point of law is to be referred to individuals not acting in a public capacity, and to whom, consequently, no responsibility attaches; although law opinions, quoting or referring to authorities, may be received from parties in support of their claims, and, if it be deemed proper by the courts receiving them, referred to their law-officers, or to those of the superior courts."—"The translations of books of law, Hindu and Muhammadan, made under the encouragement of the British government, have materially contributed to give effect to this principle, by enabling the judges of the civil courts to inform themselves upon general points of Muhammadan and Hindu law, and to investigate the expositions of the native law-officers attached to their respective courts."* Among the works that have appeared illustrative of Hindu and Muhammadan law, are two by Mr. William Hay Macnaghten, of the Bengal civil service, containing, in addition to other valuable matter, what he calls Precedents of Hindu and Muhammadan Law, that is, cases submitted to Hindu and Muhammadan law-officers of British courts, with the opinions which those officers have expressed. The care with which these cases and opinions have been brought together, will be estimated from Mr. Macnaghten's own remarks. In his work on Hindu law, he says:—"The Precedents have been selected

* Harington's Analysis, Vol. I. p. 67.

from an enormous mass of crude materials. When it is mentioned that I have examined every opinion that has been delivered in every court of judicature subordinate to the presidency of Bengal, from the year 1811 up to the present day," (his work appeared in 1829,) "it may be a matter of wonder that the selections are not more numerous and more valuable. But the task of rejection has been found very laborious. At least nine-tenths of the opinions were ascertained, on examination, to be erroneous, doubtful, unsupported by proof, or otherwise unfit for publication; while, in not a few instances, the nature of the case itself was involved in obscurity, from the circumstance of the reply alone being forthcoming; the whole record of the case having been made over to the law-officer, with a view to enable him to find out and report the law upon the point or points at issue between the parties. The admitted opinions have been carefully examined; and they will, it is hoped, be in general found to have at least the merit of accuracy." * In like manner, in his work on Muhammadan law, which was published four years earlier, (1825,) he says:—"The Precedents consist of legal expositions which have been actually delivered in the several courts of justice. I have selected such as appeared to me of the greatest importance, and those which seemed to embrace doctrinal points most likely to recur. With a view to retain the sense as far as practicable, I have left them in the original shape of question and reply; and none have been admitted but such as appeared to me, (assisted by all the legal talent I could procure,) to admit of no doubt as to their accuracy."† The cases of slavery, then, to which I am about to call your attention, are cases which have been actually brought before British courts of

* Macnaghten's Principles and Precedents of Hindu Law, Preliminary Remarks, pp. xxiii, xxiv.

† Macnaghten's Principles and Precedents of Muhammadan Law, Preliminary Remarks, p. lxxi.

law in India for adjudication; cases which the English judges of those courts have submitted to the native law-officers expressly appointed to expound the law, for their opinions; cases on which those native law-officers, under the solemn obligation which their office imposes faithfully and truly to declare the law, have formed and expressed their deliberate opinions. Still further, it is a very small selection of such cases and opinions that has been made from a great mass of materials by a judicial officer of the Bengal government, eminently competent for such a task; a selection of cases made on the principle of their importance, and the probability of their recurrence; and a selection of opinions which, amid many that were erroneous or doubtful, were deemed accurate and trustworthy. I do not know any higher security that you could desire for the correctness of my statements regarding the actual administration of the law of slavery under the British government in India. I shall give the cases in full, and the substance only of the opinions, as the latter are generally too long for quotation entire; and I shall add such remarks as may appear to be necessary for illustration. The cases and opinions relating to the Hindu law of slavery will be first given, and then those relating to the Muhammadan law.

Precedents relating to the Hindu Law of Slavery.

CASE I.

Q. "A person living in service was supposed by the inhabitants of the place to be the slave of the individual whom he served. In this case, is he to be treated as a slave from the fact of such notoriety? And if so, is the master competent to dispose of him by sale?"

This was a case which occurred in 1824, at Dacca, one of the principal cities of Bengal; and the opinion of the Hindu lawyer to whom it was referred consists simply in an enumeration of fifteen descriptions of slaves, recognised by Hindu law, and an intimation that nothing more definite can be said, on the ground that it is not distinctly mentioned in the question to what sort of slavery the individual alluded to belonged. It is evident that this information was not possessed, and the case is one similar to a very large majority of the total number of cases of Hindu slavery, in which individuals are held in bondage, and disposed of by sale, not under any known or recognised law, but by the tyrannical right which custom and notoriety are assumed to bestow. Should it ever have been made a question in a British court of justice whether such slavery shall receive a legal recognition? The Hindu lawyer administers an intelligible reproof to the British judge who could submit such a case, by refusing to acknowledge it as belonging to any of the legal forms of Hindu slavery.

CASE II.

Q. "A female slave being the property of two individuals, one of them disposed of her in marriage to the slave of another person, and ordered her to go to her husband's house, where she is still living. The other proprietor brought an action in a court of justice claiming her. In this case, does the plaintiff's right consist over half her person, or is he entitled to half the price of her person?"

This case occurred in 1818, in Chittagong, one of the eastern districts of Bengal. The opinion of the Hindu lawyer is, that one of two owners of a female slave giving her away in marriage without the consent of his coparcener, the other still retains his right, not to half her person, but to half her labor, or half her value. You will observe here the application and judicial recognition in modern times of one of the most ancient and characteristic rules of Hindu slavery viz., that a woman who is not a slave of the same master becoming the wife of a slave, thereby becomes a slave to her husband's owner, in this case only to the extent to which the consenting owner had legal property in her.

CASE III.

Q. "A slave being the property of three individuals, one of them, with his own free will, emancipated him from servitude to the extent of his legal share. In this case, is the slave released from his obligations to the other two proprietors? If not, how are the two remaining masters to claim their right of servitude?"

This case occurred in 1813, in Mymunsingh, another of the eastern districts of Bengal. The judicial decision is, that the emancipation of a slave by one of three masters does not render him free with respect to the other two, who must be served according to their shares in him. Such instances of joint partnership in a slave would appear to be common, and the decision, however equitable towards the masters, has the effect of interposing obstacles to emancipation, by rendering the consent of all the masters indispensable to its completion.

CASE IV.

Q. "A female slave, having been emancipated from servitude, suffered much for the necessaries of life, and sold herself, with her two daughters, one of them five and the other seven years of age, with her late master's consent. In this case, is the sale of daughters of such years available in law, or not? Have the daughters an option, on attaining the age of majority, to set aside the sale of their persons?"

This case occurred in 1819, in the district of Chittagong, already mentioned. The decision is, that the children of an emancipated slave, sold as slaves by their mother with her late master's sanction, are not entitled to their freedom on coming of age, and have no power to nullify the contract. The first remarkable feature in this legal opinion is, that the permanent validity of the sale of the daughters by the mother is made dependent on her late master's concurrence, although it is expressly stated that he had emancipated the mother, and apparently implied that her emancipation included that of the daughters, since, if not, the power of selling them would not have belonged to the mother, and the obligation of supporting them would have rested on the master. If the mother only was emancipated, then the daughters remained the property of her former master, and his consent became necessary to their sale by their mother for her own support. What a picture of society does this exhibit! What a depth of physical wretchedness, or of moral obtuseness, or of both! A mother emancipated from slavery again selling herself for the necessaries of life; receiving the gift of her own daughters from her former master, to be in like manner sold for the relief of her wants—sold at the age of five and seven by their own mother into perpetual slavery, perhaps to vice and infamy; and the perpetuity of the sale under such circumstances affirmed by Hindu law, and confirmed by the authority of a British court of justice!

CASE V.

Q. "A person procures a contract of marriage to be entered into between his slave and the daughter of a free person, and subsequently sells his slave's wife to another. In this case, has the master of the slave derived any right of proprietorship over the person of the slave's wife by reason of her being subject to his slave; and is the sale of such woman allowable by law?"

This case also occurred in 1819, in Chittagong; and the decision, according to Hindu law, is, that a free woman becoming the wife of a slave, becomes a slave to her husband's master, who has full power to alienate her by sale, and the sale is good and valid. This is another of those cases which, without the evidence before us, we should find it difficult to believe that the authority of the British government would be employed to enforce. A free woman, ignorant, most probably, of the law which affects such cases, is inveigled into marriage with a slave by the slave's master, who subsequently sells her for his own profit, and this sale is pronounced good and valid by the organ of Hindu law, and recognised as such by the British government and its judicial officers! Will the British people, when they know the fact, sanction it? Will not the indignation of the civilized world shame the British government into the abrogation of a law so cruel and disgraceful?

CASE VI.

Q. "Four brothers purchased a female slave, who subsequently brought forth a son and daughter. Of the four brothers, one sold his property over the slaves to the other three, while the male slave was only eleven years old, and afterwards he (the slave) married a free woman and then died. Of the three proprietors, two left no heir at their death, and one is survived by a son. In this case, is he (the brother's son) competent to sell the widow of the slave, or not?"

The date of this case is not given; the locality in which it occurred was the jurisdiction of the Dacca court of appeal. The decision is, that the slave's widow may be sold by the next heir of the deceased proprietors. This is another case in which a free woman, in virtue of her marriage with a slave, was reduced to slavery, and ultimately sold as a slave, or at least by the decision of a British court pronounced legally salable.

CASE VII.

Q. "A slave, having left his master's house, resided in another place, and supported himself by his own labor, for the period of ten or twelve years, during which time his master neither sent for him nor required his attendance, though it was known to him where the slave was living. In this case, does it follow that the master has relinquished his right of property; or, on the other hand, is a sale of the slave by the master under such circumstances valid and binding?"

Neither the date nor the locality of this case is given. The decision is, that under the circumstances described, the master has forfeited his right of ownership, and the sale is illegal. The general rule of Hindu law is that the right to movable property lapses after a period of ten years, provided there was wilful neglect on the part of the owner for that period; but not if his non-interference was unavoidable.

CASE VIII.

Q. "An inhabitant of Sylhet wishes to sell his female slave and her family, consisting of four sons and a little girl, for a fixed sum, to another person. The slaves make an application to the court, stating that they are willing to serve their own master, but that the latter from enmity has come to an understanding with the intended purchaser, to have the family removed from the place of their nativity, and the individuals sold at separate places. Can the slaves, according to Hindu law as current in Sylhet, object to such a sale? May they, in case their master is determined to part with them, select another person whom they prefer to be their purchaser? Or may they purchase their own liberty, if they can raise the sum demanded?"

This case occurred in 1825, in Sylhet, another of the eastern districts of Bengal. It was referred by the magistrate of Sylhet for the consideration and orders of the superior court, who took the opinion of their Hindu law-officers, which was in substance as follows. They state that, as has been already shown, (Letter I, pp. 17—19,) according to Hindu law, there are five sorts of slaves who cannot effect their own emancipation by paying the price set upon them by their master, since the master's right of authority in those cases extends to the property of his slaves, and consequently their possession of property applicable to such a purpose, except as an indulgence from him, is legally impossible. Of those five sorts, one is that of slaves born in the house, to which class the slaves alluded to in the question are understood to belong; and hence they cannot purchase their own liberty, while the master, in right of his ownership and free-will, can sell the slaves, although willing to serve him. But Hindu law provides a limitation to the master's power. It declares, in the words of an ancient and high authority, that "judgment is not to be formed, relying on the *Shaster* (or law) alone; for a failure of justice is produced when an inquiry is not adapted to circumstances." This principle is declared applicable to the case under consideration, and it is accordingly pronounced that if the sale of the slaves by their master to a purchaser chosen by him would occasion great misery to the slaves, then he should be required to receive the price from a purchaser chosen by the adult slave, or from any other purchaser to whom the objection does not apply. This opinion of the law-officers was confirmed by the superior court, who state "that the slaves whom it is proposed to sell to one whose intentions they suspect and dread, may be allowed to select a purchaser with whom they are satisfied, and that in this their proprietors must acquiesce." The fact that such a question between master and slave could be and was raised in a court of justice and that it was thus decided, shows in one respect the mild character of Hindu slavery in the district of Sylhet under the British government; and it also shows the severity of its character in another respect, for the answer does not go the length of stating that slaves are competent to purchase their freedom from their masters against the consent of the latter. Hindu law as administered by the British government does not enable the slave to claim his liberty on tendering the full value of his person to his master.

CASE IX.

Q. " 1. What descriptions of slaves are authorized by the Hindu law? 2. What legal powers are the owners of slaves allowed to exercise upon the persons of their slaves, and particularly of their female slaves? 3. What offences upon the persons of slaves, and particularly of female slaves, committed by their owners or by others, are legally punishable, and in what manner? 4. Are slaves entitled to emancipation upon any and what maltreatment? And may the courts of justice adjudge their emancipation upon proof of such maltreatment? In particular, may such judgment be passed upon proof that a female slave has, during her minority, been prostituted by her master or mistress, or that any attempt of violence has been made upon her person by her owner?"

The questions embraced in this case were proposed in 1809, by the Sudder Dewany Adawlut, or the East India Company's supreme court of civil judicature in Bengal, to its Hindu law-officers who are the highest in station, and may be pronounced the most learned and accomplished native lawyers in the country.

1. With regard to the descriptions of slaves authorized by Hindu law, the answer does not differ in substance from the account already given in a former letter, which need not here be repeated.

2. On the legal powers belonging to the owners of slaves, a distinction, recognised by Hindu law, is made between pure and impure work. Impure work consists in cleaning the house, the gate-way, the necessary, and the road; removing the dirt and rubbish and all other impurities; attending the master at his pleasure and rubbing his limbs; and all other work is pure. Slaves, whether male or female, and slaves only, may be legally required to perform

impure work, and in case of disobedience or fault the master may legally correct the slave by corporal punishment with a rope or the small shoot of a cane, or by ignominious exposure. If the master should inflict a severer punishment, he is liable to be fined at the discretion of the ruling power.

3. Regarding the offences that may be committed on the persons of slaves, and how legally punishable, the law-officers merely reiterate the statement that a master has no power to command the slave to do any other than the impure work already described, or to punish him in any other mode than that already mentioned, and that, in the event of his exceeding his powers, he is liable only to pecuniary fine. However extreme the offence then which a master may commit on the person of his slave, Hindu law recognises and sanctions no other punishment than pecuniary fine. If the master should wilfully occasion the death of his slave, what then is the punishment? Even in that case I do not find that Hindu law provides any other punishment than pecuniary fine. But it may be supposed that the British government has in that respect amended the Hindu law of slavery. The British government has certainly amended a similar provision of the Muhammadan law of slavery, but there is no such amendment of the Hindu law of slavery. On the one hand I find the highest judicial authority in India affirming that the spirit of the rule for observing the Muhammadan and Hindu laws is applicable to cases of slavery, and this construction formally confirmed by the governor-general in council, thereby legalizing the two systems of Muhammadan and Hindu slavery. On the other hand I find the British government enacting an amendment of the law of slavery, making a master liable to death who shall take away the life of his slave, but limiting the application of this amendment to cases that shall occur "under the Muhammadan

law." It follows that the corresponding provision of the Hindu law remains unrepealed and unamended, and that a Hindu master who shall wilfully take away the life of his slave could be legally punished only by pecuniary fine.

4. In answer to the question what offences against the persons of slaves would entitle the slave to emancipation, it is briefly and pointedly declared that there are no such offences. In certain cases, pecuniary fine may be inflicted; and if a female slave bears a child by her master, both mother and child become free; but the prostitution of a female slave, violence to her person by her master or with his permission, or any maltreatment whatever, does not affect the state of bondage, nor even give the ruling power the right to grant the manumission of the slave.

Such is the Hindu law of slavery, as expounded by the most learned and distinguished Hindu lawyers in Bengal, at the requisition of the highest judicial authority under the British government of India, by whom it is conformably administered and enforced.

Precedents relating to the Muhammadan Law of Slavery.

CASE I.

Q. "A Musalman having been sent by the ruling power to subdue some rebellious Hindus, and having obtained a victory over them, took several of their body prisoners. Among them there was one boy of tender years whom he made his own slave, and afterwards, having instructed him in the principles of the Muhammadan faith, he adopted him as his own son, and in his education and other matters he treated him with the care and consideration of a parent. Under these circumstances, can the boy so recognised as the son of the person above alluded to, be considered as his slave agreeably to law?"

In this and in all the following precedents relating to the

Muhammadan law of slavery, there is no information given respecting the time when or the place where each case occurred. The opinion of the Muhammadan law-officers on the case submitted to them is very decidedly expressed. They state, in the first place, that it by no means appears clearly from the question that the boy was legally reduced to slavery; and in the second place, the treatment of him as a son was a legal emancipation, even without any declaration to that effect, or any intention on the part of the master that such an effect should flow from it.

CASE II.

Q. "1. What descriptions of slaves are authorized by the Muhammadan law? 2. What legal powers are the owners of slaves allowed to exercise upon the persons of their slaves, and particularly of their female slaves? 3. What offences upon the persons of slaves, and particularly of female slaves, committed by their owners or by others, are legally punishable, and in what manner? 4. Are slaves entitled to emancipation upon any and what maltreatment? And may a court of justice adjudge their emancipation upon proof of such maltreatment? In particular, may such judgment be passed upon proof that a female slave has, during her minority, been prostituted by her master or mistress, or that any attempt of violence has been made upon her person by her owner?"

The questions included in this case are the same as those contained in Case IX. of Precedents relating to the Hindu Law of Slavery; and the answers may be regarded as those of the highest native living authorities on matters of Muhammadan law.

1. The answer to the first question embraces an enumeration of certain descriptions of slavery recognised by the Muhammadan law, and of certain other existing descriptions of slavery which are declared to be unlawful. The

only source of legal slavery is the capture of infidels in war, who, under such circumstances, may be put to death, or set at liberty subject to a capitation-tax, or made slaves; and in the last case they may either be sold, or given away, or may descend by inheritance. This is applicable to both sexes, and the offspring of a female slave by any other person than her master is also subject to slavery. According to this exposition, there are five, and only five, descriptions of legal slavery: an enslaved infidel captive; such a slave bought; or received in gift; or inherited; and the offspring of any such female slave, provided the master is not the father. Those kinds of actual slavery which are declared unlawful according to Muhammadan law, are the following. The custom is stated to prevail in most Musalman countries, (of which India, even at the present day, is regarded as one,*) of purchasing and selling the inhabitants of Ethiopia, Nubia, and other negroes, and the ostensible causes are either that the negroes sell their own children, or that they are taken prisoners by fraud and deceit, or that they are seized by stealth from the sea-shores. All such cases of slavery are pronounced illegal, and sales and purchases arising out of them invalid. Again, the practice among free men and women of selling their own offspring during times of famine is declared illegal, for children are not the property of their parents, and all sales or purchases of them, as of any other article of illegal property, are consequently invalid. Such sales and purchases are doubly illegal, inasmuch as the slavery they create is illegal, and it is generally created for illegal purposes, such as prostitution. Another form of slavery arises from the custom which prevails in India of hiring children from their parents for a very considerable period, such as for seventy or eighty years, and under this pretext making them and their progeny slaves. It is de-

* Harington's Analysis, Vol. I. p. 295.

clared that such a contract of hire becomes null and void when the child arrives at years of discretion, as the right of paternity then ceases. A fourth illegal form of slavery is that which is produced by a free man selling his own person either in times of famine or when oppressed by a debt which he is unable to discharge, or hiring himself for any great length of time, such as for seventy years. Such a sale is declared improper, and such a contract for service should be made illegal by limiting contracts of hire of free men to a month, one year, or at the utmost to three years.

2. In answer to the second question regarding the legal powers of the owners of slaves, it is stated that various enumerated domestic, mechanical, and agricultural services may be exacted from slaves by their masters; and that the person of a female slave, provided she has arrived at the age of maturity and has not been given in marriage to another, is subject to the will of her master. The effect however of such cohabitation is, that if the children be the avowed and acknowledged offspring of the rightful owner, they are free, and the mother becomes free also at his decease.

3. In answer to the third question regarding offences that may be committed on the persons of slaves, it is stated that if a master oppress his slave by employing him in any duty beyond his power and ability, by requiring him to do that which is unlawful, by punishing him further than by moderate correction, or by cohabiting with his female slave before she has arrived at the years of maturity and thereby seriously injuring her or causing her death, the ruling power may at discretion inflict such punishment on him as shall be deemed adequate to satisfy principles of public justice.

4. In answer to the fourth question regarding those offences against the persons of slaves which would entitle them to emancipation, it is declared that the commission of the supposed crimes by the master subjects him to punish-

ment at the discretion of the ruling power, but does not authorize the manumission of the slaves; nor has the ruling power any right or authority to grant them emancipation unless the slavery were originally illegal.

CASE III.

Q. "1. The father of Deendar Khan, (the plaintiff,) was a *Hindu*, who in a year of scarcity, out of necessity, sold his son to Budun Khan and Musummaut Asalut, to whose property Gholam Hoossein Khan, (the defendant,) lays claim. Does Deendar Khan by such sale legally become a slave or not? 2. According to law, what circumstances are essential and necessary to the ceremony of emancipation?"

This case involves two questions, unconnected with each other. In answer to the first, it is declared that no person legally free can become legally enslaved by sale in a time of scarcity; and in answer to the second, that words indicative of the act of emancipation, without the execution of any deed or the use of any formalities, are sufficient to give it effect, in whatever language expressed.

CASE IV.

Q. "It is a well known principle of law that free persons cannot on any account be sold; yet it appears to be a generally received opinion that the selling and purchasing of mankind in times of distress or difficulty are allowable. Does the latter doctrine rest on any legal foundation?"

In the answer to this case, the general doctrine is admitted to be sound and authentic that purchase confers no right of dominion over mankind, but in conformity with certain works of authority and with a tradition of Imam Muhammad, an exception to the general principle is admitted in the cases of freemen suffering under extreme distress or hard pressed by their creditors, who are permitted to dispose of their own liberties by sale. This is directly opposed to the answer given to the first question under Case II., in which it is expressly declared that "it is improper for any free man to sell his own person, either in times of famine, or though he be oppressed by a debt which he is unable to discharge. For in the first of these cases, a famished man may feed upon a dead body, or may even steal what is necessary for his support; and a distressed debtor is not liable to any fine or punishment."

CASE V.

Q. "Does the estate of *Inayut Oollah* go to the widow of *Wasil Beg*, who was educated by the deceased proprietor?"

In this question *Wasil Beg* is assumed to have been the purchased and legal slave of *Inayut Oollah*, and both master and slave being dead, the inquiry is, whether the widow of the slave, through her husband, shall be deemed entitled to inherit the estate of his master. This is not a question of slavery or no slavery, but of inheritance or no inheritance. If it had been the former, the principle recognised under Case I. would have applied, as the slave appears to have been treated by his master with much affection and regard but as a question of inheritance, it is declared that slavery is an impediment to inheritance, and consequently as the slave could not, neither can the slave's widow in his right, inherit his master's estate. The nature of this case very strikingly illustrates the mild character of domestic slavery in Muhammadan countries, and the privileges which it is supposed to confer.

CASE VI.

Q. "A prostitute hires the daughter of another woman for the sum of twenty rupees, and causes her to follow the same line of life as herself. Is such transaction lawful?"

It appears from the answer that a deed of sale passed between the parties, that the girl was only six years of age when she was let out to hire, and that the term agreed on was ninety-five years. The transaction is pronounced illegal on two grounds: first, on the ground that parents have no right to dispose of the persons or property of their children beyond the age of puberty, the extreme verge of which is fifteen years according to Muhammadan law; and second, on the ground of the illegality of the purpose for which the sale was made. The girl therefore, on attaining the age of puberty, would be at liberty to annul the contract.

CASE VII.

Q. "A person has a family by his wife, and also a family by one or two concubines to whom he was not married. These concubines were slave-girls, but it is not clear whether they were the property of the person in question or of another. The question is, can the issue of these concubines inherit the property of their father on his death?"

This question involves in fact two separate cases, according as the concubine is supposed to be the slave of the father or of another person. In the latter case, the children cannot inherit, first, because they were not born in wedlock, and their parentage cannot be established in that person; and, second, because their mother being a slave, they also are the slaves of their mother's owner, and their slavery is a bar to inheritance. In the former case, the condition of slavery was either legal or illegal. If legal, and if the father claimed or acknowledged the offspring of his slave as his children, then after his death they would be entitled to a portion of inheritance. If illegal, then concubinage was unlawful without marriage, the parentage cannot be established in the alleged father, and such children consequently are not heirs. It is here worthy of note, that in Case IV. the legality of that slavery is recognised which is created by a person selling himself when in distress or on account of debt; but in the present case, when a question is made respecting the right of inheritance belonging to the child of a slave-mother, the only legal slavery recognised is that which was created by capture in an infidel country.

CASE VIII.

Q. "The slave-girl of a Musalman, the right to whom he had acquired by inheritance, married the slave of another person, and both the wife and husband took up their abode in the house of the proprietor of the female slave, where she brought forth children in consequence of the matrimonial intercourse. The proprietor of the male slave superintended the marriage-ceremony and defrayed all the expenses attendant on the occasion, inclusive of the usual donations presented to the bride's mother. Under these circumstances, whether is the proprietor of the female slave or of the male slave entitled to the proprietory right in the issue of the marriage? Has the mother of the female slave any right to take pecuniary donations and to contract her daughter in marriage, she herself being the slave of the person who is the proprietor of her daughter?"

The answer is, that neither is the mother of the female slave entitled to dispose of her in marriage, nor has the master of the male slave any claim to the progeny. The consent of the master of the female slave can alone render the contract of marriage binding, and to him alone belongs the issue.

CASE IX.

Q. "1. According to the Muhammadan law, if a child is born of a female slave purchased by her proprietor, is such child the property of the mother or of her master? 2. Is it lawful to dispose of by sale, or to deposit as a pledge, any human being?"

These two questions have no necessary connection. In answer to the first, it is stated that, assuming the legality of the slavery of the mother, her children are the property of her master; and in answer to the second, that the sale or deposit in pledge of a free man is invalid and void in law.

CASE X.

Q. "A free woman having attained the age of majority, that is to say, being fifteen years old, voluntarily and by her own choice, contracts matrimony with a slave, and they live in the same house together as husband and wife for the space of a year and a half. Can such marriage of a free woman with a slave be considered a legal and valid contract?"

The answer is, that such a contract is legal and valid, if made with the consent of the slave's master, who is responsible for the bride's claim of dower. In satisfaction of this claim the slave-husband may be sold, and the offspring of such marriage are slaves and belong to the master of the husband.

CASE XI.

Q. "A woman of the Hindu persuasion resides in the house of a Musalman and becomes a convert to the faith of Muhammad. After such conversion, she takes up her abode with a Rajput, lives with him as his concubine, and has by him a daughter who is living, as are also both her parents. Under these circumstances, to which of the parents does the daughter belong? If the daughter belongs to the Rajput, is he entitled to sell her to another or not? If he is entitled to do so, can the purchaser of her dispose of her to another by sale; and if during her minority she lives with the purchaser, is she, on her attaining the age of puberty, at liberty to free herself from slavery or not? According to the Muhammadan law, what sort of slaves are fit subjects of purchase and sale?"

In answer to these questions, it is stated that, as between

the parents, the mother is entitled to the charge of the daughter until she attain the age of puberty; but that neither parent is permitted to sell such child, and that all transactions arising out of such a sale are null and void.

I have thus completed the view which I proposed to give of the actual administration of the law of slavery in British Indian courts of justice; and the cases and opinions I have adduced sufficiently establish not only the existence of two distinct systems of slavery in India under Hindu and Muhammadan law respectively, but the recognition, adoption, and enforcement of the main provisions of both systems by the British Indian government. The civilized world, and the British people in particular, expect, and have a right to expect, that the influence of the English government in India shall be employed to abolish barbarous and cruel social institutions, originating in ancient times, in false religions, and in governments incapable of appreciating, and little disposed to maintain, the rights of humanity; and the efforts made to abolish Hindu infanticide, and the successful abolition of the burning of Hindu widows with their deceased husbands, show that the obligation is not wholly unrecognised, and that the expectation has not been wholly disappointed. Strange to say, an exception is found in slavery, an institution against which British legislation and diplomacy for nearly the last forty years have been unweariedly directed, and in opposition to which the British government would be understood to hold its head more erect, to pursue its measures with stricter honesty and with more determined consistency, than all the other nations of Europe and America. The British trade in slaves has been abolished by the fiat of Parliament; the freedom of the slaves in the British West Indies has been purchased by the unexampled generosity of the British people; and all the world hears of the persevering efforts of the British government to interest other civilized nations to co-operate in extinguishing the traffic in human flesh ; and yet this very same government, at the very same moment, by its own sole authority, is wantonly giving life and activity to two different systems of slavery existing among a hundred million of Asiatics, subject to the imperial sway of the crown of Great Britain. I know that this is done by a delegated government, but it is not the less done by a British government. I know that this is done without the cognizance of the British people, but it is not the less done with the knowledge and implied sanction of the British Parliament. It is to be hoped that the British people, the British Parliament, and the British government will awake to the demands of justice and humanity in India as well as in Europe and America.

LETTER IV.

TO THOMAS FOWELL BUXTON, ESQ.

Ameliorations of the Law and Practice of Slavery under the British Government in India.

SIR,—The view which I have proposed to give of the law of slavery in India will be completed by considering the ameliorations that have been introduced by the British government of India. Although there are very strong grounds for judging that the sanction given by the British government to Hindu and Muhammadan slavery in India is wholly gratuitous, uncalled for, and illegal; yet the evils of the institution have been frequently and distinctly acknowledged, and measures have been from time to time adopted, with greater or less success, to limit the extension, to mitigate the condition, and to put an end to the abuses of slavery. The examination of these will show what has been done, and when compared with the practice of slavery to be hereafter investigated, will enable us the better to understand how much has been left undone.

The first of the measures referred to is the prohibition of the exportation of the natives of India as slaves. India was formerly a country exporting slaves, but I am not possessed of any information respecting the practice, except that which is contained in the government proclamation prohibiting it, under date 22d July, 1789. "Whereas information, the truth of which cannot be doubted, has been received by the governor-general in council, that *many natives*, and *some Europeans*, in opposition to the laws and ordinances of this country and the dictates of humanity, have been *for a long time* in the practice of purchasing or collecting natives of both sexes, children as well as adults, for the purpose of exporting them for sale as slaves in different parts of India, *or elsewhere*," &c.* It does not appear whether this traffic had a native or a European origin. The proclamation goes on to declare that those engaged in it shall be prosecuted with the utmost rigor in the supreme court, at the expense of the Company; if British-born subjects, the penalty is that they "shall be forthwith ordered to Europe;" and if not subject to the court's jurisdiction, they shall be apprehended by the magistrate of the place or district in which the offence shall have been committed, and kept in confinement, to be dealt with according to the laws of the country. The very mild penalty to be inflicted on British-born subjects convicted of such an offence deserves to be noted, consisting merely in sending them back to their native country; but this was at a period when public opinion against the slave-trade was not mature. A reward of a hundred rupees is offered for the discovery of every such offender, and fifty rupees for every person thereby delivered from slavery or illegal confinement. British commercial houses and private merchants are called upon to co-operate; commanders of vessels are to be refused an English pilot unless they declare on oath that they have no slaves on board; and native pilots are to be deprived of the privilege of piloting if they connive at this traffic. This proclamation, to which the force of an enactment was given, appears to have been adequate to the purpose.†

* Harington's Analysis, Vol. III. pp. 756—759, and 749, 750.

† Mr. Colebrooke, in 1812, referring to this measure, says,—"Many years ago, a clandestine export by sea to the French Islands was

I am not aware that there is any reason to believe that the natives of India have since been exported as slaves, unless we suppose an infringement of this law in the recent exportation of Hill Coolies from India to New South Wales, to the Mauritius, and to the British West Indies; but in this case the labor was hired, and the traffic open and in form legal, although the evils attendant on it and arising out of it were so serious as instantly to demand and to receive the interposition of public opinion and of parliamentary discussion for its suppression.

However undoubted the efficacy of this proclamation issued and enforced by the executive government of India, the state of the law on this subject does not appear to be satisfactory. Mr. Harington states, (Vol. III. p. 759,) that the substance of the proclamation was included in Section 74, Regulation 22, 1795; but in the revised edition of his Analysis, published four years afterwards in 1821, the following passage occurs, (Vol. I. p. 72, *note*):—"A proclamation, forbidding under penalties the exportation of natives of India to be sold as slaves, was issued by the governor-general in council, under date the 22d July, 1789. *But the existing regulations do not contain any specific provisions on this point.* I have therefore proposed in Section 19" (of a draught of a regulation suggested by Mr. Harington *for the guidance of the courts of judicature in cases of slavery,*) "to declare the exportation from the British territories of any person born in those territories to be disposed of or dealt with as a slave, a criminal offence, punishable on conviction in any of the criminal courts established under the British government; unless the person so exported shall have been produced before a magistrate, and registered

detected; and being immediately prohibited by proclamation, and the first subsequent instance which was discovered being prosecuted to punishment, it was entirely suppressed, and no surmise of its revival has since been entertained."

as a slave." Now, as far as appears, neither the law recommended by Mr. Harington, nor any similar law for the guidance of the Indian courts of judicature in cases of slavery, was ever enacted ; and if the statement of this high authority was correct in 1821, that the existing regulations did not then contain any specific provisions on this point, it is equally certain that they do not now contain any such provisions, and consequently that the exportation of the natives of India as slaves, although prohibited and effectually suppressed, is not illegal in virtue of any express enactment by the Indian government. There is no inconsistence between this conclusion and the previous statement by Mr. Harington, that the substance of the proclamation of 1789 was included in Regulation 22 of 1795, since that regulation appears to refer only to the province of Benares ;* and the absence of a general statutory prohibition of the exportation of the natives of India as slaves, while there is such a prohibition applicable to a single *interior* province, and while the traffic itself has been practically prevented, is a striking illustration of the laxity with which this subject has been treated by the government of India.

It may be proper to add in this place a reference to the provisions on this subject contained in the penal code prepared by the Indian law commissioners, and published by command of the governor-general of India in council in 1837. This code has not yet received the force of law, but is now under consideration with that view. It proposes to provide that "whoever kidnaps any person, intending or knowing it to be likely that the consequence of such kidnapping may be —— the slavery of that person, shall be punished with imprisonment of either description," (that is, either rigorous imprisonment or simple imprisonment,) "for a term which may extend to fourteen years, and must not be less than two years, and shall also be liable to fine." That kind

* Colebrooke's Digest of Regulations, Vol. II. p. 902.

of kidnapping to which this punishment is annexed, is thus defined:—"Whoever conveys beyond the limits of the territories of the East India Company, or takes on board of any vessel with the intention of conveying beyond the limits of the said territories, any person, without the free and intelligent consent of that person, or of some person legally authorized to consent on behalf of that person, or with such consent, but knowing that such consent has been obtained by deception or concealment as to the place of destination or the future treatment of that person, is said to kidnap that person from the territories of the East India Company." (Chapter XVIII. paras 354, 357.)

On this branch of the subject it may be confidently affirmed that the external traffic in slaves, that is, the exportation of natives of India as slaves, has entirely ceased, but that it is desirable that the law should be brought into greater conformity with this condition of things.

The second class of measures consists of those that have been adopted to prevent the importation of slaves into India. Slaves have been imported into India both by land and sea, and the provisions of the existing laws are different for these two branches of the traffic.

Mr. Colebrooke was of opinion that the importation by sea was very limited in extent. "The importation by sea," he says, "consisted of a very few African slaves, brought by Arab ships to the port of Calcutta. Having been led to make some inquiries into this traffic previous to its abolition, I had reason to be satisfied that the whole number of slaves imported was very inconsiderable; not exceeding annually a hundred of both sexes. I found cause at the same time to be convinced that the means by which slaves are procured on the eastern coast of Africa, for the Arab dealers who supply Arabia and Persia, and who used to bring the small number mentioned to this port, are not less abominable and nefarious than those practised on the west coast of Africa; consisting for the most part in the forcible seizure of the slaves, either in predatory war undertaken for the purpose, or by open robbery, often attended with the murder of the parents."* The language employed in the Resolutions of the honorable the vice-president in council, recorded on the 9th Sept., 1817, gives a somewhat different view of the extent of this traffic. "A traffic was carried on," says the vice-president in council, "in slaves, by importing them by sea from the eastern coast of Africa, from Madagascar, and from the Eastern Islands, into the islands and territories in the East Indies, subject to his Majesty or to the honorable the East India Company;" and this traffic, it is afterwards added, "*was in fact of a nature and tendency scarcely less objectionable than the trade which had been carried on between the western coast of Africa and the West India Islands.*"† To destroy this traffic, Regulation 10 of 1811 was enacted, to have effect within the territories immediately subject to the presidency of Fort William, and similar provisions were, at the suggestion of the governor-general in council, subsequently enacted for the same purpose within the territories immediately subordinate to the governments of Fort St. George and Bombay. By this regulation, the importation of slaves, whether by land or by sea, was prohibited under a penalty of imprisonment for six months, and a fine to government according to the circumstances of the offender, not exceeding the sum of two hundred rupees; commutable, if not duly discharged, to imprisonment for the further period of six months, on the expiration of the former part of the sentence. Persons imported as slaves were to be discharged or sent back, and captains of private ships, previously to landing their cargoes, were to be required to execute a penalty-bond of five thousand rupees not to sell slaves. In so far as this regulation

* Harington's Analysis, Vol. III. pp. 748, 749.

† Harington's Analysis, Vol. III. p. 755.

provides for the punishment of the importation of slaves by sea, it was superseded by the statute 51 George III. chap. 23, which was expressly extended to India. By the first section of this statute it is enacted "that if any subject or subjects of his Majesty, or if any person or persons residing or being within this United Kingdom, or in any of the islands, colonies, dominions, forts, settlements, factories or territories now or hereafter belonging thereto, or being in his Majesty's occupation or possession, or under the government of the United Company of merchants trading to the East Indies, shall from and after the first day of June next," (viz. 1811, but extended to the 1st January, 1812, for places to the east of the Cape of Good Hope,) "by him or themselves, or by his or their factors or agents, or otherwise howsoever, carry away, or remove, or aid or assist in the carrying away or removing as a slave or slaves, or for the purpose of being sold, transferred, used, or dealt with as a slave or slaves, any person or persons whatsoever from any part of Africa, or from any other country, territory, or place whatsoever, either immediately or by transhipment at sea, or otherwise, directly or indirectly; or shall import, or bring, or aid or assist in the importing or bringing into any island, colony, country, territory, or place whatsoever, any such person or persons as aforesaid, for the purpose aforesaid —— then, and in every such case, the person or persons so offending, and their counsellors, aiders, and abettors, shall be and are hereby declared to be felons, and shall be transported beyond seas for a term not exceeding fourteen years, or shall be confined and kept to hard labor for a term not exceeding five years nor less than three years, at the discretion of the court before whom such offender or offenders shall be tried and convicted." This is the law now in force under the Bengal presidency rendering the importation of slaves by sea felony. In the fourth section of this act, the removal of a person already a slave from one part of the West Indies to another is allowed; but this exception does not apply to the East Indies, and consequently an owner of slaves embarking at one port of British India for another on the Indian continent, or proceeding from one island to another in the Eastern Archipelago, attended by a domestic slave, subjects himself to the penalty of felony. It must be acknowledged that this is a severe provision so long as slavery itself is continued in India; and I am not aware that the exception already provided in regard to the West Indies has been subsequently extended to India, or that there has been any explanatory enactment of the provisions of the statute as meant to have operation in India and the Eastern seas. It has probably been felt that any relaxation would open the door to abuse, or give countenance to existing abuses.

It has already been mentioned, in citing the opinion of Mr. Colebrooke on the extent to which the importation of slaves by sea was carried, that Arab dealers were chiefly engaged in this traffic, for the supply not only of India, but of Persia and Arabia also; and accordingly, advantage was very laudably taken by the East India Company's government on the occasion of concluding a Treaty with the Arab Tribes of the Persian Gulf, dated the 8th of January, 1820, to introduce an article (article IX.) making the slave-trade piracy, and pledging the Arabs not to engage in it. The article runs thus:—"The carrying off of slaves, men, women, or children, from the coasts of Africa or elsewhere, and the transporting them in vessels, is plunder and piracy, and the friendly Arabs shall do nothing of this nature." It is not to be supposed that such a stipulation, unaccompanied by any sanction, and opposed to all the habits and interests of these Arab tribes, will be very rigidly observed; but the formal and authoritative declaration of a sound principle cannot be wholly valueless, were it to serve no other purpose than as a foundation on which hereafter to erect some more efficient prohibition of the trade.*

I find it also stated in your recent work on the African Slave-trade, p. 38, that "in 1822, a treaty was concluded by Captain Moresby, R. N., on behalf of the British government, with the Imaum (of Muskat,) by which the slave-trade with Christian countries was declared abolished forever throughout his dominions and dependencies; but this arrangement it must be remembered does not in any way touch upon the slave-trade carried on by the Imaum's subjects with those of their own faith."

When Regulation 10 of 1811 was enacted, the inland traffic in slaves from Nepaul was chiefly contemplated. "The importation by land," says Mr. Colebrooke, "was principally from the territories of Nepaul, whence a regular traffic in slaves appears to have been carried on; and occasionally from the western and middle parts of India, whenever a local scarcity of provisions gave a temporary impulse to a trade which was otherwise in general languid. Although the subject was brought under the notice of this (the British Indian) government by representations from the local authorities in the Nepaul provinces, it is understood that the traffic owed its existence to the oppressive administration of those very authorities, which drove the wretched inhabitants of those provinces to the sad resource of selling their children or themselves into slavery, when all other means of meeting the insatiable exactions of their Nepaulese rulers were exhausted. It was however stated that under cover of a trade which originated in this cause, kidnapping was practised; and at all events, it was highly expedient to prohibit the importation altogether, whether it gave occasion to the commission of this offence, or only served to crown the last act of extortion of Nepaulese governors from their unhappy subjects."† Regulation 10 of 1811, the provisions

* See Papers regarding the Administration of the Marquis of Hastings in India, Vol. II. pp. cxx, cxxi.

† Harington's Analysis, Vol. III. p. 749.

of which have been already summarily stated, was accordingly enacted; and as respects the importation of slaves *by land*, this regulation is not deemed by the Indian government to have been superseded by the subsequent enactment of the statute 51st George III. chap. 23. It is indeed admitted by the vice-president in council in the resolutions of 9th Sept. 1817, "that some of the terms used in the preamble" of that statute "are of a very comprehensive nature; such indeed as on the first view might lead to the inference that the bringing of slaves by land into the territories of the honorable Company, or the removal of them by land from those territories, were acts included within the penalties of the statute in question." But that such was not the intention of the imperial legislature is attempted to be shown by the following considerations. "Had the provisions of the act been intended to apply to the importation or removal of slaves by land in the honorable Company's territories on the continent of India, it cannot be supposed that the legislature would have confined the operation of the fourth section of that act exclusively to the West Indies; that it would have subjected to the punishment of transportation whole nations, amongst whom domestic slavery had immemorially existed under the sanction of laws recognised by Parliament, and this without any reference to those established laws and usages, and without repealing the acts of Parliament by which the observance of them is guaranteed to the natives; that it would, in short, have subjected the Hindu and Muhammadan inhabitants of the British territories in the East Indies to the severe punishment of transportation for acts which the fourth section of the statute renders legal in the West Indies. But if there could exist any reasonable doubt with regard to the construction of the act which this government entertains upon a general consideration of its provisions taken in connection with each other, and with all the former acts and resolutions referred to in it; it would be difficult to reconcile any other construction of the act with the letter of the sixth clause of the act. The admiralty jurisdiction vested in his Majesty's courts of justice at the several presidencies in India would enable those courts to take cognizance of all offences relating to the importation or removal of slaves by sea contrary to the act; but offences against the act which may not be cognizable by the court of admiralty can only be tried in England, in the mode pointed out by the sixth clause of the 51st George III. chap. 23. If therefore this act be construed to extend to the removal or importation of slaves by land in the territories subject to the East India Company, every native carrying or removing a slave from one part of these territories to another is liable to be sent to England, to be tried for felony in the mode prescribed by certain acts of Henry the VIII. and William the III. for the suppression of piracy. It is unnecessary to enlarge further on the difficulties which must arise from any such construction of the act."*

On this reasoning it may be remarked, that the language of the act is, and is admitted to be, clear and indisputable; that the objections to the literal construction and application of the law have reference solely to the convenience of owners of slaves who may violate the law, and in no degree to the rights of those whom the law was and is designed to protect; that when the honorable the vice-president in council asserts that domestic slavery has immemorially existed among the people of India, under the sanction of laws *recognised by Parliament*, his excellency has not specified any act or acts of Parliament recognising the Hindu and Muhammadan laws of slavery, although undoubtedly Parliament has recognised the Hindu and Muhammadan laws of succession, inheritance, marriage, and caste, and all religious usages and institutions, which have been errone-

* Harington's Analysis, Vol. III. pp. 754—756.

ously interpreted to embrace the laws of slavery; that when his excellency further alleges that the strict construction and enforcement of the act 51st George III., chapter 23, would subject whole nations to the punishment of transportation, his excellency ludicrously exaggerates, since there are not to be found in India whole nations composed of slave-owners, and that of the individuals who are such, few would have occasion to remove with their slaves from province to province, or from country to country, and fewer still, when the law was known, would choose by so doing to subject themselves to the penalties of felony; that the only inconvenience to which the strict letter of the law would subject those slave-owners who are desirous of obeying the law, would be to oblige them to travel, not with slaves, but with hired servants, in a country where labor is cheap and abundant; and that the strict enforcement of the law, by preventing the removal of slaves from place to place and from country to country, would have afforded increased facilities for the detection of imported slaves, and would at the same time have lessened the value of slave-labor, and thereby conduced to the extinction of slavery. With regard to the alleged necessity under the act of sending to England for trial natives importing or exporting slaves by land, it does not appear why this offence should not be tried by the king's courts in India as well as the offence of importing and exporting slaves by sea. Mr. Campbell, in his letter to the commissioners for the affairs of India, expresses the opinion that the act even as regards the latter offence is everywhere in the Madras territory, except at the presidency, inoperative for want of a jurisdiction by the local provincial courts to enforce its penalties concurrent with that possessed by the supreme court at Madras. Without however dwelling on these views, it is sufficient to my present purpose to state that the government of India deliberately and avowedly assumed the power of setting aside the 51st George III. chapter 23, in as far as respects the bringing of slaves by land into the territories of the East India Company, or the removal of them by land from those territories, limiting its penalties to the importation and exportation of slaves by sea, and applying the penalties of Regulation 10 of 1811 to the importation and exportation of slaves by land. The effect of this would appear to be, that the importation or exportation of slaves by sea is held by the Bengal government of the East India Company to be punishable under the act of the Imperial Parliament as felony, by transportation for fourteen years, or by confinement and hard labor for a period extending from three to five years; that the importation of slaves by land is held by that government to be punishable, under its own regulation, by six months' imprisonment and a fine not exceeding 200 rupees; and that the exportation of slaves by land is not punishable by any legislative enactment whatsoever.

With regard to Regulation 10 of 1811, which is held to be in force against the importation of slaves by land, it has been made a question whether the intent of the enactment was to prohibit the importation of slaves by land altogether, or to prohibit their importation only for the purpose of being sold, given away, or otherwise disposed of. The supreme court of criminal judicature under the East India Company's government in Bengal have construed the regulation in the latter sense; but this construction has been overruled by the decision of the government of India, "that the intent of the enactment was to prohibit the importation of slaves altogether; and not merely the importation of slaves for the purpose of being sold, given away, or otherwise disposed of."* It follows that any person bringing slaves into the territories of the East India Company, although merely as domestic attendants, is subject to the penalties of the regula-

* Harington's Analysis, Vol. III. p. 761.

tion,—a very remarkable provision in a country where slavery is legal, but justified by the abuse to which a contrary interpretation of the law would be subject.

In connection with the subject of the external traffic, it may be mentioned that the East India Company's government at the close of the Nepaul war in 1815, on the occasion of re-instating the Raja of Gurwal in Northern Hindostan in the possession of that province, of which he had been deprived by the Nepaulese, expressly stipulated that he should govern his subjects with lenity and justice, promote agriculture and commerce, *and abolish the traffic in slaves.** Such a stipulation establishes the existence at that time of such a traffic, and evinces the desire of the Indian government to put a stop to it.

Another class of the measures to which I have referred, consists of those by which ameliorations have been introduced into the letter and spirit of the law of slavery, as administered in British Indian courts of justice.

A very important amelioration has been introduced into the letter of the Muhammadan law of slavery, affording increased protection to the life of the slave. I have already had occasion to state that "according to Muhammadan law, if a man kill the slave of another, capital punishment, or, in the language of that law, retaliation of death, is incurred; but that retaliation of death in cases of murder being considered with respect to slaves the right of their masters, they are at liberty to remit the claim and forgive the offender, or to compound with the consent of the murderer for a compensation. Still farther, if a master murder his own slave, he is not liable to retaliation of death. The demand of retaliation is further barred if the person murdered be the joint slave of the murderer and others; the right failing in proportion to the murderer's share, and retaliation of death not admitting of being inflicted in part only. The

* See Hamilton's Gazetteer, Vol. I. p. 626.

same principle is applicable if the person killed be a slave appropriated by the owner to the public service, that is, capital punishment is not incurred. It must be evident that this makes the life of the slave the sport of caprice and passion without any protection from the law; and accordingly the regulations of the East India Company have enacted that in those cases in which a convicted murderer would not be liable under the Muhammadan law to suffer death by retaliation solely on the ground of the murdered person having been the slave of the murderer, or of any other person, or a slave appropriated for the service of the public, the murderer shall be sentenced to suffer death." It follows that the murderer of a slave is no longer permitted to receive a free pardon from the slave's master, nor to offer him a pecuniary compensation for the life of his slave, but must suffer the consequences of his own act according to the degree of criminality which may be determined to belong to it, just as if the slave had been a free person. In like manner if a master take the life of his own slave, he will be equally held to the consequences of his own act, without distinction of person or condition. It is deeply to be regretted that a legal sanction should ever have been given to the native systems of slavery, but while slavery continues to be legal the humanity and justice of such a provision cannot be too highly estimated. It has the obvious tendency to check that abuse of power which is incident to the relation between master and slave even in its mildest form, and to diffuse through the community a higher appreciation of human life even in its most degraded condition. It must however be observed that it is only the Muhammadan law of slavery that has been thus modified, and that the Hindu law of slavery which subjects the master, whatever may be the offence he has committed on his slave, to no other punishment than pecuniary fine, has been left unaltered. The reason no doubt is, that the Muhammadan is the only criminal code recognised by the British government of India, and that an offence committed by a Hindu master against the life of his slave would be punished under the amendment of that law which has been just explained, and not under the original law of Hindu slavery, which recognises only pecuniary fine for such an offence. But if an important provision of the Hindu law of slavery may thus be set aside without any express enactment to that effect, what becomes of the general recognition of the Hindu law of slavery by the Sudder Dewany Adawlut, confirmed by the government of India in 1798? We have thus the highest judicial and executive authorities in India declaring that the Hindu law of slavery, without any exception or limitation, is to be upheld; and on the other hand there can be no doubt that if a Hindu master were wilfully to take the life of his slave, the punishment in such case provided by Hindu law would be deemed insufficient, and, however illegally, the penalty attached to such a crime by the amendment of the Muhammadan criminal code would be inflicted—a state of things, I submit, which shows the little consideration given to the law of slavery in India and the necessity of subjecting it to a thorough revision.

The preceding is the only amelioration of the state of slavery under the Bengal presidency arising out of a modification of the letter of the law relating to it, but other ameliorations have been introduced by the milder and more protective spirit in which the law has been administered. It was shown before, that the judicial regulations of 1772, framed and enacted by the government of Warren Hastings, provided not only for the capital punishment of gang-robbers, but also for the perpetual slavery of their wives and children. This was justly characterized by the Marquis Cornwallis as "a new and very severe provision," and it disappeared in the judicial code of 1793, of which that nobleman was the principal author. Still further, the practice appears to have existed both under the native and British governments of selling offenders against the law into slavery as a mode of punishment, or as a means of lessening the expense of criminal justice. Thus we find Warren Hastings, in 1773, recommending that every convicted felon and murderer not condemned to death by the sentence of the court, and every criminal who had been already sentenced either to work during life upon the roads or to suffer perpetual imprisonment, should "be sold for slaves or transported as such." Thus also Mr. Chaplin, in his Report on the Dekhan, (p. 150, para. 283,) states that under the preceding Mahratta government "a woman of Mahratta caste committing adultery or fornication was sometimes condemned to slavery." And Hamilton (Vol. II. p. 627) states that in the provinces of Tavoy and Tenasserim, acquired from the Burmese in 1824, a great source of slavery under the Burmese government was "the sale of government criminals." He adds, that this practice was immediately abolished by the British in those provinces; and although I have no express authority to justify me in affirming its discontinuance elsewhere, yet I have no doubt that it has ceased altogether, and that no court of justice in British India would sentence a criminal to slavery as the legal punishment of his crime.

In illustration of the more protective spirit in which the law of slavery is administered under the British government than it would have been under the native government, two circumstances may be mentioned. The first regards the practice of making eunuchs of young slaves—an inhuman practice, prevalent in all Muhammadan countries, and even now more prevalent in India than is generally supposed. The Muhammadan law does not give to a master this power over the person of his slave, but the practice is so conformable to Muhammadan manners, and so necessary to the protection of the licentious pleasures of the great from invasion, that probably no Muhammadan judge would ever afford the slave any redress against his master, if the improbable case occurred of a slave complaining against his master for such an offence. The Nizamut Adawlut, or supreme court of criminal judicature under the Bengal presidency, has expressly declared that the practice is criminal and punishable by the Muhammadan law, and that its provisions will be enforced. The second circumstance regards the exercise of the power of manumission. The expounders of Muhammadan law expressly deny to the ruling power, whatever may be the crime of the master against his slaves, any authority to grant them emancipation, unless the slavery were originally illegal. But the court have assumed this power and acted upon it, having in one instance made the liberation of a female slave who had been cruelly treated by her mistress, part of the sentence against the latter.*

These ameliorations in the letter of the law and in the spirit of its administration, to whatever extent the state of society will permit them to operate, must contribute to restrain the hand of the master and to lighten the burthens of the slave.

The preceding remarks refer almost exclusively to the law of slavery and to the improvements that have been made in its letter and spirit under the Bengal presidency, the largest and most important of the three Indian governments. Respecting the state of the law under the two other presidencies, those of Madras and Bombay, for want of the necessary authorities to refer to, my information is less precise and complete. The recognition of the Hindu and Muhammadan laws of slavery is common to all the Indian presidencies, and the following are the notices that I have been able to collect respecting the amendments or modifications

* Harington's Analysis, Vol. III. pp. 761, 763, *notes*.

of those laws that have been introduced under the two subordinate presidencies.

Under the Madras government a regulation was passed in 1812, (Regulation II. of 1812,) one of the clauses of which prohibited the exportation of slaves from the province of Malabar. But after the enactment of this regulation, a reference was made to the advocate-general of Madras for his legal opinion, and the result was the formal repeal of that enactment, on the just ground that the act of Parliament of the 51st George III. chap. 23, against the slave-trade, sufficiently prohibits this traffic by sea, and that its more severe penalties supersede those previously established by the local Indian legislature. Subsequently, this reasoning does not appear to have been deemed satisfactory, for in 1826 the act 51st George III., chap. 23, was enacted into a regulation (II. of 1826) by the government of Fort St. George, and according to the meaning and definition given of that law in the regulation in question, the offence prohibited is declared to be that "of carrying or removing from any country or place whatsoever any person or persons as a slave or slaves, or for the purpose of being sold or dealt with as a slave or slaves;" and "which applies," according to the opinion of the advocate-general at Madras, "in all its consequences and penalties to all persons residing within the king's or Company's territories, including therefore the native subjects of the government." With reference to this Indian re-enactment of an act of Parliament, it may be asked, if the act of Parliament was held to be in force under the Madras presidency before 1826, what was the use of the regulation of that date? If the act of Parliament was not held to be in force until that date, and was then held to be in force only in virtue of that regulation, what becomes of the supreme authority of Parliament? With regard to the practical effect of these enactments and re-enactments, I regret to add that it is the opinion of Mr. Campbell that the slave-act, by which he designates 51st George III. chap. 23, "as it now stands, must remain a dead letter everywhere in the Madras territory, except at the presidency, until Parliament give power to the tribunals in the provinces to enforce its penalties."

An improvement that has been introduced into the law of slavery under the Madras government respects the capacity of slaves to give evidence in courts of justice. In a gross and notorious case of 76 slaves and free-born children who had been kidnapped, the depositions and evidence of the individuals themselves were objected to by the provincial court of circuit in 1812, in the absence of other evidence, of the owners of the bondsmen, and of the parents and relations of the free-born children; and the consequence was that the accused were suffered to go unpunished. This was done although there were instances of persons who had been tried and convicted of murder before the judges of the provincial court upon the complaint and testimony of slaves, and yet in the case referred to, the injured parties were held to be disqualified, by their united and consistent testimony, to prove the cruelty and oppression to which they had been subjected. To remove all doubts on this subject, and to abolish those distinctions in the Muhammadan law which excepted the evidence of slaves, whether as slaves, or because not of the Muhammadan religion, or because they were prosecutors, or stood in the situation of prosecutors from having been injured by their master or the person accused, or because they were women, or on account of any other personal distinction, Regulation VII. of 1829 was enacted by the Madras government, superseding all such distinctions, and giving slaves the right to prosecute and give evidence the same as free-born persons. Gentlemen of extensive and long-continued practical experience have declared that their evidence is to be depended on fully as much as that of free-born persons; and the admission of their evidence is another and most important check against cruelty and injustice, especially when combined with the provision which has been made under the Madras as well as the Bengal presidency, making the master amenable to punishment if he put his slave to death without a cause.*

Another evil existing in connection with the state of slavery in the Madras territories, and created by the operation of the British government, has been at least partially and ostensibly corrected, and it is mentioned here because I am desirous of giving the East India Company's government credit for all that it merely professes to do. On the Malabar coast, in the Balaghat districts, and in the western parts of the table-land of Mysore, predial slaves are held precisely under the same tenures and terms as the land itself, or rather were so held before the Company's government. They were attached to the land and never sold apart from it, and hence that fondness for their natal soil for which they are stated to be remarkable. The Company's government appears to have introduced the practice of disposing of the slaves separate from the soil, the land of their birth; private proprietors readily adopted it; and thus families are frequently broken up, husbands separated from wives, parents from children, and brothers from sisters. The occasions on which this innovation was introduced under the name and authority of the government, were in execution of judicial decrees and in satisfaction of revenue arrears. If in any litigated case a decree of court was pronounced, or if government had a claim for revenue against a slave-owner, his slaves were sold, according to the necessities of their master, in satisfaction of such claims. Some of the more humane and enlightened civil servants of the Company, and one in particular, Mr. Baber, refused to be

* Report from Select Committee, Appendix, p. 560.

made the instrument of such acts, and remonstrated against them, and in consequence orders were issued by the Madras Board of Revenue, under date the 13th May, 1819, prohibiting the sale of slaves in future on account of arrears of revenue in Malabar. The fact of such orders having been issued is creditable to the good intentions of the Board from which they emanated. But it is to be observed that these orders, proceeding from a Board of Revenue, do not and cannot embrace the case of slaves sold or liable to be sold in satisfaction of judicial decrees; that the fact of their having been issued is so little known, that Mr. Baber, though living in Malabar to the end of 1828, never heard of it, until he found it stated in a parliamentary paper laid before Parliament 12th March, 1828; and that there are good grounds for believing that the orders, limited to the single object of prohibiting the sale of slaves for arrears of revenue, are practically neglected. It is easier to introduce than to eradicate a vicious innovation which the grasping and exacting spirit of the government tends to uphold, even against its own express orders.*

With regard to ameliorations of slave-law under the Bombay presidency, my information is still more limited; but I find it stated in Mr. A. D. Campbell's answers to questions on slavery in the East Indies, circulated by the commissioners for the affairs of India, that the Bombay code contains enactments which provide that infants shall not be separated from the mother until a certain age, and which also it is believed prohibit the separation of the wife from her husband.†

In the southern Mahratta country, which is under the government of the Bombay presidency, the sale of slaves

* Report from Select Committee, Appendix, p. 564.

† See Appendix to Report from Select Committee on the Affairs of the East India Company, p. 575, ordered by the House of Commons to be printed 16th August, 1832.

was expressly prohibited by the governor-general in council under date the 18th Dec., 1819, and this, says Mr. Baber in opposition to the opinions of two of the most able and humane men India has ever produced, the Honorable Mr. Elphinstone and Mr. Chaplin. The effect of this measure or the grounds on which it was adopted in opposition to such weighty authorities, I have not been able to ascertain; but the silence that appears to have been maintained on the subject implies that this innovation on established customs in favor of the claims of humanity has not been attended with any other than salutary and peaceful results.*

It may be proper to notice in this place that the most opposite doctrines are advanced by high authorities in the Bengal and Bombay presidencies, respecting the legal effect produced by the 51st George III., chap. 23, on the rights of actual slaves in British India. On this point the vice-president in council of Bengal observes, "that none of the provisions of the acts of Parliament passed for the abolition of the slave-trade in any manner affect or profess to affect the relation between master and slave wherever that relation may exist by law. Whatever therefore was the law according to the Muhammadan and Hindu codes (for those over whom they extend) on the subject of domestic slavery before the passing of the act of the 51st George III. chap. 23, continues to be the law still; more especially as those codes have been distinctly recognised and ordered to be observed by Parliament. At the same time it is not credible that any intention existed to abrogate those codes without reference to the established laws and usages of this country, and without repealing the acts of Parliament by which the observance of them is guaranteed to the natives. The native subjects of the British government residing in the territories subordinate to the several presidencies, have in

* Report from Select Committee, Appendix, p. 565.

fact the same authority over their slaves and the same property in them that they would have had if the act in question had never been passed; and the several zillah and provincial courts are bound to receive and determine all questions of that nature which are respectively cognizable by them under the existing regulations." Another point on which the vice-president in council of Bengal has pronounced a decision, relates to the conduct which should be observed on the occasion of applications being made by the subjects or governments of neighboring states, with which the Indian government is in amity, for the restoration of slaves who have taken refuge within the Company's territories. On this point it is remarked by the Bengal government, "that the construction which has been uniformly given by the supreme government to the act of the 51st George III. chap. 23, viz., that it was only intended to apply to the importation or removal of slaves by sea, would not involve any alteration in the course of proceedings hitherto adopted in similar cases. A slave by entering the Company's territories does not become free; nor can he who was lawfully a slave emancipate himself by running away from one country where slavery is lawful to another where it is equally lawful. The property in the slave still continues in the master; and the master has the same right to have it restored to him that any native subject of our territories could have, supposing that right to be established in the mode prescribed by the local laws and regulations."

Such is the doctrine and practice of the Bengal government in the interpretation and application of this important act. Contrast with this the view given of the effect of the same statute by the advocate-general of Bombay. After quoting the words of the act, he says:—"These words certainly do not abolish slavery, for West India slavery is recognised in the same act, but they appear to me peremptorily to interdict all interference on our part as to the restoration of slaves to their masters; for I cannot see how such interference could be construed otherwise than as aiding and assisting in the carrying away the person so restored, to be used or dealt with as a slave."—"On the same principle, I think, they impose a duty on the magistrate of liberating slaves who complain of being forcibly kept in their master's service. The slave who liberates himself cannot be restored to his master without danger of felony; and I think he might prosecute any man on the statute who assisted his master to retake him for the purpose of being used as a slave."

I am content at present to exhibit, without attempting to reconcile, these conflicting opinions; but with reference to the assertion of the Bengal government, that the Muhammadan and Hindu codes, *including the law on the subject of domestic slavery*, "have been distinctly recognised and ordered to be observed by Parliament," and that the observance of the established laws and usages of the country *including slavery*, "is guaranteed to the natives," I must repeat that I have found no such parliamentary recognition order, or guarantee. As far as I have been able to ascertain, the only foundation for this allegation is contained in the statute 21st George III. chap. 70, which reserves the laws and usages of the native inhabitants of Calcutta in cases of "inheritance and succession to lands, rents, and goods, and all matters of contract and dealing between party and party, as well as the rights and authorities of fathers and masters of families;" in the judicial plan of 1772 for the provinces, which provides "that in all suits regarding inheritance, marriage, caste, and other religious usages or institutions, the laws of the Koran with respect to Muhammadans, and those of the Shaster with respect to Gentoos, shall be invariably adhered to;" and in the code of 1793, to the effect that "in suits regarding succession, inheritance, marriage, and caste, and all religious usages and institutions, the Muhammadan laws with respect to Muhammadans, and the Hindu laws with regard to Hindus, are to be considered the general rules by which the judges are to form their decisions"—*in all which slavery is not recognised, ordered to be observed, guarantied, nor even so much as mentioned.*

The only acts of Parliament in which I find express mention made of slavery and the slave-trade in the East Indies, are the felony act of 1811, just referred to, and the charter act of 1833, which may be cited as the concluding illustrations of the ameliorations introduced into the law and practice relating to slavery under the British government in India. The former prohibits the subjects of the Crown, "under the government of the United Company of merchants trading to the East Indies," from engaging directly or indirectly in the import or export slave-trade, under the penalties of felony. The latter directs means to be taken to mitigate the state of slavery, to ameliorate the condition of slaves, and to extinguish slavery throughout British India. The charter act of 1833 thus contains a distinct recognition of slavery in India, but it is not, except indirectly and by implication, an authorization of slavery, and it is solely and avowedly a recognition of it for the purpose of enjoining on the Indian government the mitigation and ultimate removal of its evils.

Such, as far as my information extends, are the modifications that have been introduced into the native systems of slavery by the British government of India. They are not all that have been proposed for its adoption. Since the establishment of the British power in India, there have been found from time to time among the servants of the East India Company able and enlightened men, a Richardson, a Harington, and a Leycester in Bengal, a Baber and a Campbell in Madras, who, penetrating below the mere surface of native society, have recognised the existence of slavery, unknown to many of their countrymen resident in India, both official and unofficial, and have devised wise and beneficent measures to remedy its evils, substantially denied by many others. They have had to contend sometimes against the opposition of their less enlightened fellow-servants, always against the apathy and ignorance of a selfish and ill-informed government and of a distant and inefficient controlling power, and almost all that they have said, and written, and done, has fallen neglected and unimproved. The views they adopted, the plans they proposed, will hereafter come under consideration; but in the mean time and in this place, although proceeding from functionaries acting under the East India Company's authority, the measures they proposed to mitigate the evils of slavery, and to lead to its extinction, can only be spoken of as ameliorations and improvements which the East India Company's government has neglected, or rejected, and wholly discouraged and discountenanced.

How strange and anomalous is that state of the law of which we have now taken an imperfect survey! First, we see the British government, which has placed itself at the head of a crusade against slavery in Europe, Africa, and America, blindly permitting a delegated government to legalize it amongst a hundred millions of British subjects in Asia. Next we see that delegated government legalizing, not one system, but two distinct systems of slavery; calling one of them out of a state of illegality which had lasted seven or eight hundred years, into a state of practical and effective legality; and legalizing both of these systems of slavery, not by a formal, well-considered, and carefully framed enactment, which would have been of course submitted for the approbation or disapprobation of the Imperial Parliament, but thus depriving hundreds of thousands of its native subjects of their personal liberty, and consigning them and their posterity to slavery, by a side-wind, by a mere interpretation, and, as I contend, by a gross misinterpretation of a rule which gives Hindus and Muhammadans the benefit of their own laws in all suits regarding succession, inheritance, marriage, and caste, and all religious usages and institutions, but which makes not the slightest mention of slavery. Next, we see two branches of this delegated government, at Madras and Bombay, professing to give full effect in all its provisions to the act of Parliament which makes the slave-trade felony, and the legal adviser of the latter government even holding that it commands the liberation of discontented slaves, and prohibits the restoration of fugitive slaves; while another branch of this delegated government, in Bengal, assumes the power, by its own sole authority, to set aside one half of the same act, that which relates to the importation and exportation of slaves by land into the East India Company's territories, in place of which it applies another enactment, with different penalties of its own, and recognises the absolute and unconditional obligation of restoring runaway slaves, not only to their masters, being British subjects, but even to the governments and subjects of foreign states. Next, we see, as an effect of these proceedings, that while under the Madras government the importation or exportation of slaves by land or sea is punishable as felony; under the Bengal government, the importation and exportation of slaves by sea only is punishable as felony, the importation of slaves by land is punishable as a misdemeanor, and for the exportation of slaves by land no legal punishment whatsoever has been provided. Lastly, while the Madras government continues to permit the sale of slaves by its own officers, at least in satisfaction of judicial decrees, and generally by private slave-owners, and while the Bengal government recognises all transfers of slaves by sale, gift, or succession in the oldest provinces subject to British sway, the provinces most familiar with the spirit and practice of the British government, and in which a prohibition of the traffic in human flesh might have been enacted with the least danger to the public order and tranquillity, and the least injury to individual rights; we see the latter government in the Southern Mahratta country, a new acquisition, where the British rule was strange, where native customs and usages were little known, where the danger and injury were likely to be the greatest, suddenly, totally, and absolutely prohibit the sale of slaves—slaves hitherto deemed "a marketable commodity," and the sale of them "an established custom"—and this done, as far as appears, without murmur or objection on the part of the people, without the slightest effervescence of public feeling. If slavery is to continue in India, it must surely be admitted that the state of the law relating to it which I have exhibited, abounding in inconsistencies and contradictions, demands investigation, revision, and amendment.

LETTER V.

TO THOMAS FOWELL BUXTON, ESQ.

Number of Slaves in British India.

SIR,—In prosecuting the design to consider the whole subject of slavery in India, I now propose to inquire into the custom and practice of slavery, as distinguished from the law relating to it. It is scarcely requisite to remark that the law is not necessarily an exact transcript of the existing state of slavery; that the law may be more rigid than the practice, or the practice harsher than the law; that the letter and spirit of the law may be strictly enforced, or that in connection with slavery usages may exist inconsistent with the law; and that the law may be administered with a proper regard to the protection of the slave from oppression, or with a blamable disregard of his rights. It will be my endeavor to supply the means of pronouncing a judgment on these points.

The first information which it is desirable to obtain in connection with the existing state of slavery is the extent to which slavery exists, the number of slaves to be found in British India. On this point the information within our reach is very imperfect and unsatisfactory. There has been no census of the whole population of British India, and consequently none of the slave-population. There is no registry of slaves. There are no protectors of slaves. There are no taxes on slave-property. There is not, as in the United States, any *quasi* representation of slaves. The only means of forming an estimate of the probable number of slaves is by collecting the separate facts that have been noted by different observers and writers, and endeavoring to deduce from the whole an approximation to the truth. This is accordingly what I shall attempt to do. The authorities I shall cite will include a reference to other circumstances connected with slavery than the number of slaves, but it is to lead to some just view of the extent to which slavery exists that they are now adduced.

Under the Bengal presidency and within the limits of Bengal proper, I find reference made to the existence of slavery in six different districts, all of them included in the eastern division of Bengal, viz., Dacca, Backergunge, Silhet, Rungpoor, Dinajpoor, and Purneah. The following details respecting slavery in these districts are derived from Hamilton's East India Gazetteer, second edition, London, 1828, dedicated to the chairman, deputy chairman, and court of directors of the East India Company,—a work of unquestioned authority, the materials from which it was composed consisting not only of printed documents generally accessible to the public, but also of manuscript records deposited at the India Board, the latter being in fact the official records of the East India Company's Indian governments, transmitted to England for the information and approval of the home-authorities.

DACCA JELALPOOR.—"In 1801, the total population" of this district "was computed at 938,712 inhabitants," (the population is stated at 1,140,000, Vol. I. p. 190,) "one half Hindu and the other half Muhammadan. A portion of this population are slaves, and the custom of disposing of persons already in a state of slavery is *common* throughout the country. On these occasions regular deeds of sale are executed, some of which are registered in the court of justice; and when an estate to which slaves are attached is sold privately, the slaves are commonly sold at the same time, although a separate deed of sale is always executed."*

BACKERGUNGE AND SILHET.—In 1801, Backergunge was estimated to contain 926,000, and Silhet 500,000 inhabi tants. In Silhet, "during the Moghul dynasty, and *even at a less distant period*, children used to be purchased as an article of commerce and resold at Dacca and elsewhere." "During the Moghul government this district (Silhet) furnished a considerable number of slaves and (as stated by Abulfazel) eunuchs for the royal seraglio. The practice of inveigling away its free natives for the purpose of selling them at Dacca, Patna, Calcutta, and Moorshedabad, *still continues*, although, from the vigilance of the British authorities, the attempt is rarely successful. An authorized traffic in slaves has existed here from time immemorial; and one of the magistrates estimated this class at one sixth of the whole population," (that is, upwards of 80,000,) "progressively increasing by domestic propagation. The transfer of slaves takes place both with and without the consent of the slaves, but in the latter predicament only the mildest treatment can secure the purchaser any benefit from his acquisition. Occasionally the poorer descriptions of free inhabitants sell themselves when in extreme distress, and a few persons, principally slaves, are inveigled away by bazeegurs" (tumblers) "and wandering fakeers," (religious mendicants.) "Women also of the poorer classes, both here and in the Backergunge district, when left widows, sell their children to procure food. Some have been hereditary slaves for several generations, and are sold along with the estate on which they reside; others are imported from Cachar, Gentiah, and other territories beyond the limits of British jurisdiction."†

* Hamilton, Vol. I. p. 475. † Hamilton, Vol. II. pp. 553, 554.

RUNGPOOR.—In 1809, after a laborious investigation, the population of this district was estimated at 2,735,000. "Among the domestics are both male and female slaves, especially towards Assam, and everywhere along the northern frontier. The people of Assam sell many slaves, and those of Cooch Behar are not unwilling to carry on the same trade. Rungpoor being a section of Camroop, (the Hindu region of sensual love,) public prostitution is so common that in 1809 twelve hundred houses were occupied by females of that profession, which has assumed the organization of a regular society, with a priesthood adapted to their manner of life. In 295 of these houses, there were found to be 460 females, between the ages of twelve and twenty-five years; 218 advanced in life, who acted as servants and superintendents; and the community also contained thirty-nine old men, thirty-five youths, and fourteen boys, all born of the sisterhood. These prostitutes, although mostly born of Muhammadan parents, affect Hindu manners, on which account they abstain from all impure food, and before the age of puberty undergo the ceremony of marriage with a plantain tree. In this district, in 1809, there were seventy-eight sets of female dancers and singers, all prostitutes. Here they are called Nutti, and belong to the same kind of institution as the common prostitutes, and have the same religious guides. *All the girls are purchased when children.* The handsomest and smartest is generally the head of the set, which usually consists of two or three girls and four or five men, who are mostly born in the caste. There are no dancing or singing boys except such as are attached to the sets which perform in honor of the gods and saints, but of these there is a considerable variety and incredible number. The number employed to make a noise on public occasions is stated in statistical tables of the Rungpoor district at 2,664."*

* Hamilton, Vol. II. p. 477.

DINAJPOOR.—In 1808, the population of this district was estimated at 3,000,000. "Slaves are very few, and were mostly purchased during the great famine of 1769 and the scarcity of 1787; but they turned out so idle and careless that their employment was found much more expensive than that of hired laborers."*

PURNEAH.—In 1810 the population of this district, after a very laborious investigation, was estimated at 2,904,380 persons, in the proportion of forty-three Muhammadans to fifty-seven Hindus. "Comprehended in the above population are *various classes of slaves*, of which one class costs from £1 15s. to £2 5s.; in another a boy costs from £1 8s. to £2 5s.; and a girl of eight years from 11s. to £1 15s. They are allowed to marry, and their children become slaves; but the family are seldom sold separately. One class of slaves are by far the most comfortable description of laboring people, and are seldom sold by their owners, although they possess the power."†

In 1824 and 1825 there were several provinces conquered from the Burmese—Assam, Arracan, and the Tenasserim provinces, including the Mergui Archipelago. The following extracts relate to the slave-trade and slavery found to prevail and still existing in those provinces; and they are taken, like the preceding, from Hamilton, with one exception, which will be noticed.

ASSAM.—The latest and probably the most correct estimate of the population of Assam makes it amount to about 800,000.‡ Hamilton states that in 1809, when Assam was an independent kingdom, a part of the value of the exports from Assam to Bengal consisted of slaves, to the amount of 2000 rupees annually. He adds:—"All the domestics are

* Hamilton, Vol. I. p. 515. † Hamilton, Vol. II. pp. 431, 432.

‡ McCosh's Topography of Assam, p. 129. Calcutta, 1837.

slaves, and they are numerous, every man of rank having several, mostly procured among the necessitous, who mortgage themselves. Some were exported, and before the British predominance, about one hundred of pure caste were annually sold in Bengal. The girls were chiefly bought by professional prostitutes, and cost from twelve to fifteen rupees. A Cooch boy," (that is, a native of Cooch Behar, a dependent principality situated at the northeastern extremity of the Bengal district of Rungpoor,) "cost twenty-five rupees, a Kolita" (that is, a member of the aboriginal priesthood of Cooch Behar) "fifty; slaves of impure tribes were sold to the Garrows."*

The Bengal government has recently called on its medical servants for reports on the topography of the districts in which they carry on their professional labors; and one of the most valuable of the productions which have been thus elicited is Dr. McCosh's Topography of Assam, published by order of government at Calcutta in 1837, and containing the following additional information respecting the state of slavery in that province. "*Slavery still continues to a very considerable extent in Assam*, and these poor creatures are bought and sold *every day* for a mere trifle. Every native in the receipt of more than ten or twelve rupees a month has one or more of them. All the drudgery of the household and the labor of the field is performed by them. Many of them have been enthralled by mortgaging their bodies for a few rupees; and for want of the means of accumulating the original sum, increased by exorbitant usury, continue in bondage for life, themselves and their descendants, from generation to generation. Slaves are believed to be kindly treated by their masters; but, as might be expected, they make frequent attempts to escape. They are valued in the market according to caste; high caste adults sell for about twenty rupees, boys fifteen, and

* Hamilton, Vol. I. pp. 72, 73.

girls from eight to twelve. Those of the lower castes do not bring more than one-third of the above estimate. No slaves are allowed to be exported from Assam."*

ARRACAN.—"In 1826, the population of Arracan, including Ramree, Cheduba, and Sandoway, was estimated at 100,000 persons."—"Slavery is tolerated *in all shapes*, and when a man wants to raise money he pawns his wife."†

TAVOY.—"In 1825, the total population of Tavoy, Ye, and Tenasserim, was estimated at 26,000 inhabitants."—"The custom of debtor-slavery or mortgaged labor *prevails universally;* another great source of slaves was the sale of government criminals; price of a slave from thirty to sixty rupees. The last was immediately abolished by the British, but the first required time, it being a matter of property."‡ On this it may be remarked that it required no time to forbid the future creation of any such property.

MERGUI ARCHIPELAGO.—This is a chain of high, bold, and generally rocky islands on the coast of Tenasserim, which with that province may be deemed to have passed under the government and protection of the British. The following is the description given of their inhabitants and of the piratical depredations to which they are exposed. "A race of men termed by the Chinese, Cholomé and Pase, are to be found scattered throughout the Mergui (Archipelago,) but their dread of the Malay pirates keeps them in constant locomotion to escape slavery. During the northeast monsoon they are obliged to remove from the vicinity of the principal birds' nest and beche de mere islands, to shun the Malays, Burmese, and Siamese, who capture and make slaves of them. Their numbers, unless collected on one spot, are quite insignificant. Their home is their boat, for they

* McCosh's Topography of Assam, p. 26.

† Hamilton, Vol. I. p. 60. ‡ Hamilton, Vol. II. p. 627.

never form settlements on shore, or cultivate, their chief employment being the collection of sea-slug, birds' nests, and other natural productions of the islands, which they barter with the Chinese traders for cloths and other articles brought from Mergui," the capital of the British province of Tenasserim, "being as yet ignorant of the value of money. They have adopted the Burmese dress and religion, but in their general habits are a harmless and industrious race. Excluding these itinerants, the Mergui islands appear almost entirely destitute of inhabitants."*

The province of Bahar joins the western boundary of Bengal, and slavery exists in at least four of the six districts into which it is divided, viz., Boglipoor, Bahar, Tirhoot, and Rungpoor.

Boglipoor.—In 1810, the population of this district was estimated at about 2,060,000. "Real slaves of the male sex are here called *nufur*, and their women *laundies*. They may be sold in whatever manner the master chooses; but they are not often brought to market, and are all either of the Dhanak or Rawani castes. The slaves here are in general industrious, seldom run away, and are rarely beaten."†

Bahar.—In 1811, the district of this name was estimated to contain a population of 2,755,150 persons. "Slaves of the description called *nufur* and *laundi* are *very numerous*, often liberated, seldom sold, and frequently, owing to the poverty of their owners, left to find a subsistence for themselves."—"The Muhammadans in the Bahar district occasionally make converts of pagans, especially by the purchase of slaves, who are treated with great kindness; but this mode of conversion goes on much more slowly than formerly, when the Muhammadans possessed the government and an enormous income, a great part of which was dissi-

* Hamilton, Vol. II. p. 226. † Hamilton, Vol. I, p. 254.

pated on this pecuniary method of propagating their faith. Still, however, there is reason to believe that within these thirty or forty years a considerable increase in the number of the faithful has taken place. By the mere exertion of fakeers, missionaries, or religious mendicants, very little has been or can be done, but by the simple processes of purchasing and procreation, any religion might in a reasonable time be extended without giving offence, a very large portion of the nominal Hindu natives being considered by the spiritual directors now in the country as not worth admission into their flocks. A conversion of this description in a temporal view would be evidently disadvantageous, and in a spiritual sense, the methods above alluded to could not with propriety be adopted. The plan, however, has succeeded perfectly well with the Muhammadans, probably more than one-half of the sect having an intermixture of Hindu blood."*

In 1837, I visited this district in the prosecution of an inquiry into the state of native education, conducted under the orders of government, and I availed myself of the opportunities and facilities I possessed to collect information on various other subjects, of which one was slavery. In one police subdivision of this district, called Jehanabad, containing a population ascertained by actual census to amount to 81,480, I found by the same means that there were 271 male slaves, and 401 female slaves, or 672 in all. If we suppose the same proportion between the slave and free population in the other police subdivisions, and that the total population is 2,755,150, the total slave population in the Bahar district will amount to 22,722.

Tirhoot.—The only information that I possess respecting slavery in this district, is derived from my own inquiries, made in 1837, on the occasion already mentioned. In

* Hamilton, Vol. I. pp. 108, 111; Vol. II. pp. 652, 653.

one police subdivision, that of Bhawara, containing a population ascertained by actual census to amount to 65,812, I found by the same means that there were 209 male slaves, and 155 female slaves, or 364 in all. If, as in the former case, we suppose the same proportion between the slave and free population in the other police subdivisions, and if, with Hamilton, we estimate the total population of the district at 2,000,000, the total slave population in the Tirhoot district will amount to 11,061.

Ramghur.—This district in 1801 was estimated to contain a population of 1,000,000. The following remarkable statement is made respecting the slave population of this district. "Theft is common throughout Ramghur; but murder more prevalent among a particular class, which are the slaves possessed by chiefs inhabiting the mountainous and inaccessible interior, and of savage and ferocious habits. When petty disputes occur, these slaves are compelled by their masters to perpetrate any enormity, and are more especially employed for the purposes of assassination. Any hesitation or symptoms of repugnance on the part of the slave is attended with instant death, which is equally his fate should he fail in the attempt. On the other hand, if he succeed, he is sought out by the officers of government, and executed as a murderer. The usual police has hitherto been unable to seize the cowardly instigator, and if recourse be had to a military force he retires to the jungles. Neither do the slaves attach the slightest idea of guilt to the murders they are thus delegated to commit; on the contrary, when taken they invariably confess, and appear to expect applause for having done their duty."*

Hamilton, in his notices of the provinces of Oude, Allahabad, Agra, and Delhi, and of the country between the Sutlej and the Jumna, Kumaon, and the Dehra Doon, in Western and Northern Hindostan, makes no mention of the

* Hamilton, Vol. II. p. 452.

existence of slavery. The subject has received so little attention that his silence does not establish its non-existence, and in the productions of two other writers I find the following notices of slavery in Gorakhpur and in the Dehra Doon.

GORAKHPUR.—This district was ceded by the Oude government in 1801, and includes two subdivisions, Gorakhpur and Azimghur, each equal to the ordinary extent of a district. I have not met with any estimate of the population. The existence of slavery in Gorakhpur appears from a communication addressed by D. Liston, Esq., a European resident in the district, to the Journal of the Asiatic Society, Vol. VI., for 1837, p. 950. This gentleman states that he had been requested by Captain Lawrence, under whose charge the survey of the eastern division of the district is placed, to furnish answers to certain statistical inquiries. In collecting the information for this purpose on the subject of the relations between landholders and those who water and cultivate their lands, he procured two documents, one a servitude bond, and the other a deed of sale of two slaves. In the former, a laborer, for a sum of 51 rupees, places himself, his children, and his plough, *always* and *for every kind of labor*, at the absolute disposal of the lender. In the latter, the owner of the slaves, for a sum of 43 rupees, sells the wife and son of his slave Bulbhader to the purchaser, and the effect of the sale is, that "wherever they go, thence they may be brought back; as slaves they are sold to perform every kind of work; wherever they may flee, thence they may be seized and brought back without objection, or complaint, or murmur; without obstacle may they be brought from under the king's or prince's throne; whoever receives these servants, Hindu or Musalman, he may (legally) be adjured—the Hindu by the sacred cow, the Musalman by Hasan," &c. These deeds are expressly stated by Mr. Liston to be "*such as are daily executed, and in full force.*"

Dehra Doon.—In 1836, the Hon. F. J. Shore published a Report on the Dehra Doon, the result of four years' residence, and originally compiled and submitted to government in 1827. The population of the Doon was then 24,527. The following remarks (p. 32) occur respecting slavery. "Slavery exists but in a small extent at present. Under the native governments, little attention seems to have been paid to either Muhammadan or Hindu law regarding slaves. The master's power was virtually almost despotic over the slave; their employment was very similar to that of domestic servants. A man and his whole family could be sold for debt or for arrears of revenue, a practice which was carried to an intolerable pitch by the Goorkas. Since the establishment of the British government, slavery here, as elsewhere, is dying a natural death." On Mr. Shore's authority, such may safely be pronounced to be the case in the Dehra Doon. That slavery in other parts of India, subject to the British government, is not dying a natural death, has been and will still further be shown.

In addition to the preceding citations, each of which has reference to a small and separate locality, the following remarks on slavery occur in Mr. Colebrooke's writings, having a general reference to the territories subject to the government of the Bengal presidency. In 1804, Mr. Colebrooke published Remarks on the Husbandry and Internal Commerce of Bengal, and in the introduction he states that when he uses that name, without any limitation, he means "all the provinces over which Great Britain exercises avowed sovereignty committed to the immediate administration of a council at Calcutta;" in other words, "the regions immediately governed by the presidency of Fort William, comprehending the whole Subas (provinces) of Bengal and Bahar; a part of the adjoining Subas of Ilahabad, Oresa, and Berar, and some tracts of country," (such as part of Morung, Cooch, and other provinces,) "which had maintained their independence even in the most flourishing period of the Moghul empire."* In the course of Mr. Colebrooke's remarks on the profits of husbandry in Bengal, he was led to contrast the cheap production and frugal manufacture of sugar in Bengal with its expensive production and manufacture by slave-labor in the West Indies; but recollecting the existence of slavery in India, he felt himself compelled to make the following admissions:—"Slavery indeed is not unknown in Bengal. Throughout some districts the labors of husbandry are executed chiefly by bond-servants. In certain provinces the ploughmen are mostly slaves of the peasants for whom they labor; but treated by their masters more like hereditary servants or mancipated hinds than like purchased slaves, they labor with cheerful diligence and unforced zeal. In some places, also, the landholders have a claim to the servitude of thousands among the inhabitants of their estates. This claim, which is seldom enforced, and which in many instances is become wholly obsolete, is founded on some traditional rights acquired many generations ago, in a state of society different from the present: and slaves of this description do in fact enjoy every privilege of a freeman except the name; or at the worst they must be considered as villains attached to the glebe, rather than as bondmen laboring for the sole benefit of their owners. Indeed, throughout India, the relation of master and slave appears to impose the duty of protection and cherishment on the master, as much as that of fidelity and obedience on the slave, and their mutual conduct is consistent with the sense of such an obligation; since it is marked with gentleness and indulgence on the one side, and with zeal and loyalty on the other."† I do

* Remarks on the Husbandry and Internal Commerce of Bengal, p. 1.
† Ibid. pp. 129, 130.

not call in question the generally mild character of slavery, as here described, in the Bengal provinces. I only wish to call your attention to the acknowledged general prevalence of agrestic or predial slavery in some form or another, "in some places," "throughout some districts," and "in certain provinces" of the Bengal presidency, although there can be no doubt,—what I am desirous neither of controverting nor concealing,—that in most provinces none but freemen are occupied in the business of agriculture.

We have the benefit of Mr. Colebrooke's testimony to the extent both of domestic and predial slavery in the Bengal provinces, delivered with still greater minuteness, in an official paper written by him in 1812, not, it would appear, entered on the public records, but quoted by Mr. Harington in his Analysis of the Laws and Regulations of the Bengal Government, Vol. III. pp. 743—748. "We find," he says, "domestic slavery very general among both Hindus and Musalmans. More trusty than hired servants, slaves almost exclusively are employed in the interior of the house, for attendance on the members of the family, and in all the most confidential services. Every opulent person, every one raised above the condition of the simplest mediocrity, is provided with household slaves; and from this class chiefly are taken the concubines of Musalmans and Hindus; in regard to whom it is to be remembered that concubinage is not among people of those religions an immoral state, but a relation which both law and custom recognise without reprehension; and its prevalence is liable only to the same objection as polygamy, with which it has a near and almost necessary connection. In the lower provinces under this presidency, the employment of slaves in the labors of husbandry is nearly if not entirely unknown. In the upper provinces, beginning from Western Bahar and Benares, the petty landholders who are themselves cultivators, are aided in their husbandry by their slaves, whom they very commonly employ as herdsmen and ploughmen; and landholders of a higher order have in a few instances the pretensions of masters over part of their tenants long settled on their estates, and reputed to be descended from persons who were acknowledged slaves of their ancestors. Their claims to the services of these hereditary serfs are nearly obsolete, and scarcely attended with any practical consequences. The serfs pay rent and other dues for the lands which they till and the pastures on which they graze their herds, and are not distinguishable from the rest of the peasantry, unless by a questionable restriction of the right of removing at choice. But those employed in husbandry by the inferior class of landholders are strictly slaves; and their condition differs from that of household slaves only as the one is occupied in out-door work, and the other in business of the interior of the house. The employment of slaves in handicraft is more rare, but not entirely unknown. It would be difficult to form a computation of the number of slaves throughout the country, or of the proportion borne to the free population. Any steps towards the preparation of an estimate which should approach to accuracy would involve inquiries which must excite alarm, and could not but be attended with circumstances offensive to the people. But taking a more general view, it may be stated, that slaves are neither so few as to be of no consideration, nor so numerous as to constitute a notable proportion of the mass of population." These views are entitled to great consideration, and it is believed are in general correct; but some of the facts already adduced show that in certain particulars they require to be qualified. That there are exceptions to the general good treatment of domestic slaves, is apparent from the Gorakhpur case, which was the sale of a wife and son apart from the husband and father; and it is very obvious that slaves must constitute a very notable proportion of the mass of population, where, as in Silhet, they amount to one-sixth of the whole, and in those provinces in which Mr. Colebrooke himself has informed us the ploughmen are *mostly* slaves of the peasants for whom they labor. Notwithstanding these exceptions, the general accuracy of Mr. Colebrooke's picture of slavery in the provinces of the Bengal presidency is unquestionable.

The first reference to slavery under the Bombay presidency that I have met with, is contained in Macnaghten's Principles and Precedents of Hindu Law, Vol. I. p. 119, *note*, where it is stated that "the question" of slavery "appears to have been a good deal discussed in the courts subordinate to the presidencies of Madras and Bombay." This merely recognises the existence of slavery within the Bombay territories and the fact of the adjudication of slave cases in the Bombay courts, without giving any information of the number of slaves or the extent of slavery.

More detailed information respecting slavery in the territories subject to the government of the Bombay presidency, is furnished in Mr. Chaplin's Report on the Dekhan, embracing most of the provinces conquered from the Mahrattas in 1818, and placed under the jurisdiction of the Bombay government. The population of these provinces was estimated by Mr. Elphinstone and Mr. Chaplin at about 4,000,000. The following statements by Mr. Chaplin in his official Report of 1822, relate to the extent to which slavery existed, and to the fact that the slave-trade was still carried on in the Dekhan at that time. "The subject of domestic slavery in the Dekhan would appear to require to be regulated by some legal sanctions, in order, on the one hand *to prevent the oppression of slaves* as well as *to check the traffic*, and on the other hand to obviate the injustice that would be occasioned to private property by any interference amounting to an absolute prohibition of the sale of *what has hitherto been deemed a marketable commodity.* From the answers" (given by the collectors of districts) "to queries" (addressed to the collectors by Mr. Chaplin), "it will be observed, that slavery in the Dekhan is *very prevalent*, and we know that it has been recognised by the Hindu law and by the custom of the country *from time immemorial.*"—"The greatest portion of slaves are reduced to that condition in times of famine, when parents sell their children for the double purpose of saving their lives and themselves from starvation. *A great number* have within these few years been imported into the Dekhan under these circumstances, and this mode of disposing of a famishing offspring seems beyond all doubt to have been the means of alleviating scarcity. One great evil has, however, resulted, *that of kidnapping children* for the purpose of *selling them in distant countries* as slaves. This is a common practice among the Lumans and Brinjarees."—"The importation of slaves from foreign states now stands prohibited by the orders of the supreme government. This, however, has increased the price *without putting a stop to the traffic.*"*

Mr. Baber, in his answers to questions on slavery in the East Indies, circulated by the Board of Commissioners for the Affairs of India, enables us to form a still more definite idea of the number of slaves in one of the divisions of the Bombay territory, viz., that "lying between the rivers Kistna and Toongbutra, and comprising the late southern Mahratta states, now partly administered by the Honorable Company, and partly by the Putwurdhun family and other principal Jagheerdars; also the dominions of his highness

* Chaplin's Report, pp. 148—151.

the Colapore Rajah." With reference to this division of the Bombay territory, Mr. Baber says: "In the Dooab or southern Mahratta country, including Colapore, the number of domestic slaves I compute at 15,000, or rather more than three-quarters per cent. of the general population, which may be reckoned at about two millions, as follows: the number, in the year 1822, in the Honorable Company's portion of the Dooab, was 684,193, and in the Jagheers 778,183, as reported by Mr. Commissioner Chaplin, exclusive of Colapore, about 250,000 more; since which period (judging from the augmented jumma, or gross annual revenue) the increase in the general population of the whole of the southern Mahratta country cannot be less than one-tenth more. The same gentleman also reported 'throughout the Dekhan slavery to be very prevalent.' In the southern Mahratta country, all the Jagheerdars, Deshwars, Zamindars, principal Brahmins and Sahookars, retain slaves on their domestic establishments; in fact, in every Mahratta household of consequence they are, both male and female, especially the latter, to be found, and indeed are considered as indispensable."*

It is under the Madras presidency that Indian slavery appears under its worst form, and it is there also that we have the most precise statements of the extent to which it prevails. It is found in the British districts of Arcot, Canara, Malabar, Bellary and Tanjore, and in the dependent native principalities of Cochin and Travancore, and of Mysore and Coorg.

Arcot.—In the Appendix to a Report from the Select Committee on the Affairs of the East India Company, ordered by the House of Commons to be printed, August 16, 1832,

* Mr. Baber's Letter, without date, but written apparently in 1832, and published in Appendix to Report from Select Committee on the Affairs of the East India Company. (Public,) p. 551.

there is an abstract of the Evidence given before the Lords' Committee, 1830, on Slavery, pp. 303, 304. In that abstract, Mr. Hyde is stated to have given evidence to the following effect:—"In Arcot there are about 20,000 slaves. They generally go with the land, and are transferred when the land is sold; they are never sold by themselves, but if the land is sold they go with it. They are so well protected by their masters, that they can scarcely be considered as slaves. The children of slaves are also slaves, but they are never sold. Enfranchisement seldom takes place. Slaves are not capable of possessing property." The two districts of Northern and Southern Arcot, to which these remarks apply, contained in 1822 a population of 1,347,312.

Canara.—Mr. Baber states that "in the Zillah of Canara, the total number of slaves, agrestic and domestic, may be fairly computed at 80,000, or about one in twelve of the gross general population, which, when I left the Malabar coast, in 1828, amounted to nearly a million of souls. In 1801, Mr. Ravenshaw, the collector of the southern division, reported the gross population at 396,672; the northern division may be calculated at one-third of this number; and Mr. Ravenshaw further reported the slave-population to be 52,122, besides 722 illegitimate children, whom, he writes, it was the custom of the Biddenore government to take possession of and sell as slaves; and also slaves imported from Arabia, of whom there were many. 'In 1819, the Honorable Thomas Harris, the principal collector of all Canara, reported the number of slaves at 82,000, of whom 20,000 were persons (or rather their descendants) who had been taken in battle, or concubines, or Brahmin and Sooder women, who had lost caste by having connection with men of inferior caste; the two last descriptions (he adds) were sold under the Musalman government, and their descendants continue slaves; and that under Mr. Baber, when magistrate here, some stop was put to this practice, but there is no doubt it exists in an underhand manner at this day.' I should here add, that Mr. Harris also stated that 'the number of slaves had never been correctly ascertained.' By a census, taken in 1807, of all Canara, the total number of inhabitants was found to be 576,640; as I have stated above, in 1827 the gross population amounted to nearly a million, making an increase of seventy per cent. in twenty years, while the slave-population has been stationary."*

MALABAR.—Mr. Baber states that "in the Zillah of Malabar, Mr. Warden, principal collector, in 1806–7, reported the number of slaves at 96,386, and in 1815–16, at 94,786; and his successor, Mr. James Vaughan, in 1819, stated the number to be 100,000, 'exclusive of Wynâd, containing about 3,000 more;' and in 1827, the late principal collector, Mr. Sheffield, ascertained the number of slaves to be 95,696, exclusive of Wynâd, as follows: Pooliar Cherumar, 48,579; Kanaka Cherumar, 20,798; Terrawa Cherumar, 20,058; Kallady Cherumar, 2,279; Vallow Cherumar, 615; Betwas or Wettowar, 3,347, (being a moiety of them, as it is only in some districts of Malabar they are laid claim to as slaves). In 1806–7, previous to which the country, as Mr. Commissioner Thackeray reported, 'had been a prey to civil wars, which burnt with a raging or smothered flame ever since the Company got that province,' the general population was, according to Mr. Warden's estimate, 700,000. In 1827, it amounted, by Mr. Sheffield's returns, to 1,003,466. In Malabar, therefore, the slave-population would seem to have been diminishing, as I find Mr. Warden has already stated in his evidence before the Select Committee of the House of

* Mr. Baber's Letter, as above, p. 551.

Lords, while the increase in the general population has been nearly as great as in Canara."*

Mr. A. D. Campbell states that "the creatures in human form who constitute, to the number of 100,000, the agrestic slave-population of that province," (Malabar,) are "distinguishable, like the savage tribes still to be found in some of the forests of India, from the rest of the human race by their degraded, diminutive, squalid appearance; their dropsical pot-bellies contrasting horribly with their skeleton arms and legs, half-starved, hardly clothed, and in a condition scarcely superior to the cattle they follow at the plough."†

Hamilton states that of the five castes into which the Hindu population is divided in Malabar, the fifth is that of "the Poliars, who are slaves or bondmen, and attached to the soil."—"The Pariar, in the plural, belong to a tribe below all caste, *all of whom are slaves.*"—"There are six sorts of Chemurs or slaves, like the Pariars of Madras, and no other tribe is bought or sold in Malabar."‡

Mr. Vaughan, as reported above by Mr. Baber, estimated in 1819 the slave-population of Wynaad, a small subdivision of the modern province of Malabar, at 3,000. Either that estimate was incorrect, or the slave-population must have been greatly reduced during the preceding nineteen years; for Hamilton states that "in 1800, the number of male slaves in this division (Wynaad), above the age of fifteen, amounted to 2,266, and the females to 2,264. The number of males below that age was 1,000, and of females 1,050," making in all 6,590. "The total number of free inhabitants at that date

* Mr. Baber's Letter, as above, pp. 551, 552.

† Mr. A. D. Campbell's Letter to the Board of Commissioners for the Affairs of India, dated 5th Nov. 1832, and published in Appendix to Report from Select Committee on Affairs of the East India Company, (Public,) p. 574.

‡ Hamilton, Vol. II. pp. 179, 181.

amounted to 8,070 persons," the enslaved being thus nearly as numerous as the free population.*

BELLARY AND TANJORE.—Mr. A. D. Campbell states:—"In the Bellary division of the ceded districts, where I firs held that situation," (the situation of collector and magistrate,) "I have already stated that no agrestic slaves whatever exist. In Tanjore, on the contrary, they amount to many thousands; but I cannot from memory give any correct estimate of their number. The house or domestic slaves in neither district can exceed one or two hundred in a population of above a million of souls, in each of these provinces respectively."†

COCHIN.—This is one of the dependent native principalities under the Madras presidency. Mr. Baber says:—"Cochin I reckon at about 150,000 souls, of whom 12,000 are slaves."‡

TRAVANCORE.—This is another of the dependent principalities. Mr. Baber says:—"The only return of the population of Travancore I have met with, is that of Fra Paulino de San Bartolomeo in his work Viaggio alle Inde Orientale, published at Rome, in the year 1796. This person resided many years in Travancore, and has certainly given a most minute account of the manners, customs, &c. of the inhabitants of that country. He estimated the whole population at 1,600,000; and judging from all I have been able to collect in the course of my inquiries among the Kariakars (ministers), and other intelligent persons, as to the aggregate general revenue as well as on this point, this estimate is probably the extent of the present population. It would no doubt have increased in the same ratio as Malabar and Canara have, but for the war of 1809–10, and

* Hamilton, Vol. II. p. 710.

† Mr. A. D. Campbell's Letter, as above, p. 573.

‡ Mr. Baber's Letter, as above, p. 552.

other political causes; and as the whole labor of wet cultivation is (as in the adjoining province of Malabar) carried on by slaves, (superintended by hired free-born persons called pannikar and chooralakar,) the number of slaves may be taken at a twelfth of the whole population."* This will make the slave-population of Travancore amount to not less than 130,000.

The Rev. Joseph Fenn, who resided between eight and nine years in the interior of the kingdom of Travancore, does not offer any estimate of the total number of slaves in that country, but states:—"In Cottayam, where the population exclusive of the slaves was between 3,000 and 4,000, I have sometimes assembled some hundreds."†

Coorg and Mysore.—These are dependent principalities. Coorg has been at least temporarily subjugated to British power, but its population has not been ascertained. In 1814 the population of Mysore was estimated at 2,171,754, since which it has been supposed to have greatly increased. Mr. Baber states that the varieties and sources of domestic slavery which he enumerates "have in former times or do now prevail more or less wherever domestic slavery is found, but chiefly in the Southern Mahratta country, both in the Company's and Jagheer portion of it, and in the Kolapore Raja's dominions; *also in those of Coorg and Mysore.*" Agrestic or predial slavery, he adds, "exists throughout, under some slight modifications, the Malabar coast, in the Balaghat district, already mentioned, *and even in the western parts of the table-land of Mysore.*"‡

* Mr. Baber's Letter, as above, p. 552.

† Mr. Fenn's Letter to the Board of Commissioners for the Affairs of India, dated 24th Sept. 1832, and published in Appendix to Report from Select Committee on the Affairs of the East India Company. (Public,) p. 549.

‡ Mr. Baber's Letter, as above, p. 551.

The following citations have a general reference to the slave-population of the entire Madras territories, and furnish additional aids to the formation of a correct opinion respecting the extent to which slavery prevails in those territories.

Hamilton says that the Pariar "are so numerous that they have been computed at one-fifth of the whole population of India south of the Krishna." The population south of the Krishna may be estimated at 15,000,000, and the Pariar would thus amount to 3,000,000. Hamilton, on the authority of Dr. Francis Buchanan, has further stated that all the Pariar "are slaves."*

Mr. Baber, after stating the opportunities and means of information he has possessed, adds, "By these means —— I have become acquainted, amongst other subjects of interest, with the *prevailing slavery* throughout, I may say, the western provinces south of the Kistna to the extremity of the Indian continent, Cape Comorin, or, properly, Kanya Coomari."†

Colonel James Welsh says:—"From Cape Comorin to Goa, including Wynaad and Soonda, I believe that there were nearly 300,000 (slaves), and from the nature of the caste distinctions, (not admitting of any kind of personal contact between the upper and lower orders of the Hindu aborigines of that country,) by far the greater numbers were field slaves."‡

Mr. A. D. Campbell says:—"In the territories under the Madras government slaves are of two distinct descriptions: the one includes the great slave-population termed 'agrestic

* Hamilton, Vol. II. pp. 6, 179; Buchanan's Travels, Vol. II. p. 493.

† Mr. Baber's Letter, as above, p. 551.

‡ Col. Welsh's Letter to the Board of Commissioners for the Affairs of India, dated Nov. 3, 1832, and published in Appendix to Report from Select Committee on the Affairs of the East India Company. (Public,) p. 570.

slaves,' or such as are usually employed in the field, though occasionally also in other labor. These consist exclusively of Hindus who become such by birth alone, in the peculiar castes which the usage of India has doomed to hereditary bondage. This species of slavery does not exist at all in the central provinces of the Indian peninsula, such as the ceded districts or Mysore, peopled by the Carnatacka nation; and I believe it is also unknown in the Northern Circars, Nellore, &c., or in the country where the people speak the Telinga language; but it is common in the southern provinces of the peninsula, or wherever the Tamil language is spoken, and it assumes its worst form on the western coast of the peninsula, or in the provinces of Malabar and Canara. The other description of slaves consists of those who may be termed domestic, from being employed only in the house itself. This kind of slavery may be found all over the Madras territory, but it is exceedingly rare."*

The preceding are all the details that I possess to guide to a just estimate of the total number of slaves in British India. In attempting to form such an estimate, we must, I think, put out of view the calculation that in Southern India there are three millions of Pariar, all of whom are slaves, since this probably does not sufficiently distinguish between those classes of natives who are socially degraded without being slaves, and those who are held as slaves in the strict and legal sense. In estimating the total number of slaves in British India, properly so called, we must also omit the estimates that have been given respecting the number in native states and jagheers, as Cochin, Travancore, Mysore, and Coorg, and the jagheers of the Southern Mahratta country which are governed by native princes and chieftains. Thus in Travancore it has been estimated

* Mr. Campbell's Letter, as above, p. 572.

that there are 130,000 slaves, in Cochin 12,000, in the Southern Mahratta country 15,000, of whom one-half may be assigned to the Mahratta Jagheers and to the dominions of the Kolapore Raja, while of the number in Mysore and Coorg no estimate has been obtained. It is however to be borne in mind, that although the British government cannot be held answerable for the existence of slavery in these dependent native states and principalities, yet its indirect influence over them is powerful, and any measures tending to the improvement of the condition of slaves or to the extinction of slavery in the neighboring British provinces, if accompanied by proper representations to the native princes and chiefs, would probably lead to the adoption of similar measures in their dominions and territories. With these omissions, the following estimates of the number of slaves in British districts and provinces would appear to be approximations to the truth:—

Silhet	80,000
Behar	22,722
Tirhoot	11,061
S. Mahratta country, (British portion)	7,500
Arcot	20,000
Canara	80,000
Malabar	100,000
	321,283

This is exclusive of the following districts and provinces, respecting which no definite estimate of numbers has been obtained; viz.:—*Dacca Jelalpoor*, where "the custom of disposing of persons already in a state of slavery is common throughout the country;" *Backergunge*, where "women of the poorer classes when left widows sell their children to procure food;" *Rungpoor*, where "among the domestics are both male and female slaves," and where all the girls belonging to seventy-eight sets of female dancers and singers "are purchased when children;" *Dinajpoor*, where "slaves are very few;" *Purneah*, where there "are various classes of slaves;" *Assam*, where "all the domestics are slaves," and where, according to the latest account, "slavery still continues to a very considerable extent;" *Arracan*, where "slavery is tolerated in all shapes;" *the Tenasserim provinces*, where "the custom of debtor-slavery or mortgaged labor prevails universally;" *the Mergui Archipelago*, where the inhabitants are hunted to be made slaves; *Boglipoor*, where slaves are stated to exist; *Ramghur*, where they are employed by native chiefs for the purposes of private revenge; *Gorakhpur*, where both bond slavery and unconditional slavery exist; *Dehra Doon*, where "slavery is dying a natural death;" *Bellary*, where domestic slaves do not "exceed one or two hundred;" and *Tanjore*, where "predial slaves" "amount to many thousands."

Upon the whole, I am of opinion that the very lowest estimate we can form of the total number of slaves, subjects of the British government in India, is 500,000; and I deem it highly probable that a thorough and faithful census would show that the number does not fall short of ONE MILLION.

LETTER VI.

TO THOMAS FOWELL BUXTON, ESQ.

The Origin and Sources of Slavery in British India.

SIR,—The next branch of the subject that I propose to consider, is the origin of slavery in India, and the means by which the slave-population has been and is supplied.

The first fact that presents itself connected with the origin of slavery in India is, that slaves in India are for the most part natives of the country. In modern times, Africa has been the great source from which a supply of slave-labor has been drawn by the European race for their settlements on the American continents and islands, and a portion at least of the slave-population of Arabia and Persia is furnished by Arab dealers from the eastern coast of Africa, obtained by the same abominable and nefarious means that are employed on the western coast, consisting for the most part in the forcible seizure of the slaves, either in predatory war undertaken for the purpose, or by open robbery, often attended with murder. But although a traffic formerly existed to some extent by the importation of slaves from the eastern coast of Africa, from Madagascar, and from the Eastern Islands into the British possessions in India, and although there are grounds for doubting whether it has been fully and effectually suppressed, yet the proportion of slaves in India of the African race is so inconsiderable that they can scarcely be taken into the account in any general estimate of their number and condition. The great body of the slave-population in India is not only Asiatic, but Aboriginal, consisting of natives of the soil, and belonging to the race which history, tradition, and observation, language, religion, manners, and institutions combine to show was probably the first that occupied the country, anterior to the Hindu, Muhammadan, and European races. This fact deserves to be prominently noticed, for important practical consequences may be deduced from it. In other slave-holding countries, the obstacles to emancipation consist not only in the supposed interests of the slave-holders, but in the alleged unfitness of the slaves for the rights and duties of freedom, and in the alleged difficulty of bringing them into a state of healthy union with the existing institutions of society and with the dominant class of the population. No such difficulty, no such unfitness, can be alleged in India. With regard to fitness for freedom, it is a remarkable fact in the civilization of India, that in Malabar, where slavery appears in its most objectionable form, the Poliar, or slave caste, however debased, are comparatively of higher social consideration than the Pariar and Niadis, who are free. Some of the Pariar are slaves, but the majority probably are free, and they are so numerous that they have been estimated at a fifth of the entire population of Southern India. The Niadis are an outcaste tribe, not numerous, but free. Both are so impure, compared with the slave caste, that if one of the latter touch them, he is defiled, and must wash his head and pray. Further; although the Poliar, or slave caste, are socially and by caste inferior to the Tiars or Tears, who are cultivators of the land and freemen, and to the Maliars, who are musicians and conjurers, but also freemen, there is no reason to suppose that they are morally and intellectually inferior to these two free castes above them, any more than to the two free castes below them, or that they are in any respect less qualified than either to enjoy the fruits of their own industry and the blessings of personal freedom. The same considerations show that slaves in the South of India, if emancipated, would continue what they now are, a separate and distinct caste, with the single difference of freedom, a caste not originally, it is probable, belonging to the Hindu race, but incorporated into that race, professing the Hindu religion, observing its usages, and obeying its ministers. In the eastern, western, and northern provinces of India, slaves are not a distinct caste, but they are for the most part domestic slaves, profess the same religion as their owners, and are certainly equal, if not superior, to a very large majority of the inferior castes of the free population, into which, if emancipated, they would naturally pass, without in any degree disturbing or interrupting the order of native society. The slaves of India, then, with comparatively few exceptions, have not been imported into the country. They are not of foreign birth and of strange aspect. They do not speak a different language, profess a different religion, practise different customs from the rest of the inhabitants. They are children of the soil. They belong to the state of society in which they are found; and their emancipation would be only one step—one of many that are necessary—towards the improvement of their condition, and that of the castes both above and below them, with which, from the necessity of their position and circumstances, they would easily and kindly coalesce.

From this view of slaves as natives of the country, the question arises, by what means they have been subjected to this condition. The origin of Hindu slavery may with great probability be traced to conquest; but a full exposition of the grounds of this opinion would lead to an amount of antiquarian and historical discussion which would be unsuitable to my present purpose. Without going into many details, it may be remarked that in the existing condition of the country there are four distinct classes of the population: first, Christians, the most recent conquerors; second, Muhammadans, whose authority the former superseded; third, Hindus, whom the Muhammadans subdued; and fourth, the Aborigines whom the Hindus conquered and subjected. These four classes include each numerous subdivisions, and they are largely intermixed, but the distinction of each from the rest is clearly marked. As far as all accessible evidence enables us to judge, the Aborigines were the first occupants of the soil, and the Hindus were their first conquerors; and in completing their conquest they drove many of the Aboriginal race into the forest and mountain fastnesses, where their descendants are still found; many they consigned to slavery such as now exists, imposing upon them at the same time the Hindu religion; and many they appear also to have incorporated with themselves as free, but still inferior and servile, castes.

That this is the origin of Hindu slavery is rendered probable by various considerations. Menu, (VIII. 415.) the great Hindu legislator, in enumerating the various descriptions of slaves recognised by Hindu law, begins with "one made captive under a standard," or in battle, as if this was the most important and most numerous class of slaves; and the commentator's illustration of this description of slavery is taken from the Mahabharat, the great national poem of the Hindus, where a Hindu warrior is represented as thus addressing a vanquished prince:—"Fool, if thou desirest life, hear from me the conditions: thou must declare before a select assembly and before the multitude, 'I am a slave.' On these terms will I grant thee life. *This is a settled rule for him who is conquered in battle.*"* That this rule was applied on a large scale, is evident from many authorities.

* Colebrooke's Digest of Hindu Law, Vol. II. p. 344.

"There are six sorts of Chemurs or slaves," says Hamilton, "like the Pariar of Madras, and no other tribe is bought or sold in Malabar. They are said to have been caught and domesticated by Parasu Rama," (the reputed Hindu conqueror of Malabar,) "for the use of the Brahmins, and are probably the descendants of the Aborigines conquered by the Chola kings and driven into the jungles, but at last compelled to prefer slavery and rice to freedom and starvation."* "With regard to agrestic or indigenous slaves," says Mr. Baber, "like those of Malabar, the only ancient books that make any mention of slaves are *Kerula-ootpati-wiwahāra Mālla* and *Vitynāna Shooriam Granddham*, and all that is narrated therein of them, to the best of my recollection, (for I have them not to refer to,) is, that they were the first and sole cultivators in *Kerula Rajium*," (in the country or kingdom of Malabar,) "having been created" (that is, created or made slaves) "for the use of the Brahmins."† This is confirmed by the following extract from the *Kérala Utpatti*, one of the books referred to by Mr. Baber, and of the first part of which a translation appears in Wilson's Catalogue of the Mackenzie Collection:—"They" (that is, the Brahman-colonists who had been settled in Malabar by Parasu Rama) "also established bondage and husbandry, and protected the slaves and husbandmen, and appointed villages and heads of villages, —— and protected and preserved them from lessening and falling." (Vol. II. p. 81.) In the same work (p. 92.) there is an enumeration of eighteen inferior castes who came from foreign countries and settled in Malabar, but among these *slaves* are not found, the reason obviously being that the dominant Brahmans obtained their slaves from among the Aboriginal inhabitants of the country whom they had subdued.

A similar process, it can be satisfactorily shown, took place in another and distant province, and in more modern times.

* Hamilton, Vol. II. p. 181. † Mr. Baber's Letter, as above, p. 565.

"The province of lower Behar, as at present divided, contains a considerable extent of that range of hills that runs across the greater portion of Hindoostan from the Ganges to Malwa and Goojrat. This line of mountainous country has long been known to be peopled by various tribes, whose origin, whose difference from each other, and whose absolute alienation from the Hindus, have been matters of curiosity and are as yet a mystery to all researchers. The press of population upon the adjoining plains has driven multitudes of Hindu families to settle by force or by sufferance in these yet uncultivated pergunnahs; and many of these emigrations are sufficiently recent for the local authorities to obtain a tolerable account of the origin and progress of the settlers in their new position. Of some instances," says Mr. Augustus Prinsep, from whose papers this extract is taken, "I propose to give a brief sketch. The facts have been collected by personal acquaintance with the country, and I was induced to observe the customs of this district with attention from the same motive that now leads to a publication of these remarks—a belief that a similarity with the early practices of India might be discovered, and, if discovered, might be useful to those who may have to guide our future territorial policy." For the sake of illustration I shall quote only one of the instances which Mr. Prinsep has adduced :—

"At the beginning of the seventeenth century, or a little more than two hundred years ago, a scion of one of the families of the Bhojpoor Raja, whose estates lay near Rhotas in Shahabad, being urged by the spirit of adventure, and probably discontented with his subdivided heritage, proclaimed his intention of seeking lands above the Ghāts, or beyond the range of hills that rise on the south side of the river Soane, and invited followers to join in the undertaking. Some thousands of Rajpoots collected round the standard raised by Bhugwant Roy, who (in the year 1021, Fussily, as the tradition of the pergunnah fixes the date) led his army into that part of the Ramgurh district which has been ever since and was perhaps before called Palamoo One encounter with the inhabitants was sufficient to insure the conquest of the country, which, containing several cultivable and some already cultivated plains between the lines of hills, became a valuable prey to a multitude in search of a vacant territory. The chief of the invaders, assuming territorial dominion, proceeded to divide the lands of the pergunnah between himself and his followers, who, increasing in numbers, as the fame of his success spread abroad, took possession of all existing villages, to the exclusion of their former occupants. *The revolution has been so complete, that at the present day the original and wilder inhabitants of the pergunnah are found to have no fixed interest or property in the soil, and earn a livelihood* ONLY BY SLAVERY AND HIRED LABOR."—"Such was the condition of this province when taken possession of by" (the British) "government, as purchaser at auction, in the year 1814." —"The household of the Raja, and of every considerable jageerdar, was a perfect feudal establishment. It was a matter of pride to be surrounded by a train of *vassals* under the titles of *burkundauzes*" (guards,) "*fakeers*" (devotees,) "*shikarees*" (huntsmen,) "and *bhats* or *bad feroshes*" (family poets or bards,) "and a still larger retinue of *serfs* called *kumeas*, whose state of bondage is the counterpart to the condition of the *servi* of the eighth and ninth centuries in Europe." Such is the most probable origin of Hindu slavery; and that Muhammadan slavery originated in a like cause, is still less doubtful, since, according to Muhammadan law, "they *only* are slaves who are captured in an infidel territory in time of war, or who are the descendants of such captives. Perhaps there is no point of law which has been more deliberately and formally determined than this."—*Macnaghten's Principles and Precedents of Muhammadan Law, Preliminary Remarks*, pp. xxx, xxxi.

The practical consequences deducible from this view of the origin of Hindu and Muhammadan slavery are of great importance, since we thus see the enormous amount of long-standing injustice and cruelty which has been virtually sanctioned and ratified by the British government in legalizing these two systems of slavery. Neither the origin nor the administration of the British power in India is faultless, but it is a wholly gratuitous and useless supererogation of demerit to endorse the oppression and fanaticism of the Hindu and Muhammadan conquerors of India, by upholding and perpetuating the slavery which they respectively created, however unjust and cruel to the Aborigines, an important subdivision of the native population, and however inconsistent with the spirit and practice of British institutions. In reasoning and legislating on this subject, exclusive consideration has been given to the supposed rights of the Hindu and Muhammadan slave-owners, as if the rights of the enslaved natives of India and of the free people of Great Britain were not equally worthy of attention. When the beleaguered fortress of an enemy is taken, is it not the captor's first business to liberate the prisoners in the dungeon? The Hindu and Muhammadan conquerors had no better right to enslave than the English conquerors have to emancipate, and emancipation would appear to be the natural consequence of the overthrow of the oppressors. This appears to have been the legal effect of the Muhammadan conquest, for although the custom of Hindu slavery probably continued to exist under the Muhammadan government, there is no evidence that its legality was ever recognised; while the legality of Hindu slavery has been revived and that of Muhammadan slavery has been continued by the British government which should have equally refused its sanction to both. It is not the rights of the slave-population only that have been neglected; the feelings and the principles of the government and people of Great Britain have also been outraged. While Great Britain is moving heaven and earth to abolish slavery and the slave-trade in the West, is it, among other objects, to extend, to perpetuate, to confirm Hindu and Muhammadan slavery, that she delegates to a few individuals the powers of government over the many millions that acknowledge her sway in the East? The government and the people of Great Britain are called upon to adopt immediate practical measures in order to repel an imputation, for which appearances have hitherto afforded too much ground.

The next prolific source of slavery in India is the sale of free children by their parents. The existence of this practice is so notorious, that it seems scarcely necessary to support the statement by any authority. Mr. Colebrooke says:—"The number of slaves continually diminishing, a demand constantly exists for the purchase of them, which is supplied chiefly by the sale of children by their parents in seasons of scarcity and famine, or in circumstances of individual or peculiar distress."* This must be understood to refer to the Bengal presidency; and with reference to the Madras territory, Mr. A. D. Campbell states that "individuals generally become domestic slaves by being sold when children by their parents, in years of scarcity approaching to famine, for famine itself in the British territories is happily now nearly unknown."† Unhappily the incorrectness of the last assertion may be established by the most conclusive evidence, for there is perhaps no country in the world that has been subjected in modern times to so many severe and heart-rending famines as British India, and we may hence infer how considerable the number of those who by means of slavery have been preserved from starvation, and in times of famine have been consigned to

* Harington's Analysis of the Laws and Regulations, Vol. III. p. 747.

† Mr. Campbell's Letter, as above, p. 572.

slavery. Mr. Colebrooke very properly vindicates the motives of the parents in selling their children on these occasions. "During a famine or a dearth," he says, "parents have been known to sell their children for prices so very inconsiderable, and so little more than nominal, that they may in frequent instances have credit for a better motive than that of momentarily relieving their own necessities, namely, the saving of their children's lives by interesting in their preservation persons able to provide nourishment for them. The same feeling is often the motive for selling children when particular circumstances of distress, instead of a general dearth, disable the parents from supporting them." He is however mistaken when he goes on to state that "there is no reason to believe that they are ever sold from mere avarice and want of natural affection in the parent. The known character of the people and proved disposition in all the domestic relations, must exempt them from the suspicion of such conduct. But the pressure of want alone compels the sale, whether the immediate impulse be consideration for the child, or desire of personal relief. So long therefore as no established fund or regulated system for the relief of the indigent exists, it does not seem practicable to prevent or restrain the disposal of children by their parents, which is lawful by their own laws."*

That in India, whence an enormous revenue is drawn, and where numerous expensive establishments are maintained, there is no established fund or regulated system for the relief of the destitute, is one feature of the British government of that country. That in the absence of such a provision, slavery, which implies so many evils and produces so many more in the state of society where it exists, is held to be a good, and furnishes the only means by which indigent parents in times of famine and distress can rescue

* Harington's Analysis, Vol. III. pp. 747, 748.

themselves and their children from starvation, and that this resource is employed to such an extent that the sale of children under such circumstances constitutes, in Mr. Colebrooke's opinion, at least under the Bengal presidency, the chief source of domestic slavery,—these are other features of the same system of government. But surely these facts do not lessen the abhorrence of slavery which every civilized and free man must entertain, but tend rather to increase the conviction of the pernicious working of a system of government under which that which is evil in itself, the effect of evil, and the cause of evil, becomes by dire necessity a comparative good.

In the preceding extract, Mr. Colebrooke has expressed the opinion that the selling of children by their parents is "lawful by their own laws," and that "there is no reason to believe that they are ever sold from mere avarice or want of natural affection in the parent." In opposition to this view, and in illustration of the evils to which the mere existence of the state of slavery leads, the following passages may be cited form a high native authority, being extracts from a legal opinion delivered by the law-officers of the Sudder Dewany Adawlut in 1809. "With regard to *the custom prevailing in this country*" (*India*) "of hiring children from their parents for a very considerable period, such as for seventy or eighty years, and *under this pretext making them slaves, as well as their progeny also*, under the denomination of *Khanazad*, (domestic slaves,) the following laws are applicable: It is lawful and proper for parents to hire out their children to service; but this contract of hire becomes null and void when the child arrives at years of discretion, as the right of paternity then ceases."—"*It is customary* also among women who keep sets of dancing girls to purchase female children from their parents, or by engagements directly with the children themselves. Exclusively of the *illegality* of such purchases, there is a further evil resulting from this practice, which is, that the children are taught dancing and singing for others, and are also made prostitutes; both of which are extremely improper and *expressly forbidden by the law.*"*

The illegality of the sale and purchase of free children is here unequivocally declared; and it thus appears that the existence of the state of slavery not only opens a door for the relief of the destitute in times of famine and distress, but also affords a pretext and facility to unnatural parents to sell their children and their children's children into perpetual servitude and prostitution. There are other purposes sometimes answered by the purchase of children, such as initiation into a particular sect or religion. Thus, among the Hindus, there are certain "religious orders, the members of which purchase children to bring them up and initiate them in the religious order to which they themselves belong. Being restricted in their selection of subjects to the higher castes of the Hindus, they do not readily find persons of the requisite caste willing to part with their children, and being in general opulent from the union of the commercial with the religious profession, they are able to tempt the cupidity of parents by a large pecuniary consideration, and often by a provision for life."† In like manner Muhammadans are represented as having largely recruited their ranks by the same means, particularly in the district of Bahar, (Hamilton, Vol. II. pp. 652, 653); and with reference to the Madras presidency, it is stated by Mr. Campbell that "under the spirit of proselytism which characterizes the Musalman faith, a male infant is no sooner purchased than it is circumcised; and whether male or female, it is invariably brought up in the Muhammadan creed, which, if it be a Hindu (as is usually the case,) irrevocably excludes it from all return

* Macnaghten's Principles and Precedents of Muhammadan Law, pp. 314, 315.

† Harington's Analysis, Vol. III. p. 748.

to its parents or relations."* Christian missionaries and philanthropists in India have also established institutions for the reception of native orphans and of children whose parents are willing to part with their offspring, who are brought up and educated as Christians. There have no doubt been instances, probably many, in which, at the same time that the care of the child was undertaken, money was given to the famishing parents, which they may have regarded as the purchase-money of their offspring, although it was not so considered by the donor.

The result is, that from various motives on the part of parents, sometimes from the strength of natural affection, and sometimes from the weakness and want of natural affection, children are sold by their parents; and that for various purposes on the part of those who buy them, sometimes from pure benevolence for the preservation of life, sometimes from sectarian zeal, and sometimes for the degrading occupation of vice and prostitution from their earliest youth, orphans as well as the children of living parents are bought. It does not appear that any good or benevolent purpose contemplated in these transfers might not be, and would not be, equally effected if slavery did not exist; while at the same time the existence of slavery affords an apparent and reputed legal shield under which profligate parents may throw off the obligations of humanity towards their children, fanaticism make its unwilling converts, and vice secure and retain its youthful victims. Is this a state of things which the civilized world will not exclaim against? Is this a state of things of which the religious and moral, the free and slavery-hating people of England will not instantly and loudly demand the abrogation?

The next source of slavery in India to be noticed is kidnapping, an evil the extent of which cannot be fully known,

* Mr. Campbell's Letter, as above, p. 572.

but which evidently owes much of its activity to the existence of slavery. Mr. Colebrooke says:—"The greatness of the reward" offered by certain religious orders in India for children, "has been supposed to lead to kidnapping in some instances of this nature, though not frequently, since the purchaser requires to be ascertained of the parentage of the child."* Slaves as well as free persons are kidnapped in the district of Silhet. "A few persons," says Hamilton, Vol. II. p. 554, "principally slaves, are inveigled away by bazeegurs and wandering fakeers."—"The practice of inveigling away its free natives for the purpose of selling them at Dacca, Patna, Calcutta, and Moorshedabad, still continues, although, from the vigilance of the British authorities, the attempt is rarely successful." This crime appears to be practised at the present day, under the very eye of government, and in the very heart of Calcutta. "A correspondent informs us," says the Calcutta Christian Advocate of August 24, 1839, "that the practice of enticing away young native widows, and of kidnapping and purchasing young destitute native children, for the vilest bazar purposes, is daily carried on to a considerable extent in Calcutta." Cases of this nature sometimes come before the courts of criminal justice. In the annual statements connected with the administration of criminal justice for the lower provinces (Bengal and Behar,) for the year 1836, it appears that in those two provinces, in that year, there were seven cases of "child-stealing, for the purpose of selling in slavery," for which two persons were convicted and sentenced by the magistrates of districts, and ten persons by the commissioners of circuit and session judges. In the same provinces and in the same year there were thirteen cases of "illegal purchase or sale of slaves," for which twenty-one persons were convicted and sentenced by the magistrates. The distinc-

* Harington's Analysis, Vol. III. p. 748.

tion between these two classes of crime would appear to be, that in the former case *free* children were stolen for the purpose of being sold in slavery, and that in the latter case persons *already slaves* were illegally purchased or sold, previous to which it would seem that they must have been taken by force or fraud from their legal owners. These twenty cases and thirty-three convictions occurred in one year in two provinces, exclusive of those which may have occurred within the jurisdiction of the judges and magistrates of Calcutta, and exclusive also of similar cases in the Eastern and North-Eastern, Western and North-Western provinces of the Bengal presidency. Moreover, it is by no means to be assumed that *all* the cases of the kidnapping of free children or the illegal sale of slaves that actually occurred in Bengal and Behar in 1836, came under judicial cognizance and trial.

Mr. Chaplin's Report (p. 150) shows that in the Mahratta country subject to the Bombay presidency, the practice of kidnapping has arisen out of the sale of children by their parents in times of famine. "The greatest portion of slaves," he says, "are reduced to that condition in times of famine, when parents sell their children for the double purpose of saving their lives and themselves from starvation. A great number have within these few years been imported into the Dekhan under these circumstances, and this mode of disposing of a famishing offspring seems beyond all doubt to have been the means of alleviating scarcity. One great evil has however resulted, that of kidnapping children for the purpose of selling them in distant countries as slaves. *This is a common practice amongst the Lumans and Brinjarees;* but it may be prevented by forbidding the sale of all children of whom a satisfactory account of the manner of procuring them is not given." It is in this province that the sale of slaves has been expressly prohibited, but slavery still exists, and it is probable that the sale and kidnapping of children also continue.

In the Madras territories also, kidnapping exists to a great extent. Mr. Baber states that while he was in India, his duties led to constant official intercourse, upon a variety of subjects, with the political residents at the courts of the neighboring states of Mysore, Coorg, Cochin, and Travancore, some of which related "to slaves who had been kidnapped in Travancore," a native state, "and sold to British subjects; and even to free-born children of various castes of Hindus, subjects of the Cochin or Travancore Rajas, reduced to slavery in the Honorable Company's dominions, who had been procured by the most fraudulent and violent means, and deprived of their caste by cutting off the lock of hair (the distinguishing mark of their caste), by making them eat prohibited food, and otherwise disguising and polluting them." He further states, that one of the varieties and sources of domestic slavery in the western provinces south of the Kistna to Cape Comorin, is "kidnapped persons brought by Bingarries and other travelling merchants from distant inland states, and sold into slavery." In 1787, when Fra Paulino wrote his account of Travancore, "several thousands of persons were being sold annually like cattle, and sent out of the country;" and in 1811, Mr. Baber relates that he discovered and suppressed a traffic consisting in the kidnapping of slaves and free-born children from the Cochin and Travancore states, and importing them into Malabar, and this traffic he states had been carried on for a period of twelve years by the overseer of the Company's plantation in Malabar, and under authority alleged to have been granted by the Bombay government. In that year, 123 persons who had been stolen were liberated. This, however, was but a small portion of the number originally supplied, many having absconded, and more than half having died, as ascertained from the survivors. The native agent employed acknowledged that in 1811 no less than 400 children had been transported to Malabar. This is a traffic which Mr. Baber affirms to have been carried on by an agent of the Company's government, under the authority of the Company's government, for the purposes of the Company's government; to have been continued for twelve years; and to have been suppressed in 1811 only after considerable opposition on the part of the local authorities. The Company's agent asserted in his own justification, and Mr. Baber thinks with truth, "that he would produce hundreds of them (slaves) in every town in Malabar, there being few Moppilla (Muhammadan) and Christian houses in which there were not some of them;" and the provincial court judges, who opposed Mr. Baber's benevolent efforts, admitted "that numbers of the inhabitants of Travancore had been introduced in a state of slavery, and but too often reduced to this situation by the most criminal means, into Malabar and the adjoining province of Canara." While Mr. Baber was exerting himself to suppress this traffic in Malabar, the Company's province to which the kidnapped persons were brought, the political resident at the court of Travancore, the native state from which they were taken, with equal humanity and firmness insisted upon the punishment of those British subjects who were carrying on the traffic in human flesh; "and there can be very little doubt," adds Mr. Baber, "that without such interference, the slave-trade would be revived with all its horrors."*

Mr. A. D. Campbell also states, that "there can be no doubt that children are sometimes kidnapped and sold as slaves without the knowledge of their parents. As superintendent of police at Madras, I succeeded in restoring several such children to their parents, among the lowest and poorest of the Hindus; and their anxiety to recover infants whom

* Mr. Baber's Letter, as above, pp. 550, 551, 552, 553, 556, 557.

they in all probability found it very difficult to support, would have done honor to the highest classes of European society. I may add, that from Malabar, a province on the western coast of the peninsula, where the ancient institutions of the Hindu government have descended to our own times nearly unimpaired, I recollect one trial having come before the Sudder Foujdary court in 1830, in which the members of a high-caste Hindu family, to conceal the disgrace to which they would have been exposed from retaining one of the daughters, whose chastity was more than suspected, forcibly carried her off to a distant province, where they were taken up on account of endeavoring to dispose of her as a domestic slave."*

While these pages are passing through the press, the London Times of January 23d, 1840, communicates the following flagrant case, on the authority of a letter, dated Madras, Nov. 15, 1839, from the superintendent of marine police at that place:—"I have the honor to be for the present beach magistrate and superintendent of the marine police, and on the first inst. I detected a party smuggling off eight young children to a native brig; these were rescued, and the parties brought to my office. I sent off a constable, who searched the brig, and rescued five more. The vigilance of the police found ten children secreted in a house in the Black-town. Pursuing our search and investigation, I proceeded myself to a house, suspicious that four children were there concealed, and captured one; the other three were discovered on the following day. From information which I obtained while the search was proceeding, I sent again on board the brig, and two very young urchins were brought on shore. In all we have rescued twenty-eight, two of them girls, and all between the ages of three and ten years. It appears by all the evidence adduced, that

* Mr. Campbell's Letter, as above, p. 572.

these poor children have been stolen, decoyed, and purchased; two from Bimlipatam, twenty-six from Caliogapatam; and I have no doubt, if the case is properly handled in the supreme court, that the nacoda, or master of the vessel, his owner, and his passengers, all Musalmans, will be convicted as slave-dealers, and the brig, the Magdien, will be confiscated. The children have deposed that they were brought away by the above parties; some of them say they were stolen, some that they were decoyed away, and a few that their parents sold them; they have given their former names, and their present names as fixed by their masters; they are all Gentoos; they have been converted, or rather forcibly changed, by their masters from that caste to Musalmans. I have the owner, nacoda, the passengers, and crew, in custody; the children are under my office, under my special care, and are as happy as possible; the brig is under my charge. Government have approved and confirmed all my proceedings, and the collectors of Ganjam and Vizigapatam are duly apprized and have orders from government to prosecute the most vigilant inquiries throughout their jurisdiction. The whole case is new and very important."

The only remark I will make on these facts is, that kidnapping is in several instances directly traced, and probably in all instances is traceable, to slavery; that if there was no slavery, there would be no kidnapping; and that while slavery continues, kidnapping must be expected. Kidnapping is one of the sources of slavery, and increases the number of slaves; but it is also one of the fruits of slavery, for it exists only in slave-holding countries, or is practised in free countries to recruit the number of slaves in slave-holding countries. This is one of those instances in which the *legal* violation of the rights of human nature is practically and morally condemned by the base interests, the bad passions, and the flagitious crimes which it produces, and by which it disorders and outrages society which law is designed to protect and to regulate. There can be no effectual suppression of kidnapping, however much we may profess to abhor it, while we cherish or even only tolerate its cause in the institution of slavery.

The next source of slavery in India is the importation of slaves either by land or sea. The law relating to the importation of slaves has already been considered, and however imperfect and inconsistent its provisions, there can be no doubt that they evince a desire to prevent the traffic. There are, however, grounds for suspecting that it is still carried on, although probably only to a limited extent.

Formerly the importation of slaves by land into the Bengal presidency was chiefly from Nepaul, Assam, and Gurhwal. Assam has now become a British territory, in which slavery continues to exist, and the trade in slaves, to whatever extent it may be carried on from province to province, is an internal and clandestine traffic, like that which Hamilton (II. 554) states still continues between Silhet and the other districts of Bengal. Gurhwal is under British protection, with a stipulation for the discontinuance of the slave-trade; and I have no reason to believe that the importation from Nepaul has been revived since the original prohibition. Hamilton, however, writing in 1828, states that some slaves "are imported from Cachar, Gentiah, and other territories beyond the limits of British jurisdiction" into Silhet, showing that at that time, according to his authorities, the importation by land, although prohibited, had not ceased.

The case is the same under the Bombay presidency. Mr. Chaplin says:—"The importation of slaves from foreign states now stands prohibited by the orders of the supreme government. *This, however, has increased the price without putting a stop to the traffic;*"* that is, with-

* Chaplin's Report, pp. 150, 151.

out putting a stop to it in the Dekhan, to which his whole report refers. When Mr. Chaplin speaks of the traffic not having been put a stop to, it is not clear whether he means the importation of slaves from native states by land, or from abroad by sea. It is in the former sense that I here understand him. Under the Madras presidency, the importation of slaves by land appears to have been principally carried on from the territories of the Rajas of Cochin and Travancore, under the instigation of British subjects, and its suppression in 1811 and 1812 is ascribed entirely to the superintending presence and firm conduct of the British resident, Col. Munro, without which Mr. Baber anticipates its revival. I have no means of knowing whether the British authorities in Malabar and the political resident at Travancore continue to be on the alert to prevent the renewal of this traffic in human flesh.

Slaves were formerly imported by sea, by Arab dealers, from the eastern coast of Africa, from Madagascar, and from the Eastern Islands, and there are grounds for believing that this traffic has not wholly ceased, although it is now probably limited to importation from the coast of Africa. In confirmation of this statement I have to remark that, although a very large majority of the slave-population in India is native and aboriginal, yet it is equally certain that there is a small proportion of African birth and blood, loosely denominated *Caffrees* and *Hubshees*, or Cafres and Abyssinians. I knew an Armenian family in Calcutta in which there were four such slaves, and although from this single example it would be wrong to infer that the practice of slave-holding prevails generally among the Armenians in India, yet the subject deserves inquiry, as I have no reason to believe that the family referred to was peculiar. I may mention also as an additional circumstance, that during part of the time I was resident in Calcutta, I was a tenant of a house belonging to an Armenian landlord, formerly occupied by an Armenian family, and situated in Amratola street, in which and in its neighborhood there are several Armenian families: one of the appurtenances of the house was a *Gholam-Khana*, or slave-keep, a roomy and not uncomfortable apartment, but with wooden bars and a padlock on the door like the cages of wild beasts. I have also been assured that African slaves are not uncommon in Muhammadan families, and I found a confirmation of this statement in the fact that by a census which I made of the population of the city of Moorshedabad, in 1836, under the authority of government, it was shown that there belonged to the household of the Nuwab of Moorshedabad sixty-three eunuchs, stated by the retainers of the Nuwab's family, from whom the information was obtained, to be of Abyssinian birth. It is not necessary to assert that all the slaves in India of African birth have been imported since the prohibition in 1811; but as most of them are young, and many of them, old as well as young, are eunuchs, it is difficult to believe that all were either imported, or are the children of those who were imported, before the prohibition.

From these facts alone I should infer that the importation of slaves from the coast of Africa into the Bengal presidency has not even now wholly ceased; and I proceed in support of this inference to state a case of actual importation which came within my own knowledge in 1826, implying the probability of previous importations to a greater or less extent by the same individual. This is the case of the Arab ship Adramytte, master Ruhim Seyud, which arrived in the port of Calcutta in the month of October, 1826, bringing for sale three slave-girls, one Greek and two Africans, belonging to one Hajee Durvesh, a passenger on board the vessel. This person had been known to make frequent voyages to Calcutta, but he had never brought, as far as could be ascertained, any legal merchandise, and, although professing to be a merchant, had on all occasions apparently come without any cargo, consignment, or shipment of any kind. A person who had occasion to go on board this vessel was assured by two of the Lascars or native sailors belonging to it that there had been three slave-girls brought in the vessel to Calcutta, one of whom was a Christian, and that they had been taken on shore by night a few days after the arrival of the ship at Calcutta. The two Lascars offered to come on shore and give evidence, if required, to that effect; and the information they gave was communicated to Mr. Constantine Pandazie, a Greek gentleman resident in Calcutta, whose feelings were interested by the fact that one of the slaves was a Greek. Mr. Pandazie applied to me for my advice and assistance, and our first object was to get positive and direct information as to the facts from the Lascars, but leave to go ashore was uniformly refused to them. After some days, however, Mr. Pandazie informed me that a Malay woman, who had for many years associated with the Greeks in Calcutta, and could speak the modern Greek, and was also acquainted with Hajee Durvesh, had in his absence called at the house in which he kept his slaves, and had seen one of the African girls, and conversed with the Greek girl, who stated that she had been bought as a slave by the Hajee, and was kept by him in a state of slavery and restraint, and entreated that means might be employed to set her at liberty. On the following morning I went to Mr. Pandazie's house, expecting to see the Malay woman, to take down her statements in writing and prepare an affidavit to to which she should be sworn with a view to ulterior proceedings; but in the mean time the Hajee, learning the nature of the evidence that had been obtained against him, had come forward and offered to surrender the Greek girl to the Greeks, which he accordingly did in my presence, at the house of Mr. Lucas, another Greek gentleman who had co-operated with Mr. Pandazie in the matter. He however denied that he had the two African girls, although when the Greek girl was interrogated she affirmed that he had brought them also with him to Calcutta. I was accordingly desirous of employing her evidence to prove the fact, but was disappointed to find that my Greek friends, having obtained the liberation of their country woman, were unwilling to proceed any further. Having failed to remove their objections, I laid the whole affair before government, who referred me to Mr. R. C. Barwell, chief magistrate of Calcutta, whom they had instructed to investigate the matter. This officer required me to prepare and swear to an affidavit of the principal facts as above detailed, and then told me that he would not proceed any further in the business, for this reason, that if he should fail to establish the criminality of Hajee Durvesh and those who aided and abetted him in the alleged importation of slaves, the rule of the government in such case was to make him pay the expenses of the unsuccessful prosecution, and that consequently without the certainty, which did not in this case exist, of obtaining a conviction against the accused, he would not hazard a prosecution at all. I will not remark here upon the spirit or tendency of such a rule; but will only say that, however reluctant to drop the subject, I felt myself unable to proceed with it any further, although fully persuaded in my own mind that the case might have been successfully established and the actors convicted and brought to condign punishment. All the inquiries I made satisfied me that the importation of slaves from the coast of Africa is still covertly carried on, and the extent can be ascertained only by a more thorough investigation than it was possible for a private, a single, and an unaided individual to attempt.

With regard to the Bombay and Madras presidencies, it may be remarked, that the whole line of the western coast of India, by its proximity to the coasts of Africa and Arabia and to the ports of the Red Sea, presents facilities for importation, which are increased by the existence on that coast of the Portuguese settlements of Goa, Damaun, and Diu, under the flag of which nation the slave-trade has continued to be carried on elsewhere. That African slavery exists at Goa is shown by the statements of Captain Henry Bevan to the commissioners for the affairs of India. "In the year 1821," says this gentleman, "as adjutant of the corps of pioneers, while employed in the neighborhood of the Portuguese territory of Goa, I enlisted several *African slaves or Caffres* who offered themselves as pioneers, having an impression that the act was perfectly allowable. A few days after they had joined the battalion a letter was received by the officer commanding the corps, from the governor of Goa, directing their restoration to the *Portuguese families* from whom they had eloped, being their slaves, and therefore considered in the light of private property." They were accordingly restored, and Captain Bevan adds:—"I witnessed some months afterwards the marks of harsh treatment endured by these unfortunate beings, who had been most cruelly lashed at intervals, and their wounds rubbed each time with red pepper and salt to make their sufferings more refined and excruciating, which was ordered by their masters as a punishment for their having absconded, and as a warning to *deter others from committing a like act.*" This clearly implies not only the existence of African slavery at Goa, but the existence of an African slave-trade by which the supply of slaves may be obtained; and the escape of the above-mentioned slaves from Goa shows the ease with which slaves may be and probably are smuggled from the Portuguese to the British territory. The continued existence of the slave-trade between Africa or Arabia and India is further confirmed by the facts brought out in the trial at Bombay, about ten years ago, of Captain Hawkins, to the details of which I regret that I have not at present the means of referring.

These statments are abundantly confirmed by the information contained in your recent work on the African Slave-trade, resting on the authority of Captain Cogan, of the Indian navy, accredited agent in England of the Imaum of Muskat, and on that of Mr. Erskine, political resident at Kattewar, in the province of Guzerat, under the Bombay government. On the authority of Captain Cogan you state that by means of the reserved trade carried on by the Imaum's subjects with those of their own faith, slaves are exported from Africa "to the north-west coasts of India." Now the north-west coasts of India are occupied, exclusive of the Ameers of Scinde who exercise an independent sovereignty, by the Baroda and Cutch governments, by the numerous chieftains of Kattewar and Guzerat, and by the Abyssinian chiefs of Jinjeera, Jafferabad, and Sucheen, all of them protected, tributary, or in some form dependent on the paramount authority of the British government, and their different ports presenting unobstructed inlets to the slave-trade. The Portuguese ports on the same coast, already mentioned, are equally open both to receive and to export slaves. In a despatch to the court of directors from the Bombay government, dated 12th May, 1838, Mr. Erskine says, that "a considerable importation of slaves takes place at Dieu (Diu), both directly from the Arabian Gulf, and from Goa and Damaun, from whence they are brought into the province (of Guzerat). For this I may confidently say I see no remedy whatever, as it rests entirely with the British government to say how far they consider it politic to interfere with their allies, the Portuguese, on this important question." There is happily no doubt now of the manner in which this question is regarded by the British government.

Mr. Baber, enumerating the various sorts of slaves found

in the western provinces of the Madras territory, specifies, with others, "persons imported from the ports of the Persian Gulf, in the Red Sea, or from the African coast;" and in another place, after noticing other descriptions of domestic slaves, he adds:—"The rest of the domestic slaves are persons, or their offspring, natives of Arabia, but chiefly of Abyssinia, and called Wadawar and Goolams, who came over with and are either the personal attendants of their masters the Seyuds (who pride themselves upon being descendants from the prophet, and who are very numerous on the coast,) or employed in navigating the Arab, Moppilla, or Lubbee vessels, or in the service of the tanguls or high priests of the Moppillas, in all the great Moppilla and other Musalman families in the towns of Mangalore, Munjeeshwar, Coombla, Bekkul, Cavar, Paiangady, Belliapatam, Cananore, Tellichery, Cuilandy, Barragurry, Calicut, Parperengady, Tirniwangaddy, Condooty, Ariacotta, Kootai, Parony, Panany; and *in fact in all the great towns throughout Malabar and Canara, these descriptions of slaves are to be met with.*" Here the existence of a large and widespread class of slaves in the British provinces of Malabar and Canara, who are either natives of Arabia and Abyssinia or the offspring of such, is expressly affirmed, and it may, I think, be at least asserted as highly probable, that the majority of those who are natives of Arabia or Abyssinia must have been imported since the importation ceased to be legal.*

These statements and authorities are the grounds on which I have been led to suspect that the importation of slaves into British India by land and by sea has not entirely ceased; and if they do not fully establish the fact, they at least make out a case for thorough and searching investigation. I may add that the employment of African slaves

* Mr. Baber's Letter, as above, pp. 551, 557.

in Muhammadan families in India is rendered the more probable because it is the custom in the neighboring Muhammadan countries. Mr. Lane, in Note 13 to the first chapter of his Translation of the Arabian Nights' Entertainments, says:—"The slaves of the Arabs are mostly from Abyssinia and the Negro countries; a few in the houses of very wealthy individuals are from Georgia and Circassia." —"Those called Abyssinians appear to be a mixed race between negroes and whites; and are from the territories of the Gallas. They are mostly kidnapped and sold by their own countrymen."—"Most of them" (of the eunuchs) "are Abyssinians or negroes."

Another source of slavery has been the sale of criminals, outcastes, and their offspring. I have already had occasion to notice the disallowance, by the criminal code of 1793, under the Bengal government, of the regulation proposed by Warren Hastings in 1773, for the sale of criminals and their offspring into slavery, and the discontinuance of the same practice in the Tenasserim provinces after their acquisition by the British. In like manner in the Dekhan, under the Mahratta government, Mr. Chaplin informs us that "a woman of Mahratta caste committing adultery or fornication was sometimes condemned to slavery;" and it is to be inferred that this mode of punishment is not employed under the British government. In the Madras territories, the practice appears to have prevailed under the native government of selling illegitimate children and outcastes into slavery. Mr. Baber mentions, as one description of slaves, "outcaste Hindus, who had been sold into slavery under or by former governments." Mr. Ravenshaw, the collector of the southern division of Canara in 1801, states that it was the custom of the Biddenore government to take possession of illegitimate children and sell them as slaves. In 1819, Mr. Harris, the principal collector of all Canara, estimated that of the total slave-population "20,000-

were persons (or rather their descendants) who had been taken in battle, or concubines, or Brahmin and Sooder women, who had lost caste by having connexion with men of inferior caste; the two last descriptions (he adds) were sold under the Musalman government, and their descendants continue slaves; and that under Mr. Baber, when magistrate here, some stop was put to this practice; *but there is no doubt it exists in an underhand manner at this day;*" that is, as I understand the statement, concubines and outcaste females still continue to be sold into slavery clandestinely by private individuals. Mr. Baber further states that, besides kidnapped persons and imported natives of Arabia and Abyssinia and their offspring, "the domestic slaves of Malabar consist of the descendants of outcaste persons who had been excommunicated either through some aberration from caste rules, such as eating with, or the food cooked by, men of low caste, or from cohabitation with men of lower caste than themselves, or within the prohibited degrees of kindred; and of Brahmins convicted of robbery and theft, who had been sold by former governments into slavery, to Chetties, Moplas, and to whomsoever would purchase them."* It follows from these statements that while the British government does not itself sell into slavery criminals, outcastes, concubines, and illegitimate children, it confirms the acts of former governments by perpetuating the slavery of such persons and of their descendants.

Another source of slavery is the sale of freemen by themselves, either for a sum of money or in redemption of a debt previously incurred. This practice prevails extensively in the countries and provinces east of Bengal. "The custom of debtor-slavery or mortgaged labor," says Hamilton, "prevails universally" in the Tenasserim provinces; and according to him no attempt has been made to restrain it. It exists in Bengal itself:—"Occasionally," says Ham-

* Mr. Baber's Letter, as above, pp. 551, 556.

ilton, writing of Silhet, "the poorer descriptions of free inhabitants sell themselves when in extreme distress.' Mr. Liston, in the Journal of the Asiatic Society of Bengal for 1837, has given a copy of a servitude-bond, such as he states is daily executed and in full force in the district of Gorakhpur, by which a native, for a loan of fifty-one rupees at twelve per cent. interest, comes under an obligation to give his own labor and that of his family to the lender at all times and in all forms, for an indefinite period, until the amount of the loan shall be repaid, principal and interest, in full. The effect of such an agreement would be, on the death of the father, to leave the children in bondage. The Muhammadan lawyers whose opinions Mr. Macnaghten has quoted in his Principles and Precedents of Muhammadan Law, after mentioning the practice of parents selling their children, refer also to the practice of freemen selling themselves:—"A freeman who has reached the years of discretion may however enter into a contract to serve another, but not for any great length of time, such as for seventy years, as this also is a mere pretext, and has the same object of slavery in view."—"Reverting to contracts of hire for service for a long period and the nefarious practice of subjecting freemen to a state of bondage and slavery under this pretence, it appears expedient to provide against such abuses; and with this view, to restrict the period of service, in all contracts of hire of freemen, to a month, one year, or at the utmost to three years."* The statement of these native lawyers both establishes the reality of the practice and denounces it as nefarious and deceptive, and designed to create and perpetuate slavery. Mr. Chaplin states that in the Dekhan "debtors have sometimes become slaves to their creditors." Mr. Baber in the western provinces of the Madras territory recognises one class of

* Macnaghten's Principles and Precedents of Muhammadan Law, pp. 314, 315.

slaves as consisting of those "persons who, in consideration of a sum of money or in discharge of a security for the payment of a debt, have bound themselves by a voluntary contract to servitude either for life or a limited period;" while Mr. Campbell considers that this description of servitude can scarcely be classed as slavery. "Besides the purchase of children in years of scarcity," says Mr. C., "I have heard of natives, to cancel a debt, voluntarily selling themselves as domestic slaves for a certain number of years; but this is unusual; and though classed as a species of servitude, it more resembles that of persons serving under written articles in Europe, than slavery of even the most qualified description." Mr. Campbell overlooks that the existence of the state of slavery in India, and its non-existence in Europe, wholly destroy the comparison between bond-servitude and service under written articles. According to Hindu law, the sale of a freeman by himself not only creates slavery, but the most degraded form of slavery. According to Nareda, an ancient and authoritative Hindu legislator, "that low man, who, being independent, sells himself, is the vilest of slaves: he cannot be released from slavery."* We have further the testimony of the respectable native Muhammadan lawyers above quoted, that the practice of contracting for a service of seventy years is adopted by freemen as a mere pretext to sell themselves into slavery. Even where such an intention does not exist, such bond-servitude must often practically become perpetual slavery by the inability of the bond-servant to discharge the pecuniary obligations he has incurred to his master. Moreover, the bond-servant, as appears from the Gorakhpur case, contracts not only for his own services, but those of his family, whom, until his pecuniary obligations are redeemed, he condemns to the same doom of slavery with himself. The authority of the native lawyers, whose acquaintance with

* Colebrooke's Digest of Hindu Law, Vol. II. p. 347.

the customs of the country cannot be questioned, and the concurring tenor of Mr. Liston's servitude-bond, prove beyond dispute that this species of servitude is practically one of the sources of slavery in India, and that provision ought to be made against such an abuse.

The only other source of slavery in India to which I shall refer, is descent from a slave parent or parents. In the actual condition of Hindu and Muhammadan society, as well as in the language of Hindu and Muhammadan law, one of the most common descriptions of slavery is that which consists of those who are born in the house, that is, born of female slaves in the houses of their masters. The rule is, that if a female slave should bear offspring by any other than her legal lord and master, whether the father be a freeman or slave, and whether the slave of the said master or of any other person, in any of these cases, such offspring is subject to slavery. With reference to this source of slavery, Mr. Colebrooke remarks:—"Neither the disposition of the people nor their accustomed mode of treating their slaves, tends to impede the rearing of children by any discouragement to marriage. I of course except the instances of concubines and prostitutes. In other cases a sense of propriety leads very usually to provide a match for the household slave; and the offspring following the condition of the mother, and the child of a female domestic slave being considered to be attached to the family by a stronger tie than the simple relation of slave to a master, no requisite indulgence is wanting to enable the mother to devote due care to the rearing of her progeny."* Mr. Chaplin states that in the Dekhan slaves "become domesticated in the houses of the upper classes, who treat them with affection, and allow them to intermarry with the female slaves; and the offspring of this connection, though deemed baseborn, if males, are often considered free, but if females, they

* Harington's Analysis, Vol. III. p. 746.

remain slaves. Marriage, however, is equivalent almost to emancipation, because when married slaves become rather an incumbrance to their owners."* These remarks might probably be extended to the domestic slavery of the Madras presidency, but it is to domestic slavery there or elsewhere that they should be strictly limited. Mr. Campbell expressly states that the children of agrestic slaves "are doomed to hereditary slavery."† This is doubtless at present the chief source of the predial slavery to which the aborigines of the soil are subject, particularly in Southern India. Hindu, Muhammadan, and Christian conquerors have successively swept over the land, but only to rivet their chains, to perpetuate their servitude, and to condemn them to propagate from generation to generation a race of slaves, so thoroughly debased, that the unjust and inhuman institution of which they are the victims wears in their estimation the character of an inevitable necessity, such as we ascribe to the laws of nature and of God.

Of the various sources of slavery that have been mentioned, there is not one that every Englishman, every subject or citizen of a free government, must not condemn. The enslavement of captives in war, the sale of free children by their parents, the kidnapping of children, the importation of slaves, the sale of criminals, outcastes, concubines, and their offspring, the sale of freemen by themselves—all are either expressly forbidden by law, or are the customs of barbarous times and governments to be mentioned only to be denounced. Can it be consistent with justice and humanity, by perpetuating slavery, to perpetuate the operation and effect of causes which justice and humanity must and do condemn?

* Chaplin's Report, p. 149. † Campbell's Letter, as above, p. 576.

LETTER VII.

TO THOMAS FOWELL BUXTON, ESQ.

Occupations and Treatment of Agrestic Slaves—Domestic Slaves—in British India.

Sir,—Having inquired into the probable number of slaves and the various sources from which the supply of slaves is obtained, I shall now examine into the occupations in which slaves in India are engaged and the treatment which they receive from their masters. This touches the real essence of slavery, and is necessary to enable us to understand the nature of the institution as it exists in India.

The first and most important class of slaves consists of those who, being chiefly employed in the labors of the field, are called agrestic or predial slaves. Mr. Colebrooke says that "in the lower provinces under this (the Bengal) presidency, the employment of slaves in the labors of husbandry is nearly, if not entirely, unknown." This is not quite correct. Thus Hamilton says that in the district of Dacca, "when an estate *to which slaves are attached* is sold privately, the slaves are commonly sold at the same time;" and the inference is that slaves are attached to estates only for the purpose of cultivation. In like manner in Silhet some slaves are stated by the same authority to have been "hereditary slaves for several generations," and it is added that they "are sold along with the estate on which they reside." In the same district of Bengal one of the magistrates estimated the class of slaves at one-sixth of the whole population, and considering the very remarkable subdivision of landed property in that district, many of the slaves are most probably employed in the cultivation of the ground for or with their masters. In Assam, according to Dr. McCosh, "all the drudgery of the household *and the labor of the field* is performed by slaves." Mr. Liston states that in the Gorakhpur district the landholders, in order to water and cultivate their lands, employ bond-servants; and the servitude-bond of which he has given a copy purports to have force over the bond-servant and over his whole family "for the driving of a plough and for remaining always at hand to execute every kind of labor that may occur." In the upper provinces, according to Mr. Colebrooke, beginning from Western Behar and Benares, there would appear to be three descriptions of predial slaves. The first are bond-servants by whom throughout some districts the labors of husbandry are chiefly executed. The second are the slaves of the free peasantry or petty landholders. In certain provinces the ploughmen are mostly slaves of this sort. The masters or owners are themselves cultivators, and are aided in their husbandry by their slaves, whom they very commonly employ as herdsmen or ploughmen. Those who are employed in this manner in husbandry by the inferior class of landholders are strictly slaves, and their condition differs from that of household slaves only as the former are occupied in out-door work and the latter in business of the interior of the house. The third class are a species of serfs on the estates of the larger landed proprietors. In some places the landholders have a claim to the servitude of thousands among the inhabitants of their estates, reputed to be descended from persons who were acknowledged slaves of their ancestors. They are to be considered rather as villains attached to the glebe than as bondmen laboring for the sole benefit of their owners.

With regard to the treatment of predial slaves under the Bengal presidency, I have met with very few facts directly illustrating their condition. The claims of the large land-holders on the services of the hereditary serfs just mentioned are stated by Mr. Colebrooke to be nearly obsolete, and scarcely attended with any practical consequences. Slaves of this description, he considers, do in fact enjoy every privilege of a freeman except the name. They pay rent and other dues for the lands they till and the pastures on which they graze their herds, and are not distinguished from the rest of the peasantry " unless by a questionable restriction of the right of removing at choice." This certainly is a very important restriction on the privileges of a freeman; but if in the progress of society the authority of the master is so far relaxed that it is the only restriction on the liberties of this class of serfs—the only remaining link of their chain—and if even this restriction has become questionable, as Mr. Colebrooke states, then it is clear that the time has more than arrived for breaking this link also, and for putting them in full and undisputed possession of all the rights of freemen. The slaves of the free peasants or petty land-holders are further described by Mr. Colebrooke as being " treated by their masters more like hereditary servants, or like mancipated hinds, than like purchased slaves," and as " laboring with cheerful diligence and unforced zeal." That this is often true, I think very probable; that it is universally the case, is much to be doubted. It is this description of slaves, as I understand, that Hamilton tells us are sold in the districts of Dacca and Silhet with the lands to which they are attached; and with reference to the latter district he adds that " the transfer of slaves takes place *both with and without the consent of the slaves;* but in the latter predicament only the mildest treatment can secure the purchaser any benefit from his acquisition." Mr. Liston also informs us that in the Gorakhpur district "a slave-holder may sell a whole family or what part of it may suit his convenience," and the deed of sale which he has published records the sale of a wife apart from her husband and of a son apart from his father. Mr. Liston also enables us to form some idea of the treatment of the bond-servants who are employed by the Zamindars of the Gorakhpur district to water and cultivate their lands. They "are paid *at half a cooly's rate*, and are at the same time liable to fine in case of absenting themselves from their superior's work." A cooly is the very lowest description of free laborer, and the rate of wages he receives in the country, out of large towns, probably never exceeds two annas or fourpence sterling per day. Half a cooly's rate will enable a bond-servant to purchase only a very scanty supply of the coarsest rice and pulse, without any salt, or fish, or vegetables, except of the last what he can pick up wild in the fields, to make them palatable. With these specific facts and statements resting on sufficient authority—the starvation-allowance given to bond-servants, the power sometimes at least exercised of selling separately members of the same family, and the practice of selling slaves, like chattels, with the lands which they cultivate, with or without their own consent—it is impossible to believe that the predial slaves found under the Bengal presidency receive universally that gentle and indulgent treatment which Mr. Colebrooke alleges.

But it is under the Madras presidency that predial slavery in India is presented in its worst forms; and in the letters of Mr. Baber and Mr. Campbell to the board of commissioners for the affairs of India, we have a complete view of it. In the following account I shall chiefly aim to give a clear and connected summary of their statements.

Predial slavery does not exist at all in the central provinces of the Indian peninsula, such as the ceded districts or Mysore, peopled by the Carnatacka nation, and it would appear to be unknown also in the northern Circars, Nellore, &c., or in the country where the people speak the Telinga language; but it is common in the southern provinces of the peninsula, or wherever the Tamil language is spoken, and it assumes its worst form on the western coast of the peninsula, or in the provinces of Malabar and Canara.

In order to form a just notion of the nature and extent of slavery in the peninsula of India, we must not confound predial slaves with those rude tribes that are inferior to them in social consideration, but are notwithstanding free and independent; such as the Moola or Kadda Cooramer, inhabiting the forests that separate Wynad from Mysore, the Naiadees in Malabar, inhabiting the more open parts of the lowland country, the Palgât Malaseers, chiefly inhabiting the Anamalla forests, and the Mallakooder tribe of mountaineers in Canara. Those tribes, the remnants of the Aborigines of the country, are in a most deplorable state of ignorance and barbarity, living almost in a state of nature, deemed unworthy of contact or association with even the slave-castes, unacquainted with the regulations of civilized society, and yet rendered amenable to its laws and sanctions. The condition of these tribes demands the earnest consideration of the philanthropist; but they do not yield obedience to any superior, they are not liable to be bought or sold, they are the unredeemed sons of the forest, wild men of the woods; in short, they are not slaves, and therefore are not embraced by our present inquiry. I hope that the time is not far distant when the civilization of the numerous mountain and forest tribes scattered all over India will be deemed a legitimate object of government; but in the mean time their claims to attention are sufficiently distinct from those of the predial slaves, although both probably belong to the same aboriginal race. The freedom of the one class and the slavery of the other constitute the distinction that is here contemplated.

The next circumstance to be noticed is, that there are certain tribes who, by submitting to a sort of qualified servitude, form a link between the independent aboriginal tribes and those that have been reduced to absolute slavery. In the upper country of Wynad, the Koorcher, Kooramer, Kadder and Pannier tribes or castes are agrestic slaves, or more properly conditional laborers. The Koorcher inhabit the Ghaut mountains, and with the Kadder attend to the cardamum cultivation, and cultivate a variety of hill products under the name of Koomeree. The Kooramer cultivate both the hills and lowlands, and also work in the gold mines in Parakameetel. Both the Koorcher and Kooramer are claimed as slaves by the hill proprietors, but they are never sold, and in fact they barely yield obedience to their *yejaman* or lord. The Kadder or Kādar are more submissive, though they also are never sold, and invariably desert if beaten or otherwise ill-treated. The Pannier alone, of these four tribes, are liable to be sold, but never out of the country of their birth. Their employment is to cultivate the rice-lands.

There is an important difference also, not to be overlooked, between the agrestic slaves of the eastern and those of the western districts of the peninsula. In the Tamil country the agrestic slaves are entitled to a certain proportion of the harvest reaped on the land they cultivate, and to prescribed fees in grain at each stage of the previous cultivation, as well as at certain national festivals. Some of them who are outcastes possess also a right to all the cattle which die from disease; and they eat the flesh of such animals as well as that of snakes and other reptiles. In general their food is the coarsest grain, but if a judgment may be formed from their appearance, which is generally that of stout athletic men, it is not deficient either in quantity or quality. Besides food and clothing, the latter of which is scanty, the master also defrays the expense of the marriage of his slaves, and presents them with small gifts on the birth of each child. A slave too may with his master's permission enlist in the army as a native soldier, or may enter the service of an European gentleman, (and many have done so without permission,) exercising all the rights of a free-man; but of late years the enlistment of slaves or Pariar in the native army has been prohibited by the government. On the western side of the peninsula agrestic slavery assumes a far worse aspect, particularly in Malabar. In Malabar the permission to take other service than that of his master does not appear to be conceded to the slave, except for the master's profit. The creatures in human form who constitute the agrestic slave-population of that province are distinguishable, like the savage tribes still to be found in the forests of India, from the rest of the human race by their degraded, diminutive, squalid appearance; their dropsical pot-bellies contrasting horribly with their skeleton arms and legs, half-starved, hardly clothed, and in a condition scarcely superior to the cattle they follow at the plough. The chief cause assigned for the superiority of the agrestic slave on the eastern coast over his unhappy brethren on the western side of the peninsula is, that the landed tenures on the eastern coast vest most of the land, and of the agrestic slaves who cultivate it, in the hands of corporate village communities and of Hindu temples or other bodies, and not in the hands of individual landowners, as on the opposite coast, although it does not very clearly appear in what manner this cause operates to produce such an effect. The vicinity of some of the Tamil slaves to Madras, where the existence of the British code renders slavery altogether unknown, and the facility with which some have taken refuge there and entered into the service of Europeans, appear also to have contributed to raise them above their brethren on the other coast; and in general amongst the slaves in the vicinity of large towns, a growing spirit of industry and independence has been observed, which, but for the countenance their masters have received from the British government in their unnatural acquisitions, would, it is believed, have long ago ripened into an assertion of their liberty.

Even on the western side of the peninsula agrestic slaves are not all treated with equal harshness. The two principal British slave-holding provinces on the western side are Malabar and Canara, and in most parts of the latter slaves are in general better off than in the former. In Canara, though not allowed to enter the house or to touch the persons of the free castes, they are permitted to approach them; and it is only early in the morning, after Brahmins have bathed, and before meals, that slaves are obliged to leave the road to avoid contaminating them. In Malabar, on the contrary, a slave must not approach any of the free castes nearer than a distance of ninety-six steps, and if he wishes to speak to any of them he must stand at that distance and cry aloud to them. In Canara too the slaves are allowed to possess a small slip of ground of their own, and they have occasionally a few articles of value about their persons; but in Malabar, although the slaves sometimes sow dry grains and cultivate yams, and although they are found also to have a few plantain trees and now and then a solitary jack-tree in the ground adjoining their huts, the fruits of which they enjoy, yet the right in the soil and in the trees is in the master. In the southernmost subdivisions of Canara, called Coombla and Neelesheram, the local prejudices are everywhere the same as in Malabar, and if possible even more inveterate than in that province, in consequence of the chief portion of the people consisting of Nairs, the name by which the Hindu military caste is distinguished in the south of India. In the native states of Travancore and Cochin, there is no reason to suppose that slaves are better treated than in Malabar, except that the inhabitants are more lightly assessed than in the British province, and consequently in better circumstances, and able to treat their slaves with greater indulgence.

Another distinction is between the predial slaves of the Hindu and Muhammadan divisions of the native community, and also between those who reside in the vicinity of the sea-coast and in the inland districts. The treatment of slaves belonging to Muhammadan masters generally is more liberal than that which the slaves of Hindu masters receive, and the difference is ascribed to the former being more frugal and industrious, having fewer ceremonies, and being in better circumstances than "their more generous though too improvident Hindu neighbors;"—the meaning of which is, that Hindu slave-owners expend all their generosity on themselves, and allow the effects of their improvidence to fall upon their slaves. Agrestic slaves in the vicinity of the sea-coast and large towns are much better off than those in the inland districts, in consequence of the opportunities they possess, when their masters do not require their services, of subsisting themselves by working for strangers, cutting and selling grass and fuel, and serving as porters. In the inland districts no such opportunities occur, and when their master has no work for them to do, and their usual scanty allowance is either lessened or altogether withheld, the slaves are reduced to extreme destitution. Even on the sea-coast, masters very often refuse permission to their slaves to work for themselves; and in those instances when without work and allowances from their masters, they are in as great distress as those in the inland districts.

A general feature belonging to agrestic slavery under the Madras presidency is, that the slaves are all Hindus in name, however rude the forms of the Hindu religion which they practise, and that they become slaves by birth alone in certain castes which immemorial usage has doomed to hereditary bondage. These castes are believed never to have stood in any other relation to the free castes than that in which they now stand, and they are believed to be destined to stand in the same relation to the remotest posterity. One effect of this relation is, that apart from the servitude which each slave owes to his own master, all agrestic slaves are considered, as far as relates to caste distinctions, under bondage to all Hindu free-born persons; but those distinctions are confined to leaving the road and other external marks of inferiority, which of course would cease with slavery itself. These distinctions are rapidly wearing away, especially in Canara, and in north Malabar they are much less attended to than in the southern division, where, at Calicut, though it is the seat of a British court and the head station of the principal collector, they are perhaps even more prevalent than during the period of the native government. Mr. Baber shows that these invidious distinctions have led to unjust pecuniary exactions from the slaves, to affray, and even to murder.

Another effect of this relation is, that agrestic slaves are liable to be called upon to perform certain acts of servitude to the whole Hindu community, and also to the government of the country. On behalf of the community, they are required to drag the enormous cars of the idols round the villages or temples, for which purpose immense cables, drawn by many thousands, are necessary. In Tanjore, in particular, from the great number of the temples and frequency of the festivals, this is a very onerous duty. The slaves are called to this duty by the official requisition of the government collector or magistrate, issued to their masters; and in one province, the omission, probably intentional, of the magistrate to enforce the attendance of any slaves on this duty, greatly impeded the Hindu festivals, and created a religious enthusiastic hostility dangerous to the government, which nearly broke out into open rebellion. Orders were therefore issued to cause their attendance as usual. Even those of the slaves who, under the instruction of Catholic or Protestant missionaries, have become Christians, are not exempted by the magistrate from this part of the long-established civil duties, common to the whole class of slaves. In another instance, after thirteen of the slaves who were dragging the car lost their lives by the wheels passing over them, government directed that the practice of pressing them into this service should be discontinued; but in some provinces, at least, it is still enforced. A servant of the East India Company states that in the province of Tanjore alone there are "not less than four hundred thousand people compelled year by year to leave their homes, and proceed often ten, twenty, or thirty miles, without any provision or remuneration, for the purpose of dragging the idol cars of the province;" and that "unless government were to enforce their attendance, not a man of them would come, nor would they when arrived pull the cars, were it not for dread of government, and of the whip applied by the government servants to compel their exertions."* This extract, it may be remarked in passing, seems also to indicate the probable number of slaves in Tanjore, of which I have not met with an estimate elsewhere. If the number of persons above mentioned compelled to draw the idol cars is correct, and if, as Mr. A. D. Campbell seems to imply by his statements, slaves only are required to perform this duty, it follows that the number of slaves in Tanjore alone does not fall short of 400,000.

It is not for the Hindu community only that slaves are required to perform compulsory and unrequited services. The English rulers of the country make still more numerous and severe exactions on their own account. They are called on by the requisition of the collector or magistrate, issued to their masters, to aid in stopping any sudden breach in the great works of irrigation conducted at the expense of govern-

* See Memorial to the Madras Government, Appendix, D. p. 36.

ment; and they are pressed in gangs to make or repair the high roads, to carry the baggage of the public servants and their establishments, of marching regiments, and of travellers, to carry treasure-remittances from the several subordinate stations for the collection of revenue to the collector's treasury at Calicut, ("and scarcely a week passes," says Mr. Baber, "that parties of 10 to 100 of these slaves do not arrive,") to bring stolen property with parties of robbers sent in to the head station by the different police officers, and to carry the Company's tobacco, of which the government has a monopoly, from the several depots for sale to the subordinate stations—on all which occasions they are guarded by armed men to prevent their running away. The seizure of slaves in this manner was one of the most prominent causes of the discontents that led to the disturbances in the mountainous region of Wynâd in 1812, and a pledge was then given that this oppressive practice should be discontinued; but the pledge has been disregarded, and the practice is justified by the local authorities, and countenanced by the government itself, as a necessary evil. Of the extent to which this evil at present exists an idea may be formed by a fact which Mr. Baber states, that the native superintendent of police at Kuddalore in Wynâd "threw up his appointment rather than be instrumental in such oppression and cruelty." Little as the native officers of government in general sympathize with the sufferings of their own countrymen, there are occasionally found some, it appears, who are repelled from the service of the English government by the rapacity and exactions of which the system would make them the tools.

The agrestic or field slaves in the Tamil country are employed by their masters in every department of husbandry; the men in ploughing the land and sowing the seed, and in all the various laborious works necessary for the irrigation of the land upon which rice is grown, the women in transplanting the rice plants, and both sexes in reaping the crop. Their labor is usually confined to the rice or irrigated lands; the lands not artificially irrigated, watered only by the rains of heaven, and producing what in India is technically called dry grain, being seldom cultivated for their masters, whose stock is concentrated on the superior irrigated soils, and any cultivation by the slaves in unirrigated land is generally as free laborers for others, or on their own independent account. They work in bodies together, the village accountant registering the work executed by them, which he inspects; but they are not personally superintended by any one, nor placed under any driver. They usually work from about sunrise till sunset, with the intermission of a couple of hours for their meal during the middle of the day. They are not exempted from work on any particular day of the week, but obtain holidays on all the great native festivals, such as on those fixed for consecrating implements, the new year, and other great days. No particular task-work is assigned to them daily; it is sufficient that the slaves of each master execute the work necessary for the cultivation and irrigation of his lands. The lash is never employed by the master against his slave in the Tamil country.

In Malabar and Canara, as well as in the Tamil country, all the wet-grain lands are cultivated almost exclusively by the slaves, under the direction of hired laborers, and in Malabar the lash is employed, and its legality has been recognised. Their labors in the field are not confined to manuring, ploughing, sowing, harrowing, hoeing, reaping, and thrashing, but they are likewise employed in fencing, tending cattle, watching the cattle by night, and even in carrying agricultural produce, it not being customary to use carts or cattle in the transportation to market, and when the harvest is over, in felling trees and preparing materials for house-building, &c., and this without intermission for a single day, so long as their master can find employment for them. They not only have no days of rest during working seasons, but they work by day and keep watch by turns at night in sheds erected on an open platform in the centre of the paddy field, several feet under water, exposed to the inclemency of the weather, to scare away trespassing cattle, or the wild animals with which every part of Malabar, excepting the vicinity of populous places, is infested.

The food, clothing, and habitations of the field-slaves are on the lowest possible scale. With respect to their dwellings, Buchanan states that they erect for themselves small huts that are little better than large baskets; and so very impure are all castes of slaves held that they are obliged to erect them at a distance from the habitations of the free castes. In Malabar the allowance of clothing consists of a waist-cloth to men, and a fragment to females which is just large enough to wrap round their loins, and is of the value of 6*d*. to 1*s*. In some districts this is given but once a year, but more generally twice. As a substitute for these waist-clothes it is very common with slaves, especially in the retired parts of the country, to wear bunches of leaves, generally of the wild plantain tree, supported by a fibre of some tree or vine. In Canara the allowance of clothing is six cubits of cloth, a blanket, and a cloth to cover the head, for a man; four cubits of cloth for a woman; and four cubits for a child. Hindu female slaves, according to established custom, wear no upper garments; but female slaves, particularly those belonging to Muhammadan masters, adorn their persons with necklaces of cowry shells, glass beads, brass bracelets, and finger and ear rings. In Canara the daily allowance of food to a male slave is one and a half sers, or about three pounds, of coarse rice, two rupees' (say a dollar's) weight of salt, and a little betel-nut and leaf, the three last-mentioned articles being optional; to a female slave one ser, or two pounds of rice; and to a child three-fourths of a ser, or a pound and a half. In Malabar the allowance to a male slave is from one and a half to one and three-quarters sers of rice, that is, from three pounds to three pounds and a half; and to a female slave from one to one and a quarter sers, that is, from two pounds to two pounds and a half. The young and aged are generally allowed half of what able-bodied men and women receive, provided they do some work. The daily wages of a field-laborer who is a freeman is about a third more than that of a slave, and moreover he works only till noon, whereas the slave has to toil from morning until evening, with no other sustenance than his morning's rice-water and his evening meal, after which he has to keep watch by turns at night. When the slaves are not regularly employed, the daily allowance of food is seldom more than half of what it is in working seasons, and very often even that scanty allowance is withheld, which obliges them to seek work from strangers; or if residing in those remote parts where there is no demand for their labor, they are left to eke out a miserable existence by feeding upon wild yams and such refuse as would be sought after only by extreme wretchedness, and not unfrequently they are tempted by the cravings of hunger to rob gardens of their fruit. Mr. Græme, recently acting governor of Madras, uses the following language:—"The slave in the interior is a wretched, half-starved, diminutive creature, stinted in his food, and exposed to the inclemencies of the weather, whose state demands that commiseration and amelioration which may confidently be expected from the humanity of the British government." Alas! the expectation, however confident, has hitherto been vain and fruitless! In Tanjore, indeed, the government humanely attached to the house of each of the slaves, in common with the other householders who are not landowners, a small piece of land as garden, tax-free; and this is the only instance of care for the personal comfort of the slaves that I have found on record, and to this the government was stimulated by the benevolence of one of their own servants. It should also be mentioned that on occasion of marriages, deaths, and other extraordinary events either of joy or sorrow, small presents are made to the slaves by their masters, of money, clothes, oil, pepper, salt, and tobacco, but the two latter, especially the tobacco, though a necessary of life in a humid climate like Malabar, (where the annual fall of rain averages 140 inches, being more than three times what it is in the adjoining province of Coimbatore, or in any part of the Coromandel coast), are less common than formerly, owing to the greatly enhanced price to the consumer, especially in the vicinity of the Ghaut mountains, *since the establishment by the Company of a monopoly in those two articles.* Thus we see the East India Company's government, under temporary and individual influence, increasing the comforts of the slave in Tanjore; and under the permanent influence of its own grasping and monopolizing spirit, lessening those comforts in Malabar.

By the ancient laws of Malabar a proprietor is accountable to no person for the life of his own slave, but is the legal judge of his offences, and may punish them by death. At the present day all slaves are under the nominal protection of the law. Masters cannot take their lives without incurring the penalty of murder. They are also perfectly competent witnesses in all cases, civil or criminal, whether against freemen or others; and yet the evidence is strong that the law, in its actual administration, does not extend its shield over them. Mr. Græme, already quoted, says that "the interference of the magistrate" for the protection of slaves "is so systematically withheld, that they could not with any prudent regard to the interests of themselves and families resort to a higher power." "How stands the fact between the slave and his master?" asks Mr. Baber. "Can it be denied that their excluded condition, their ignorance, their poverty, their impurity, compared with the ability, the affluence, the influence, and high bearing of those they have to contend with, do present insuperable obstacles in the way of their getting redress, unless their masters step forward to see justice done to them?" And is it to be expected that their masters will step forward to see justice done to their slaves against their own injustice? In like manner Mr. Campbell states that violence and cruelty on the part of the master are punishable; but he does "not think that the civil magistrate has sufficient summary power to interfere for their due protection." The usual modes of punishment are flogging, putting in the stocks, and working them in chains. Formerly the practice prevailed of cutting off the noses of the slaves, and although this is now illegal, the practice has not wholly ceased. Mr. Baber tried a case in which it was proved that four slaves, belonging to the same owner, had had their noses amputated, and that although the case had come before the magistrate, no steps had been taken to bring the perpetrators of such horrid barbarities to justice. The slaves themselves preferred no complaints, for having no means of subsistence independent of their owners or employers, their repairing to and attending upon a public court is a thing physically impossible. Even if those provisions of the Regulations that require all complaints to be preferred in writing were dispensed with in favor of the slaves, and they were exempted from the payment of tolls at the numerous ferries they would have to pass, and an allowance were made to them by government during their detention at the courts, still, unless forfeiture of the right of property over slaves was the penalty for ill-usage, their situation would only become more intolerable than it was before they complained. Slaves are thus practically at the mercy of their masters and beyond the pale of the law. "There is hardly," says Mr. Baber, "a sessions of gaol delivery the calendars of which (*though a vast number of crimes are occurring which are never reported*) do not contain cases of wounding and even murdering slaves, chiefly brought to light by the efforts of the police; though generally speaking they are the most enduring, unresisting, and unoffending classes of the people."

There is another fact which speaks a very intelligible language as to the treatment which they receive from their masters and the protection they receive from the laws, and that is, that the practice of slaves in the British districts of Malabar and Wynâd deserting their owners and taking refuge in the native states of Coorg and Mysore is not unfrequent. It is only from those parts which border upon Coorg and Mysore that slaves take refuge in those countries. Many others further removed make the attempt, but they have been almost always overtaken. The consequence is, that the slaves in those parts of Wynâd and Malabar which border upon the states of Mysore and Coorg are better fed, better clothed, and better housed than in any other parts of those districts. It has been coolly proposed to the Madras government, by one of its revenue collectors, that the native rulers of Coorg and Mysore should be required to make pecuniary compensation to the owners of the slaves for the loss of them, although it is not pretended that the desertions are encouraged by those princes, or take place with their cognizance, or that any of their subjects entice the slaves, unless giving them employment and paying them for their labor can be so called. There are in Upper Canada several villages of free negroes who have escaped from their former owners in the United States: What would be thought in England of a demand for pecuniary compensation on account of those negroes made by the United States government and addressed to the government of Upper Canada? Mr. Baber remarks that flight is the only way the slaves have of showing their sense of ill-treatment and enjoying security of life and limb, and it would be cruel in the British government, and an aggravation of their hard lot, so long as the British tribunals are hermetically closed against them, if the government were to throw any obstacle in the slaves' way, or look to the rulers of those countries for any indemnification to their tyrannical masters. The laws do not extend to them adequate protection, and they consequently seek an asylum in the neighboring states. No people in the world, miserable as their condition is, are more attached to their natal soil than they are, and they would be the last to leave it and their families if they were permitted to live in security and enjoy that comfortable state of existence which they might acquire by their labor and are entitled to from their masters.

These desertions are by no means so numerous as to account for the fact that the slave-population in Canara and Malabar is stationary or diminishing, while the general population in the same provinces is rapidly increasing. By a census taken in 1807 of all Canara, the total number of inhabitants was found to be 576,640, and in 1827 the gross population amounted to nearly a million; making an increase of 70 per cent. in 20 years, while the slave-population has been stationary. In like manner in 1806–7 the general population of Malabar was, according to Mr. Warden's estimate, 700,000, and in 1827 it amounted, by Mr. Sheffield's returns, to 1,003,466. The increase in the general population has thus been nearly as great as in Canara, while, according to Mr. Warden's evidence before the select committee of the house of lords, the slave-population of Malabar has been diminishing. How are these facts to be explained except on the supposition that the increase of the slave-population has been checked by scanty fare, hard work, and cruel treatment?

The institution of marriage is observed among the slaves, but the man may separate from his wife, and also, provided

16

he has her consent, part with her to another on paying back to his master the marriage expenses. These separations are not by any means common, and when they do happen are less owing to themselves than to their masters. When the slave of one master marries the slave of another, it is usual for the female slave to reside with her husband; but it is optional to the master to allow this, and instances occur in which it is prevented, and in which the husband also is prevented from visiting his wife. The consequences have been stolen visits by the husband, frequent absences from his master's work, and severe chastisement ending in murder.

Masters possess the legal right of manumission, but it is never exercised in favor of agrestic slaves. A slave of the highest class may be hired from his master for seven and a half fanams per annum, equal to 3*s.* 9*d.* The lowly Pooliar Cherumar, who compose more than half the aggregate slave-population, may be hired for two and two and a half fanams per annum, equal to 1*s.* and 1*s.* 3*d.* The average annual hire of a slave is estimated at five fanams, equal to 2*s.* 6*d.* The sale-prices are correspondent. A slave of the highest class will fetch 250 old gold fanams, equal to 6*l.* 5*s.* A man of the lowest class will fetch 48 fanams, equal to 1*l.* 4*s.*; a woman, 30 fanams, equal to 15*s.*; a boy, 20 fanams, equal to 10*s.*; and a girl 15 fanams, equal to 7*s.* 6*d.* The average selling price of all castes, of which twenty are enumerated, is 132 old gold fanams, equal to 3*l.* 6*s.* Such is the market value of human cattle in British India. The sale of agrestic slaves is common. They may be sold for the debts of their master; but in the Tamil country the removal of them from their village, and consequently from their families, would be contrary to ancient usage; and hence the practice of transferring them with the land when it is sold, which, though not necessary in law in Mr. Campbell's judgment, is in the Tamil country almost invariably adopted. On the western side of the peninsula, on the other hand, the people, except immediately on the sea-coast, are nowhere congregated in villages. Each landlord there is resident on his own estate, and the slaves may be removed from one estate to another however distant. Even in Malabar, Mr. Baber considers that the practice of selling the slaves apart from the land is decidedly at variance with and in innovation of the law as observed in ancient times—an innovation which has been introduced since the Malabar coast provinces came under the Company's government. In this opinion he is borne out as well by the traditionary legends of the origin of the slave-castes, as by the fact that slaves are held under precisely the same tenures and terms as the land itself, although they are in general transferred in a deed separate from that disposing of the land, and sometimes without any deed at all. The innovation that has been introduced is moreover inconsistent with the due observance of their religious ceremonies, every part of Malabar having its tutelary deity, and all classes of slaves having their household gods, to whom on particular days they perform the same ceremonies that all other castes who are free-born do to theirs. They likewise cherish the memory of their ancestors, by consecrating a spot of ground where all the members of each caste meet and make offerings of meat and liquor—practices which, it would seem, could not have arisen unless they had been attached to the soil.

How the innovation referred to arose, does not clearly appear, but it is probable that it originated, and it is certain that it was confirmed, by the objectionable measure of realizing the public dues by the seizure and sale of slaves off the land in satisfaction of revenue arrears, or compelling their owners, the revenue defaulters, to sell them. Slaves were thus sold away from the estates where they were born and bred; husbands and wives, parents and children were separated; and all the nearest and dearest associations and ties of our common nature were severed—and all this done by authority, in execution of judgments and in satisfaction of revenue arrears. The extent to which this practice has been carried under the authority of government is shown by the statements of Mr. Vaughan, a collector of revenue under the Madras government, and a defender of such proceedings. "Why government," says this officer, "should give up a right which every proprietor enjoys, is a question worthy of consideration."—"The sale of cherumars," that is, slaves, says the same officer, "both in execution of decrees for arrears of revenue and by mutual and private contracts, is as common as the sale of land." And how common is the sale of land for arrears of revenue, appears from the statements contained in Sir Thomas Munro's Report, dated July 16, 1822, that in one single talook (or estate) out of 63 in Malabar, 1330 plantations and rice-fields were sold in order to satisfy public balances. In consequence of repeated remonstrances from benevolent and public-spirited servants of the government, the Madras Board of Revenue in 1819 issued orders prohibiting the sale of slaves in future on account of arrears of revenue in Malabar; but the sale of them has not been prohibited in execution of decrees, and of course slave-owners continue to exercise the right, to which the example of government has accustomed them, of selling their slaves indiscriminately one to another apart from the lands to which they belong, and even still, as is alleged, in discharge of revenue arrears. When proprietors are in want of cash to pay the revenues, the effect is the same to the slaves whether they are sold by the direct authority of government, or privately by their owners, to satisfy such demands.

In the preceding sketch of the incidents belonging to predial slavery under the Madras presidency, there are many circumstances which cannot but be regarded with shame by every British subject possessed of the common feelings of humanity; but the sale of slaves away from their birthplace and their families for arrears of revenue to the government furnishes the last touch to the dark picture. When the people of England are informed, on the undoubted authority of trusted and experienced servants of the East India Company, that the enormous revenue of that company is not only wrung from an abjectly impoverished people, but that up to 1819 it was in part obtained by the open and authoritative sale of slaves belonging to revenue defaulters, involving the permanent separation of parents from each other and from their children; and that at the present day the sale of slaves, not by the government, but by their masters, for the payment of government revenue, is still practised, it may be hoped that public indignation will be so distinctly expressed as to draw attention to the entire system of Indian government of which this is only one feature.

The next subdivision of the slave-population in India is that which consists of domestic slaves. The following description of domestic slavery under the Bengal presidency is from the pen of Mr. Colebrooke.* "We find domestic slavery very general among both Hindus and Musalmans. More trusty than hired servants, slaves almost exclusively are employed in the interior of the house for attendance on the members of the family, and in all the most confidential services. Every opulent person, every one raised above the condition of the simplest mediocrity, is provided with household slaves; and from this class chiefly are taken the concubines of Musalmans and Hindus, in regard to whom it is to be remembered that concubinage is not among people of those religions an immoral state, but a relation which both law and custom recognise without reprehension, and its prevalence is liable only to the same objection as poly-

* Harington's Analysis, Vol. III. pp. 745—747.

gamy, with which it has a near and almost necessary connection."—"A sense of propriety leads very usually to provide a match for the household slave; and the offspring following the condition of the mother, and the child of a female domestic slave being considered to be attached to the family by a stronger tie than the simple relation of slave to a master, no requisite indulgence is wanting to enable the mother to devote due care to the rearing of her progeny. It is not necessary to suppose the number of children born and reared to be deficient, for the sake of accounting for the call for a supply from other sources, of foreign importation, and home sale of free children. Opulent persons, in whose families more slaves may be born than they are desirous of retaining in their employ, do not sell, but emancipate those whose services they do not require; and persons of reduced circumstances, no longer needing nor able to employ so many domestic slaves as before, are not less unwilling to dispose of slaves by sale, which is a highly discreditable act, but give them their freedom without a price, however acceptable the value might be to them in their actual state of indigence. The manumission of slaves, being deemed an act of piety and an expiation of diverse offences, frequently takes place from religious motives, without either of the inducements before described; and slaves are often redeemed by purchase either expressly for that purpose, or from a less laudable impulse, as attachment to a courtesan, or some other cause."

I have before expressed my opinion of the general accuracy of Mr. Colebrooke's account of slavery in Bengal, but a much more thorough investigation into details would be necessary before pronouncing on its perfect correctness. With the imperfect information at present possessed, my conviction is that the kind treatment of domestic slaves, although I hope general, is not universal; and that the sale of them is not uncommon. With regard to the sale of domestic slaves, how improbable must it appear that their owners in times of distress would refrain from selling them, in a country and in a state of society where one of the great sources of domestic slavery is the sale of children by their parents and of freemen by themselves. In Arracan, where Hamilton tells us slavery is tolerated in all shapes, and where when a man wants to raise money he pawns his wife, how improbable that he would hesitate to pawn or sell his slave. Mr. Liston states that the deed of sale of slaves he has placed on record is such as is daily executed and in full force in Gorakhpur. In Dacca, according to Hamilton, the custom of disposing of persons already in a state of slavery is common throughout the country. In Silhet, according to the same authority, the transfer of slaves takes place both with and without the consent of the slaves. Hamilton further states that in Purneah slaves are allowed to marry and their children become slaves; but he adds, "the family are seldom sold separately:" it follows that they are sometimes sold separately and more frequently together; but whether separately or together, the fact of their being sold is undoubted. In Assam, according to Dr. McCosh, slaves are bought and sold every day for a mere trifle. In Boglipoor, Hamilton says slaves may be sold in whatever manner the master chooses, but they are not often brought to market: it follows that they are sometimes brought to market. In Bahar, we farther learn, on the authority of Hamilton, that slaves are very numerous, often liberated, *seldom sold*, and frequently, owing to the poverty of their owners, left to find a subsistence for themselves: it follows that they are sometimes sold, and this inference is confirmed by the fact, that in this district Muhammadans often purchase slaves for the purpose of initiating them into Muhammadanism. From these scattered facts and authorities I draw the general conclusion that the sale of domestic slaves under the Bengal presidency is not so unusual as Mr. Colebrooke's remarks imply.

I am equally doubtful of the uniform good treatment of domestic slaves. Although I do not question the kindness and lenity with which in a majority of instances they are regarded, yet there are several facts and considerations which prevent this admission from being made without exception. It is scarcely conceivable that the absolute authority which the master possesses over the slave should not frequently be abused, and accordingly many of the cases brought before the courts are cases of maltreatment of various kinds and in various degrees. Exclusive of cases of this kind brought before the Company's courts, I recollect that during my residence in Calcutta a Muhammadan lady was tried before the supreme court for the murder of a slave-girl, and I should add was acquitted, according to my recollection of the case, but the proof of cruel treatment was overwhelming. Another consideration is, that, according to Mr. Colebrooke's statement, it is chiefly from the class of domestic slaves that the concubines of Musalmans and Hindus are taken; and that, in conformity with the law of slavery, the persons of all unmarried female slaves are at the absolute command of their masters. It is impossible to doubt that such a relation must produce much degradation and suffering to the female slaves. Then, again, the profligate sisterhoods of Rangpur, described in a former paper, all of which consist of girls purchased when young, and to be reckoned as domestic slaves, no doubt are contented with their lot, but it is contentment with prostitution and infamy. If we turn to the male domestic slaves, we shall find many of them equally degraded and maltreated. A considerable class of them is composed of eunuchs—a name which describes them as objects of the most barbarous and inhuman cruelty. Still further, in Ramghur male slaves are employed by their masters for purposes of revenge and assassination; if they succeed and are apprehended, to be sacrificed to the laws, if they fail and return to their masters, to be sacrificed by them. To all this, it is necessary only to add that the custom of the Gorakhpur district gives the master the power to sell the members of a slave-family apart from each other; and we shall be convinced that the treatment of domestic slaves under the Bengal presidency is by no means universally of that mild and considerate character which it has been described to be.

The following is Mr. Chaplin's official report on the state of domestic slavery in the Dekhan under the Bombay presidency. "The subject of domestic slavery in the Dekhan would appear to require to be regulated by some legal sanctions, in order on the one hand to prevent the oppression of slaves as well as to check the traffic, and on the other hand to obviate the injustice that would be occasioned to private property by any interference amounting to an absolute prohibition of the sale of what has hitherto been deemed a marketable commodity. From the answers to queries it will be observed that slavery in the Dekhan is very prevalent, and we know that it has been recognised by the Hindu law, and by the custom of the country, from time immemorial. It is, however, a very mild and mitigated servitude, rather than an absolute slavery, and it differs essentially in many particulars from the foreign slave-trade, which, to the honor of humanity and of the British character, (though with little effect towards diminishing the extent of the evil,) has been discontinued by British subjects. Slaves are treated by the Hindus with great indulgence, and if they conduct themselves well, are considered rather as hereditary servants of the family than as menials. They become domesticated in the houses of the upper classes, who treat them with affection, and allow them to intermarry with the female slaves; and the offspring of this connection, though deemed base-born, if males, are often considered free, but if females they remain slaves. Marriage, however, is equivalent almost to emancipation, because when married slaves become rather an incumbrance to their owners. Many respectable Brahmins have one or more slave-girls as servants, and in a Mahratta household of any consequence they are indispensable. The female slaves are termed Laundees, and the offspring of Laundees by a Brahmin is designated Sindey. They do not however acquire the character of pure Mahratta blood till the third generation, though they call themselves Mahrattas from the first. The children of Mahrattas by a Laundee take the family name of the father, but the stain of blood is not wiped out till after the expiration of three generations. A slave-girl could not quit her master without his consent, but the master was obliged to clothe and feed her, and provide for the children whom she might bear him. The master could chastise his slave with moderation, but if death ensued from his severity he was punished severely by fine or otherwise, according to the pleasure of the government. A master could sell his slave, but in the upper classes it was not considered respectable to do so." Mr. Baber also, referring to the provinces of the Dekhan, says that "all the jagheerdars, deshwars, Zemindars, principal Brahmins and Sahookars, retain slaves on their domestic establishments; in fact, in every Mahratta household of consequence they are, both male and female, especially the latter, to be found, and indeed are considered as indispensable."

Notwithstanding Mr. Chaplin's description of the very mild character of domestic slavery in the Dekhan, some of his own statements suggest a somewhat different conclusion. It has already been mentioned that the sale of slaves in the provinces of the Dekhan, contrary to the recommendation of Mr. Chaplin, has been expressly prohibited by government; but although he considered that slaves should continue a marketable commodity, he also thought that domestic slavery should be regulated by some legal sanctions, in order to prevent the oppression of slaves as well as to check the traffic. It seems a legitimate inference from this view, that without such legal sanctions the traffic in a marketable commodity was not very inactive, and the oppression of slaves not wholly unknown. Mr. Chaplin also informs us that domestic slaves, *if they conduct themselves well*, are considered rather as hereditary servants of the family than as menials. How they are treated *when they conduct themselves ill*, appears from the additional statement that death sometimes ensued from the severity of the chastisement inflicted by the master on his slave. I do not mean to call in question the general accuracy of Mr. Chaplin's representation of domestic slavery in the Dekhan, but his account implies facts which tend very essentially to qualify the mitigated character which he has ascribed to it.

Under the Madras presidency nearly all the domestic slaves are Muhammadans, and they are confined principally, although not exclusively, to Muhammadan families. A Hindu who buys a child treats it not as a slave but as a servant, to whom food and raiment are due, and whose wages have been advanced to maintain the existence of the authors of its being, authorized by nature to contract for its service until it is old enough to confirm or cancel such compact. The text of the Hindu law, as well as its practice, clearly maintains such compacts to be temporary only, for it expressly mentions the gift of two head of cattle as annulling them, and entitling the child to legal emancipation. But such fine is entirely nominal; it is never practically exacted, and on the child attaining maturity it is in practice as free amongst Hindus as amongst Britons, unless long habit or attachment induces it voluntarily to acquiesce in a continuation of its service. The Muhammadan law is entirely opposed to the purchase of free children for the purpose of reducing them to a state of bondage; yet in practice, compacts such as are described above confer permanent rights on the Muhammadan purchaser, for under the spirit of proselytism which characterizes the Muhammadan faith, a male infant is no sooner purchased than it is circumcised, and whether male or female it is invariably brought up in the Muhammadan creed, which, if it be a Hindu, (as is usually the case,) irrevocably excludes it from all return to its parents or relations. The slaves are thus at once amalgamated with the family itself, who treat the males indulgently with somewhat of that privileged familiarity allowed in all countries to those who are permanently attached to a family, and are rather its humble members by adoption than its servants or slaves. They are well fed, well clothed, and employed in domestic offices common, except in families of the highest rank, to many of their master's relatives. The free communication with others, and facility of access to the British tribunals, which the want of all restraint over egress from the house ensures to the male domestic slaves, combine with the indulgent treatment of their masters to qualify their bondage so as nearly to exclude it from what the term slavery implies.

Such, however, is not the lot of the female domestic slaves, employed as attendants on the seraglios of Musalmans of rank; they are too often treated with caprice, and frequently punished with much cruelty. Once admitted into the harem, they are considered part of that establishment, which it is the point of honor of a Musalman to seclude from all communication with others. Mr. Campbell, from whom most of these statements respecting domestic slavery in the Madras territory are derived, states that the complaints made to him, as superintendent of police at Madras, against the nabob of Arcot, and subsequently, when magistrate of Bellary, against the brother of the nabob of Kurnool, gave him an insight into transactions committed in the recesses of the female apartments of these two personages, which has left on his mind a strong impression of the cruelty and wanton barbarity with which this class of female slaves are subject to be treated. The murder of more than one female slave alleged to have been committed by the brother of the nabob of Kurnool, induced Mr. Campbell repeatedly to address the Madras government; nor was it until he added to them the murder of his own wife that he was confined as a state prisoner, instead of being brought to trial for his life, as Mr. C. suggested. Indeed, little doubt can be entertained that the seclusion of female slaves in the harems of Musalmans of rank too often precludes complaint, prevents redress, and cloaks crimes at which Europeans would shudder.

Mr. Baber presents substantially the same views. He considers it difficult to determine with accuracy what the treatment is of the domestic slaves, how employed, clothed, or subsisted, amongst a people like the natives of India, who, whether Hindus or Muhammadans, observe a watchful jealousy in all that regards their domestic economy, and consequently of whose family arrangements and habits, and indeed domestic character in general, we can know very little. Generally speaking, however, male and female slaves are employed as menial servants; and a great many are kept for purposes of state. As the male slaves of a family possess the advantage of approaching freemen, and thereby the means of making their complaints known in case of any very severe treatment, there is no reason to suppose that their condition is particularly grievous, though it must be obvious that, under the most favorable circumstances, a state of perpetual servitude, whether employed as menials and kept for the purpose of saving the greater expense of free labor, or, *what is almost universal with respect to female domestic slaves,* for sensual gratifications, must at best be but a life of pain and sorrow, and, as such, as repugnant to humanity and morality as it is to the principles of British rule.

Such is predial and domestic slavery practically under

the British government of India. So little has the subject attracted attention, that the Court of Directors, the governing body in England, so recently as the 12th of Dec. 1821, say in one of their dispatches to the Indian government, "*We are told* that part of the people employed in the cultivation of Malabar (an article of very unwelcome intelligence, they add) are held as slaves; that they are attached to the soil; and marketable property;"—and this is said fourteen years after the appearance of Dr. Francis Buchanan's Journey through Mysore, Canara, and Malabar, published in London, under the authority and patronage of the directors themselves, familiar to every one who has the slightest interest or curiosity in Indian affairs, and containing a complete development of the system of slavery prevailing in the western provinces of the peninsula. Dr. Buchanan's work was not only published under the authority and patronage of the Directors, but the investigation into the resources of the three above-mentioned provinces which it records was performed under the orders of the Governor-General of India, and at the expense of the East India Company. Authentic information is collected at great expense to the state, and with much labor to the agent employed, and still these provinces continue to be governed, or rather misgoverned and neglected, just as if no such information was possessed.

If the government has been remiss, there are some of its servants who have not been indifferent to the claims of humanity, but who have endeavored to rouse the government they served to a sense of the obligations they owe to the slave-population. An inquiry into their recommendations, and into the reception they met with, will help to show what ought to be done, and will at the same time convince us that nothing will be done by the government of the East India Company without the powerful stimulus of enlightened public opinion.

LETTER VIII.

TO THOMAS FOWELL BUXTON, ESQ.

Unsuccessful attempts to ameliorate the Law and Practice of Slavery in British India—Abolition of Slavery.

SIR,—There is one other view of slavery in British India remaining to be presented. A bad law may not be justly estimated from the want of a clear perception of the various injurious relations which it bears to life and society. A bad institution may not be justly estimated from familiarity with its hurtful effects, and from the habit of regarding them as belonging to the natural and established order of things. The correction of these errors may be aided by examining the views of those who, by their official position, have been obliged strictly to consider the letter of the law, and to trace its effects to their cause, and who, under a sense of official obligation, have employed their earnest efforts to amend the law and to lessen its injurious influences. The ameliorations which good, and wise, and experienced men, holding high and confidential employments under the East India Company's government, have from time to time proposed, will enable us to appreciate the spirit of the law and the actual working of the institution of slavery in India, and not less the spirit and working of the government which has rejected or neglected recommendations proceeding from such sources. My information on this branch of the subject is principally derived from Harington's Analysis of the Laws and Regulations, revised edition, Vol. I. pp. 68—73, *note;* and from Mr. Baber's and Mr. Campbell's Letters in reply to the Circular of the Commissioners for the Affairs of India, already quoted.

The first person whose attention appears to have been strongly called to the necessity of amending the provisions and operation of slave-law in British India, was Mr. Richardson, who, in 1808, as judge and magistrate of Bundlecund, addressed a letter to the East India Company's supreme judicial authorities in Calcutta, enclosing the draft of a regulation proposed by him, and entitled "a Regulation for checking and reforming the abuses that have crept into practice and at present exist with respect to Slavery within the British dominions subordinate to the presidency and government of Fort William." The very title, it will be observed, of Mr. Richardson's proposed regulation assumes the existence of abuses that have crept into the practice of slavery, and recognises the necessity of legislation to check and reform them. In his letter of the 23d of March, 1808, after forcibly stating the evils of slavery and contrasting this condition with that of voluntary servitude, he offered the following suggestion:— "Aware of the great importance and convinced of the caution with which innovations should be attempted, or the ancient laws, customs, or prejudices of a people should be infringed, I presume not even to sketch out the mode or to fix the period of general emancipation; and perhaps the sudden manumission of those now actually in a state of bondage, though abstractly just, might be politically unwise. But there can exist no good reason, either political or humane, against the British government's prohibiting the purchase or sale of all slaves, legitimate or illegitimate, after a specified time; and likewise ordaining and declaring that all children, male and female, born of parents in a state of slavery, shall from a like date be free." The subject appears to have remained under consideration or in abeyance until March of the following year, when certain questions regarding the laws of slavery were put to the Muhammadan and Hindu law-officers of the Sudder Nizamut Adawlut, or the East India Company's supreme court of criminal judicature in Calcutta, by the judges of that court; the same questions, it is believed, which, with the substance of the answers to them, have been already quoted in Letter III., under Precedents relating to the Hindu Law of Slavery, Case IX., and Precedents relating to the Muhammadan Law of Slavery, Case II. Copies of the questions put to the Muhammadan and Hindu law-officers of the court, and of the answers received from them, were furnished to Mr. Richardson about the end of March, 1809, with instructions, if, under the information contained in those papers, any further provisions or modifications of the existing laws of slavery should appear to him requisite, to prepare the draft of a regulation, in conformity with the rules prescribed for such an occasion. Mr. Richardson's letter in reply, dated the 24th of June, 1809, after stating his sentiments on the expositions of the Muhammadan and Hindu laws which had been communicated to him, and giving his reasons for setting aside the Hindu law of slavery as supposed to have been long dormant under the Muhammadan government, and allowing operation only to the strict provisions of the Muhammadan law as the established system enforced by British criminal courts, not only in cases affecting personal freedom, but even in such as extend to life and death, concludes as follows:—"I am still of opinion that great alterations are indispensable in the application of the law and in the practice with regard to slaves throughout the dominions dependent on the Bengal government, whether we consider the question either as a measure of justice and policy, or as spreading wider the blessings of personal freedom and increasing the stock of human happiness. On the above considerations I solicit and rely upon the aid of the Court of Nizamut Adawlut to supply my deficiences to promote so great a purpose as that of liberating a great portion of our fellow-creatures from bondage and preventing slavery throughout the British dominions in future."

With the above-mentioned letter Mr. Richardson submitted the draft of a regulation which assumes in the preamble that "no reason exists why the state of slavery throughout the British possessions should not be determined by the Muhammadan law; the British government having acquired the right of legislation from a Musalman power in previous possession of these territories for centuries, and having adopted the Muhammadan laws particularly in all criminal cases, and indeed in all judicial cases except those of heirship, marriage, caste, or matters connected with religion;" and on this basis proposes the enactment of rules, the principal of which are in substance as follows: *First*, That all claims and disputes respecting slavery be made cognizable by the magistrates in the first instance, subject to the established control of the courts of circuit, instead of being primarily referred to the slow, vexatious, and expensive process of the civil courts. *Secondly*, That the Muhammadan law as expounded by the Musalman law-officers of the Sudder Dewany and Nizamut Adawlut (supreme civil and criminal courts) be made the standard for regulating the magistrates' decisions in all claims and disputes respecting slavery, whether the claimant be a Musalman or Hindu. The effect of this would be to emancipate all slaves held under Hindu law and all slaves held contrary to the strict letter of Muhammadan law. *Thirdly*, That when the claimant and also the person claimed as a slave are not Muhammadans, the claim be dismissed and the alleged slave declared free. This is a necessary consequence of the exclusive recognition of Muhammadan slave-law. *Fourthly*, That a similar judgment be given when the claimant may be a Muhammadan and the person claimed as a slave is not a Muhammadan, unless the former's right of property over the latter be proved according to the letter and spirit of the Muhammadan law. *Fifthly*, That the sale of children as slaves, whether by their parents or others, be prevented, and that measures be adopted through the police officers for rendering this prohibition effectual; that the theft and fraudulent sale of children by persons not their parents, as well as the purchase of such children, knowing them to have been stolen, be declared punishable by the courts of circuit; and that parents selling their children and the purchasers of such children be likewise subject to a fine equal to the price given for the child in each instance. It is scarcely necessary to remark that these provisions distinctly recognise the sale of children by parents and kidnappers as a prevalent practice requiring to be prevented by law. *Sixthly*, That proclamations be issued by the magistrates half-yearly for five years, and afterwards annually, notifying the rules enacted respecting slavery, and inviting all persons detained wrongfully in bondage, contrary to the letter and spirit of the Muhammadan law, to apply to the local magistrate for emancipation; and that any forcible means or severities practised by claimants to slaves for the prevention of such applications be punishable by fine or imprisonment. These provisions recognise the fact that there are persons detained wrongfully in bondage, and anticipate the probability that forcible means or severities would be employed to prevent them from making their wrongs known and from claiming their liberty. *Seventhly*, That the decisions of the magistrates under the proposed regulations be open to revision, in all cases of a written application for that purpose, by the judge of circuit holding the district or city jail delivery, or by the court of circuit at the chief station of the division.*

Such is the substance of the amendments of the law of slavery in India proposed by Mr. Richardson in 1809, and the leading idea which they embrace is the exclusive recognition of the Muhammadan law of slavery by the British government, and the strict application of the letter and spirit of that law to all existing cases of slavery. Mr. Richardson did not propose the formal abolition of slavery, but there can be no doubt that the effect of the adoption of the measures he recommended would have been nearly equivalent to abolition. All slaves held by Hindus, Christians, and all others except Muhammadans, and even all those slaves held by Muhammadans except such as could be legally proved to have been taken prisoners in war against infidels, or to be the descendants of such captives, would have been instantly emancipated by the mere *fiat* of the law. It does not appear to have occurred to Mr. Richardson that, on the basis which he himself lays down in the preamble to his proposed regulation, it was not necessary to recognise even the Muhammadan law of slavery. The rule to which he refers, and which he has incorrectly stated in his preamble, is not that the British government has adopted the Muhammadan laws particularly in all criminal cases, *and indeed in all judicial cases* except those of heirship, marriage, caste, or matters connected with religion, but that † the British government has adopted the Muhammadan laws with respect to Muhammadans and the Hindu laws with regard to Hindus in all suits regarding heirship, marriage, caste, and matters of religion, and that in all other cases (of which slavery is one) it has left itself free to legislate for all, and to judge between man and man on the principles of equal

* Harington's Analysis, revised edition. Vol. I. pp. 68—73, *note*.

† See Harington's Analysis, Vol. I. pp. 20, 67; and Reg. IV. of 1793, § 15, re-enacted for Benares by Reg. VIII. of 1795, § 3, and for the ceded provinces by Reg. III. of 1803, § 16.

and impartial justice. It is evident that, according to this rule which the British government has prescribed to itself, and which it has presented to its native subjects at once as a boon and a pledge, there is no ground for the institution of slavery to rest upon, except the mere will of the government, which has unhappily, arbitrarily, and ignorantly been pronounced to rivet the chains of the slave and to perpetuate the unjust dominion of the master.

Mr. Richardson first submitted his views on this subject in March, 1808, and with benevolent zeal reiterated them in June, 1809. In January, 1816, copies of the proposed regulation and of Mr. Richardson's letters were submitted to Government, with some other papers on the subject, and the Court at the same time intimated their intention of preparing and transmitting the draft of a regulation concerning slavery at a future period. It does not appear why Mr. Richardson's letters and papers had lain neglected during a period of more than six years.

In a letter from the Secretary to Government in the Judicial Department, dated the 24th May, 1816, the Court were desired, in preparing a draft of the proposed regulation regarding slavery, to "take into their consideration the expediency of requiring that the future purchase or transfer of slaves should be regularly registered, and that any breach of the rules which may be framed for that purpose shall entitle the slave to demand and obtain his freedom." This, it will be noted, is a formal admission by the Government that there is no registry of slaves in India. In 1816, also, Mr. Leycester, a judge of circuit, made a report to the superior court suggesting the abolition of slavery. On this report the Court of Nizamut Adawlut passed resolutions under date the 12th June, 1816, in which they state that "they fully participate the sentiments expressed by Mr. Leycester in abhorrence of hereditary slavery, and earnestly wish it could be discontinued with regard to all children born under the British protection. But whilst it is allowed to remain with respect to the progeny of existing slaves born under the British government in the West Indies and South Africa, the abolition of it on general principles of justice and humanity could not, the Court apprehend, be consistently proposed for India, where it has from time immemorial been sanctioned by the laws and usages of the country, and where, it may be added, the state of slavery is not so injurious to the object of it as in other countries where it is still maintained." These arguments for the continuance of slavery, which the Court notwithstanding cordially join in abhorring, will hereafter be considered. The facts are now mentioned only in justice to the memory of Mr. Leycester, and for the purpose of bringing into view his opinions as those of one who was not contented with expressing his abhorrence of hereditary slavery and then discouraging all efforts for the removal of the evil, but who stepped out of the routine of office to propose its abolition.*

The next public officer whose sentiments and recommendations come under review, is Mr. Harington. In 1817 we find Mr. Harington, the chief judge of the high court to which Mr. Richardson's communications were addressed, gravely announcing that the court over which he presided had "long had under their consideration the draft of a regulation proposed by Mr. J. Richardson,"† &c., from which it may be inferred that up to that time, whatever may have been said or written, nothing whatever had been done. In the month of November, 1818, Mr. Harington, in his capacity of chief judge of the Nizamut Adawlut, being then absent from the presidency, transmitted to the court a minute containing his sentiments upon the regulation proposed by Mr. Richardson, with the draft of a regulation suggested by himself *for the guidance of courts of judicature in cases*

* Harington's Analysis, Vol. III. p. 762, *note*.
† Ibid. Vol. III. p. 761. Calcutta, 1817.

of slavery. First:—In this minute Mr. Harington expresses his entire concurrence in Mr. Richardson's recommendation that all claims and disputes respecting slavery should be tried summarily by the magistrates in the first instance, and he enforces this recommendation on the grounds that years may elapse before the cause can be tried and decided in the civil court; that in the mean while the owner is deprived of his slave's services; that he continues to feed and clothe him; that the refractoriness of his slave may have subjected him to the costs and expenses of a civil suit which the slave can never reimburse him; that slaves are possessed of and can acquire no property to enable them to institute or defend a suit; and that such slave, it may be, is kept in actual confinement, or continues subject to such degree of restraint as his bail may think necessary to impose upon him. *Secondly:*—Mr. Harington objects to Mr. Richardson's leading principle that the Muhammadan law should be made the standard for regulating the decision in all claims and disputes respecting slavery. He admits that the law and usage of slavery have no immediate connection with religion, the full toleration of which has been guaranteed to the natives of India by the British government. He further admits that the rule which the British government has laid down to administer to Muhammadans Muhammadan law, and to Hindus Hindu law, in suits regarding succession, inheritance, marriage, and caste, and all religious usages and institutions, is not directly and strictly applicable to questions of personal freedom and bondage. But he adopts, without argument, simply as an authoritative decision, the interpretation of that rule pronounced by the Sudder Dewany Adawlut and confirmed by the Governor-General in Council in 1798,—"that the spirit of the rule for observing the Muhammadan and Hindu laws was applicable to cases of slavery, though not included in the letter of it;" and he successfully contends against Mr. Richardson that the fair and impartial application of this rule so interpreted will require the same regard to the Hindu as to the Muhammadan law of slavery when the claimants may be of either persuasion. The fallacy consists in adopting an interpretation, however high and authoritative, which has condemned hundreds of thousands of human beings to slavery by discovering in the spirit of the law what is neither directly nor indirectly contained in its letter,—something which is additional to and wholly different from that which the letter expresses; and if this interpretation is rejected, as it ought to be, it would carry with it not only Hindu but Muhammadan slavery also. *Thirdly*:—Acknowledging both the Hindu and Muhammadan laws of slavery, Mr. Harington would acknowledge those only. Slavery not being sanctioned by any system of law which is recognised and administered by the British government except the Muhammadan and Hindu laws, he was of opinion that no claim to the property, possession, or service of a slave should be admitted and enforced except in behalf of a Musalman or Hindu claimant. This would emancipate all slaves held by Christian masters, of whom there are some. He would not, however, prevent persons of full age and in every respect competent from entering into contracts of hire and service either for a limited period or for life, either for wages or for maintenance; provided, however, that no person subjecting himself to voluntary slavery should thereby entail bondage upon his children, though if another maintain them he may be allowed to engage their services for a period sufficient to provide an ample remuneration for their support. In proposing to legalize contracts of hire and service even for life, including the services of children for a period sufficient to provide an ample remuneration for their support, Mr. Harington overlooked the gross abuses to which the Muhammadan law-officers of his own court had shown that this practice is liable, as a pretext for creating slavery both of parents and children. How strongly does such a recommendation, or the actual absence of all regulation of such contracts in British India, contrast with the orders in council of September 7, 1838, which are the supreme law in the British crown colonies, to the effect "that no contract of service made out of the colony shall be of any force or effect in it; that no contract of labor shall remain in force for more than four weeks unless it be reduced to writing; and that no written contract of service shall be binding unless signed by the name or mark of the persons contracting in the presence of a stipendary magistrate, nor unless the magistrate shall certify that it was made voluntarily and with a full understanding of its meaning and effect; *nor can any written contract remain in force for more than one year*."* These are the provisions which the ministers of the crown have enacted to guard the new liberties of the freed men of the West Indies: the East India Company have not yet devised a single such provision to prevent the free-born subjects of the crown under their government from being entrapped into slavery. *Fourthly*:—As no parent can have a legitimate right to impose the yoke of slavery upon his children or their descendants in perpetuity, Mr. Harington supports Mr. Richardson's proposition to prohibit the sale of children as slaves, whether by their parents or others; but at the same time recommends that parents and guardians having the care of children under the age of fifteen years, the age of maturity fixed by the Muhammadan and Hindu laws, should be expressly empowered to contract for the support and service of such children, when indispensably necessary for their maintenance, provided that the contract shall not extend in any instance beyond the expiration of the twenty-fifth year of the age of the child so contracted for. This is recommended as a means by which parents or guardians

* See Orders in Council of Sept. 7, 1838, chapter fourth, cited in Emigration to Guiana, pp. 8, 9. Boston, 1840.

18

may provide for the preservation and support of their children and wards in times of famine and distress, but its probable abuse at other periods is wholly overlooked. *Fifthly:*—Mr. Harington further regards it as obviously repugnant to every principle of natural justice, and inconsistent with the common rights of mankind, that any person should be deprived of his personal freedom during the whole of his life without his consent, and without having committed any offence subject to so heavy a punishment, and he therefore proposes to destroy the hereditary character of slavery by providing for the future emancipation of slaves hereafter born under the protection of the British government, at the expiration of a period when their services may be presumed to have fully compensated for all expense incurred in their support during infancy, viz., at the age of 25 years. This provision would be wholly insufficient for the purpose contemplated. A female slave at the age of 25, according to the customs and habits of native life, would be the mother of a family of children, who, being born in slavery, would be slaves, and obliged, like their mother, to work out their liberty till the age of 25, and so on throughout successive generations. It must be evident that this would not be destroying, but perpetuating, the hereditary character of slavery. *Sixthly:*—Mr. Harington supports the suggestion of a registry of slaves, and recommends two distinct registers, one of slaves, and the other of hirelings. *Seventhly:*—Mr. Harington proposes the emancipation of slaves and hirelings in certain cases of maltreatment by the owner or master. *Eighthly:*—In certain cases of kidnapping children and selling them as slaves, unaccompanied by any circumstances of extenuation, Mr. Harington proposed that the punishment attached to that crime should be increased beyond that which was then prescribed by the law. *Ninthly:*—The existing regulations not containing any specific provision forbidding the exportation of natives of India to be sold as slaves, Mr. Harington proposes that this omission should be supplied. *Tenthly* :— Regulation X. of 1811 being superseded by the statute 51st George III. chap. 23, as far as regards the importation of slaves by sea into British India, Mr. Harington recommends that the provisions contained in sections second, third, and fourth of that regulation, held to be still in force with respect to the importation of slaves by land, should be declared to extend to the prohibition of the importation of any person whatever to be sold or otherwise disposed of or dealt with as a slave, excepting only persons who may have been possessed by the importers as their domestic slaves for a period of at least one year before importation, and who may be produced and registered as such within six months after their importation.*

Upon the whole, Mr. Harington, although doubtless influenced by the most benevolent intentions, appears to have taken neither a comprehensive, nor, as far as it extended, a just view of the means of lessening the evils of slavery in India; and the weight of his character and authority was thrown into the scale against the most important recommendations of Mr. Richardson and Mr. Leycester, which struck at the very root of those evils. His recommendations were probably perceived by the government to be inadequate, while his objections were of sufficient force to defeat the more thorough measures proposed by Mr. Richardson and Mr. Leycester. Nothing consequently was done, and as far as my information or the books of reference I possess enable me to speak, slavery, under the Bengal presidency, in law and in practice, is in substance the same at the present day as when Mr. Richardson, in 1808, first proposed to check and reform its abuses. A period of thirty-two years—an entire generation of the human race—has passed away, and slavery in Bengal is unchecked, unreformed, and unremedied.

* Harington's Analysis, revised edition, Vol. I. pp. 68—73, *note*.

No one has more honorably distinguished himself in the west and south of India, on behalf of the slave, than Mr. Baber, who resided a period of thirty-two years in India, and who was actively employed during that time in every department of the public service, revenue, police, magisterial, judicial, and political, in various provinces both of the Madras and Bombay territories where domestic and agrestic slavery prevails. I have already had occasion to refer to some of his meritorious labors, and I shall here only notice the official recommendations he offered and the opinions he expressed either for the total abolition of the state of slavery, the mitigation of the law relating to it, or the improvement of the condition of the slave.

In 1812, disturbances amounting to incipient rebellion occurred in the mountainous region of Wynâd in Malabar, consequent on the additional burthens that had been imposed upon the people by the tobacco and salt monopolies, stamp-duties, &c. &c., the oppressive mode of administering the revenue department in general, and the practice of the native servants of government seizing the slaves and cultivators and making them to serve as coolies, and demanding supplies of every kind from those of the inhabitants who had not the means of providing them. Tranquillity was restored by Mr. Baber's zealous exertions, and on occasion of fresh symptoms of resistance to the authority of government in the same district, his interference as magistrate of North Malabar was equally prompt and effectual. Among other necessary measures for securing the public tranquillity from future interruption, Mr. Baber took the earliest opportunity, after he had re-established the authority of government, of introducing into the body of a general police regulation a few rules which appeared to him urgently called for, to put a stop to the horrible traffic in human flesh at that time so prevalent, as well as for the amelioration of the condition of the slaves in general by restraining their owners from selling them out of the country of their birth and from separating families, and also by rendering it compulsory on them to make the slaves a suitable provision in food, clothes, and habitation, in sickness or health, young and old, at all times and in all seasons. He subsequently repeatedly reported to his superiors the necessity of some such measure, but unfortunately it was not supported by those in whom the legislature had reposed the controlling authority over the acts of the executive administration. On the contrary, he had to contend even against their systematic opposition to his endeavors to bring to public justice individual acts of violence and cruelty, the board of revenue at Madras evincing a strong disposition to palliate glaring instances of neglect of duty and of oppressive abuse of power, and Mr. Baber's fellow-civilians, Mr. Vaughan and Mr. C. M. Lushington, with the countenance of the board, insolently protesting against and ridiculing in their official communications his endeavors to prevent the system of perpetual labor and the indiscriminate sale of slaves away from their families and the country of their birth. Even a conspiracy was formed against his life through the machinations of the principal slave-owner, and in 1823 he was deserted by the government itself, by an avowal of their unwillingness to repeat the expression of their approbation of his conduct, lest it should aggravate this distempered feeling, as the struggle between the ardent zeal of an individual and the selfish views of a party was called. "Since that time," says Mr. Baber in 1832, "I have confined myself to occasional notices of the condition of the Malabar slaves as often as my public attention has been drawn to the subject, but with little or no benefit to the unfortunate slaves, who continue the same reprobated people as ever, as their half-famished persons, their sieves of huts, and the diminution of their numbers, while every other class of the people is increasing, abundantly testify." To this it is important to add that Mr. Baber does not hesitate to declare his sentiments to be in favor of an unqualified abolition of slavery in India. I should not have presented the preceding view of the language and conduct of the Madras government on this subject, of the board of revenue of that presidency, and of individual servants of that government, if Mr. Baber had not presented the same view in his own name, supported by facts and authorities which, as far as I am aware, have been uncontradicted and unrepelled.*

The next public officer whose exertions on behalf of the slave are most prominent under the Madras presidency, is Mr. A. D. Campbell, who resided in India twenty-two years, and who at different periods held the official situations of secretary and subsequently member of the board of revenue at Madras, superintendent of police at the presidency, registrar to the Foujdary Adawlut or supreme criminal court of that presidency, judge of circuit in the provinces, and principal collector and magistrate in Tanjore, and in the Bellary division of the ceded districts.

In January, 1818, Mr. Campbell, who appears then to have been acting as secretary to the board of revenue at Madras, induced the board to call for information from the several provinces for the purpose of defining by a legislative enactment the power to be exercised by masters over their slaves, and thus preventing abuse or oppression; and with respect to those on the western coast in particular, a legislative enactment was suggested to prevent their being removed against their will from the place of their nativity, or being exposed to sale by auction in execution of decrees of court, or in realization of arrears of revenue. In his subsequent letter of the 23d Dec. 1819, the practice of selling slaves for arrears of revenue, against which Mr. Baber had repeatedly remonstrated, was directed by the board of revenue to be

* Mr. Baber's Letter, before quoted, pp. 552, 558, 569, 570.

discontinued in the only district (Malabar) under the Madras presidency where the practice had occurred. Respecting this, however, it is to be remembered that the order of the board could only prohibit the revenue-officers acting under its authority from selling slaves for arrears of revenue; that it did not and could not prohibit the sale of slaves in execution of decrees of court which belong to the judicial department of government; that it did not and could not prohibit proprietors from themselves selling their slaves to meet the demands of government for revenue; and that it received so little attention and publicity even within the limited sphere of its operation, that Mr. Baber, though living in Malabar to the end of 1828, never heard of it till he saw the fact stated in a parliamentary paper after his arrival in England.

In laying before the government of Madras, on the 13th of December, the proceedings of the board of revenue of Nov. 25, 1819, with the information which had been received from the provinces, the board, at Mr. Campbell's suggestion, proposed that by an enactment of the Madras government it should be declared, *First*, that the purchase of free persons as slaves should be illegal, and of course subject to penalties. The highest court of judicature at Madras have since made a similar proposal. *Secondly*, that the children of all slaves born after a certain date should be free, contemplating, of course, a registry of slaves and of their children born previously to such date. *Thirdly*, that voluntary contracts to labor for a term of years or for life should bind the individual alone, and not his wife or children after the years of discretion. *Fourthly*, that slaves should be competent to possess and dispose of property independently of their master. *Fifthly*, that the purchase of children to be brought up as prostitutes should be subjected to special penalties. The late Mr. Munro supported this proposal by his recommendation, but it has been opposed by Mr. McLeod, apparently on the ground that parents or guardians cannot be prevented from assigning children in the customary modes to be brought up as dancing women. To this it may be answered, that the object of the proposal is to subject to special penalties *the purchase of children* for that purpose. *Sixthly*, that the local civil officers should by a summary proceeding have power to cause masters to provide wholesome food and decent clothing for their slaves, and to prevent their neglecting them in sickness, age, or infirmity. Mr. Baber advocates a similar provision. *Seventhly*, that the power of corporal punishment should be transferred from the masters of slaves to the local civil officers. *Eighthly*, that slaves bought by their masters should by repayment of the purchase-money recover their liberty. Mr. Græme, when a member of the government at Madras, supported a similar proposal. *Ninthly*, that all slaves attached to lands or estates escheating to government should be declared free. There is an inference deducible from this recommendation to which special attention should be called. As neither this nor any of the other proposals has been adopted; as lands and estates with slaves attached to them are assumed to be, and in fact are, from time to time escheating to government; and as the rule is to retain such lands and estates in the possession of government, it follows by the clearest implication that the proprietors of East India stock are in their own right, as a chartered and incorporated company, the owners and masters of the slaves attached to those lands and estates, that they are the only slave-holders in Great Britain, and that the half-yearly dividends which they draw from India are in part the direct and indubitable produce of slave-labor, and suffering, and degradation. *Tenthly*, that slaves on being ill-treated by their masters should be allowed to claim the privilege of being sold to another; and that the breach of any of these rules by the master should, at the option of the slave, entitle him to liberty. The latter part of this recommendation has received the concurrence of Mr. Græme and Mr. Baber. It was also recommended that the share of the harvest granted to the agrestic slaves in the Tamil country should be augmented at the expense, not of the masters, but of the government itself. Mr. Campbell, having soon afterwards left Madras for duties in the provinces, remained ignorant of the fate of these suggestions until, after his arrival in England, on reference to the papers on Indian slavery printed by order of the House of Commons, he perceived that by the Madras government they were merely "ordered to be recorded," *i. e.*, put on the shelf—consigned to oblivion.

In the letter to the Board of Commissioners for the Affairs of India, from which these details have been taken, Mr. Campbell offers other recommendations which should not be overlooked. *First*, he considers it desirable, as regards the slaves on the western coast, that the government of Madras should pass enactments similar to those contained in the Bombay Code, which provide that infants shall not be separated from the mother until a certain age, and also prohibit the separation of the wife from her husband. Mr. Warden proposed an enactment embracing the latter provision, but the Madras government saw no necessity for it. It also receives the support of Mr. Baber. The proposed prohibition of the separation of infants from their mothers and of wives from their husbands, proves the existence of these cruel usages in the estimation of Mr. Campbell, Mr. Warden, and Mr. Baber, who are all three eminently practical and experienced men. *Secondly*, Mr. Campbell considers that in any future act of Parliament on the subject of India, a modification of the slave-act 51st George III. chap. 23 is imperatively called for. Offences against it by traffic in slaves by sea may take place in any part of the extensive coast either on the Coromandel or on the Western side of the peninsula under the Madras government, and by natives of distant provinces many hundred miles from the presidency. The removal of such persons with the witnesses on either side from their own peculiar climate, as, for instance, from Malabar to Madras, would be attended by an inevitable mortality, similar to that of Europeans if sent for trial to the deadly climate of Sierra Leone; yet the slave-act makes all offences under it, even when committed by natives in the provinces, cognizable only by the distant admiralty or king's supreme court of judicature confined to the presidency itself, to the criminal jurisdiction of which they are otherwise not amenable. The local provincial courts possessing power of life and death in matters of the highest criminal jurisdiction, ought, in Mr. Campbell's judgment, as regards a breach of the slave-act by natives in the interior subject to their jurisdiction, to have power concurrent with that of the king's court of admiralty; for to carry into effect the law as it now stands in this respect, would in such cases be no less inhuman than revolting to the prejudices of the people. Indeed, like all laws at variance with the feelings of the people, the slave-act as it now stands must remain a dead letter everywhere in the Madras territory, except at the presidency, until Parliament give power to the tribunals in the provinces to enforce its penalties. In doing so, however, the punishment to be annexed to the breach of its provisions in the provinces should be proportioned to the punishment for other offences in the interior. Death is there the punishment of murder alone; transportation is the next grade of punishment, but never takes place except for life, on account of the great civil forfeiture of caste by which in India it is ever attended; and confinement in fetters or hard labor for fourteen or seven years respectively, alone are the punishments equivalent to transportation from England for these several periods. *Thirdly*, Mr. Campbell, recognising the injustice of interfering with the private property which masters possess in their slaves, and the danger of too suddenly disturbing the long-established relations in society subsisting between these two orders, has nevertheless ever been of opinion that British policy ought to be directed, not only to the immediate practical amelioration of East India slavery, but to its ultimate though gradual abolition.*

The preceding view of some of the most prominent attempts to mitigate the law of slavery, and to improve the condition of the slaves in the Bengal and Madras presidencies of British India, suggests some considerations, the development of which will bring me to the conclusion of these letters.

We see more distinctly what slavery is both in law and practice by the attempts made to lessen its evils, to control the master, and to protect the slave. When men of high official station, of acknowledged sound judgment, and of extensive local experience and intimate acquaintance with native institutions and customs, in different and distant provinces, without communication with each other, earnestly and repeatedly urge on the government they serve the adoption of certain modifications of the existing law of slavery to remedy certain alleged evils,—in the very terms of the recommendations they offer, and of the descriptions they give of the evils to be remedied, we have their testimony to the existence and reality of those evils, perhaps in one of the most natural and unforced, the most authentic and impressive, forms in which it could be conveyed. Bearing this in mind, let us look back on the various suggestions of Mr. Richardson and Mr. Harington in Bengal, and of Mr. Baber and Mr. Campbell in the Madras presidency, and we shall see such a picture of slavery as, independent of all other evidence, may well arrest the attention of the government and people of England. According to Mr. Harington, there is no law in Bengal against the exportation of natives of India, to be sold as slaves; and according to Mr. Camp-

* Mr. Campbell's Letter, before quoted, pp. 572—577.

bell, the act 51st George III. chap. 23, making the slave-trade felony, is a dead letter throughout the Madras territory, and offences against it by traffic in slaves by sea may take place with impunity along the whole line of the Coromandel and Malabar coasts under the Madras government. The additional fact established by Mr. Baber, that domestic slaves, partly natives of Arabia, but chiefly of Abyssinia, are found in fact in all the great towns throughout Malabar and Canara, proves not only that the slave-trade may take place, but that slaves actually are imported at least on the Malabar coast, although probably in small numbers at a time and only for domestic purposes, and introduced under the guise of personal attendants of their masters or as sailors employed on board Arab, Moppilla, or Lubbee vessels. The argument of Mr. Richardson against the continued recognition of Hindu slave-law, and in favor of the rigid interpretation and enforcement of the letter of Muhammadan slave-law, and Mr. Harington's defence of the continued maintenance of both systems of slave-law by the British government, prove that they are in fact recognised, maintained, enforced, and administered by that government, if any additional proof of that fact were required after the perusal of Mr. Macnaghten's Principles and Precedents of the Hindu and Muhammadan laws of slavery. With regard to the actual state of slavery and slaves in India, the various recommendations and suggestions of these public officers of the East India Company's government for the reform of slave-law, prove that parents sell their children as slaves; that children are kidnapped to be sold as slaves; that girls are purchased to be made prostitutes; that men and women sell themselves for life, and involve their families in the same doom; that slaves are sold by their owners to provide means for the payment of arrears of revenue to the government, and by the government in execution of decrees of courts of justice; that by these sales slaves are removed from the places of their nativity, parents are separated from their children, and even mothers from their infants, husbands from wives, and brothers from sisters; that the East India Company, by the escheating of lands and estates and of the slaves attached to them, become and are slave-holders; that agrestic slaves in particular are ill-fed, ill-clothed, and ill-housed, and that they are neglected in sickness, age, and infirmity by their masters; that their masters have the power of corporal punishment in their own hands; and finally that many, Mr. Macnaghten says thousands, are wrongfully detained in bondage, contrary to the letter and spirit of the law. Such is slavery in British India according to the clearly implied testimony of those who have benevolently but unsuccessfully employed their official station and influence to rouse the government to remedy its most direct and flagrant evils.

The reforms of the law and practice of slavery that have been unsuccessfully proposed by the good and wise in India, enable us to estimate the spirit and operation of the East India Company's government in connection with that subject. However uninformed and apathetic the majority of European residents in India may be respecting slavery, its evils are known and acknowledged, undenied and undeniable, by the government. The persevering and disinterested representations of some of the most enlightened and philanthropic servants of the East India Company have left the government no excuse on the plea of ignorance; and to remedy the admitted evils of slavery in India only two methods can be proposed, viz., regulation or abolition. All the reforms that have been enumerated, contemplate regulation—not without a view to abolition ultimately, and by gradual approaches—but primarily and principally regulation of an existing institution still to be maintained and enforced. Now it is a fact that since 1808, when Mr. Richardson under the Bengal presidency, and since 1812, when Mr. Baber under the Madras presidency, first endeavored to awaken the attention of government to the claims of humanity in connection with this subject, the law and the practice of slavery under the British government in India have remained essentially the same, without improvement or mitigation, up to the present year, 1840. During the whole of that period nothing whatever has been done to control the power of the master, to protect the rights, to lighten the burthens, and to increase the comforts of the slave, or to prepare the way for placing master and slave in a different relation to each other. This fact would seem to admit of different explanations. It may be that the governing powers both in India and England deemed that slavery originating in crime and violence, maintained by cruelty and oppression, and productive only of vice and misery, did not admit of regulation, and that its only effectual cure was abolition—extinction—the immediate and complete emancipation of the slave. No such idea appears to have entered their minds. Slavery has continued to be the law of the land, and therefore necessarily in some measure a subject of regulation; and not a single movement has been made towards the enfranchisement of the slave-population. It may be that the governing powers in India and England, dissatisfied with the inadequate reforms of Messrs. Richardson, Harington, Baber, and Campbell, which would have unquestionably left much evil unremedied, have been engaged in devising and discussing and settling other and more searching and effectual measures of their own. It might have been expected that such deliberations would have produced some fruit before the year 1840, stimulated as they ought to have been by the express requisition of the Imperial Parliament in 1833, addressed to the government of India, to mitigate the state of slavery, to ameliorate the condition of slaves, and to extinguish slavery in India as soon as practicable. But the fact is, that, with the exception of occasional calls for information from the subordinate local officers of government, official letters in reply to these calls written amid the pressure of current revenue, police, or judicial business, and abstracts of these letters by a clerk, or reports founded on them by an under-secretary, only to be added to the mass of papers already existing on the subject unread and unregarded—with these exceptions the East India Company's government have equally neglected the recommendations of their own ablest servants and the requisitions of the Imperial Parliament. The painful and disgraceful truth is, that the East India Company, admitting—compelled by the testimony of their own most trustworthy servants to admit—the existence of slavery and the reality of its evils, have been content to continue to legalize slavery, to tolerate its evils, and to discourage, reject, or consign to forgetfulness every suggestion dictated by justice or benevolence for their removal or mitigation. In this matter they have deliberately and systematically disregarded and neglected a grave and solemn duty of government, involving the rights and liberties of hundreds of thousands of British subjects placed under their authority, and they have thereby, so far, shown themselves unworthy of the high trust reposed in them by the Crown and Parliament of Great Britain—unworthy of the respect and confidence of the friends of humanity and civilization throughout the world.

The consideration of the whole subject has strongly convinced me that the immediate extinction of slavery and emancipation of the slaves is the wisest, the justest, and the most humane course that can be pursued, and the only effectual means of remedying acknowledged evils. Mr. Richardson and Mr. Harington did not extend their proposed reforms further than the regulation of slavery with a view to its very gradual but ultimate extinction, while Mr. Leycester proposed its total abolition. Mr. Campbell advocates its ultimate though gradual abolition, while Mr. Baber declares his sentiments to be unhesitatingly in favor of an unqualified abolition. The latter at the same time suggests to the commissioners for the affairs of India and to both Houses of Parliament the expediency of appointing "a committee both in England and in India, the latter to be composed partly of natives, those who are most intelligent, most enlightened, and most influential from property in land and slaves, to inquire and report upon the measures best calculated to extend the blessings of freedom to this most wretched, most helpless, and most degraded portion" of the Indian subjects of Great Britain. The utility of such a committee would depend on the instructions they should receive, the basis on which their inquiries should be conducted, the object at which they should aim. If that object is merely the regulation of slavery, it may be safely affirmed that the appointment of such a committee would be a useless waste of the public money. If regulation could be effectual, sufficient information is already possessed to show what reforms and changes are indispensably necessary to restrain the master and to protect the slave. But all mere regulation, however searching and stringent, would leave the root of the evil untouched, for slavery is in itself essentially and inherently an evil, and you might as well talk of regulating by law any of the most notorious and infamous violations of the indefeasible rights and obligations of nature and society, such as murder and robbery. Besides, whatever regulations might be devised, must be adopted and enforced by the East India Company's government, and the experience of the last thirty-two years has shown what confidence should be reposed in that government in connection with the subject of slavery. Abolition, then, the immediate abolition of slavery in India, is the only legitimate object at which the friends of humanity should aim. Abolition is the only basis on which such a committee as Mr. Baber proposes could usefully conduct its inquiries; and to frame the requisite arrangements preliminary to abolition with a view as far as possible to reconcile all conflicting interests, is the only purpose that would justify the appointment of such a committee, and that would make its labors honorable to the nation and beneficial to society.

This subject cannot be satisfactorily dismissed without examining the objections that have been advanced to the immediate abolition of slavery in India, or the arguments in favor of its continued legal recognition by the British government.

In 1816, the existence of West India slavery was employed as a plea for the maintenance of East India slavery, by the court of Nizamut Adawlut, in reply to Mr. Leycester, who had proposed its abolition. "Whilst it (hereditary slavery) is allowed to remain with respect to the progeny of existing slaves, born under the British government in the West Indies and South Africa, the abolition of it on general principles of justice and humanity could not, the court apprehend, be consistently proposed for India." To ordinary observers the connection between West India and East India slavery is not so close as readily to suggest the conclusion that the one must stand or fall with the other. If the abolition of West India slavery were now urged as a reason for abolishing East India slavery, the argument would appear and be sufficiently flimsy, and yet such reasoning was not stronger or more substantial when employed for a contrary purpose. The court which assigned this reason was the same that pronounced the opinion "that the spirit of the rule for observing the Muhammadan and Hindu laws was applicable to cases of slavery, *though not included in the letter of it*," and which has thereby legalized and perpetuated Hindu and Muhammadan slavery from 1798 to the present day.

The governor in council at Madras in 1825 argue against direct interference with slavery on the part of government, trusting to the gradual operation of justice and police administered in a spirit favorable to personal liberty. The following is an extract of a letter in the revenue department, from the governor in council of Fort St. George, to the Court of Directors, dated 30th Dec. 1825. "In Malabar a numerous class of laborers employed in agriculture have not the free disposal of their own industry, but are in a peculiar state of servitude. Their condition may therefore with more propriety be regarded as dependent on the treatment which they receive from their masters than as capable of being improved by government. But the consideration of the measures proper to be taken with respect to the kinds of slavery found to exist in India relates to a subject of great delicacy and considerable difficulty; and we are of opinion that it is a matter in which more good is to be expected from the gradual operation of justice and police administered in a spirit favorable to personal liberty, than from direct interference on the part of government." That slaves should be left wholly in the hands of their masters, without any direct interference on the part of government, is a doctrine that must be very convenient and agreeable, at least to the masters, although it is not a doctrine we should have expected to be preached by a government which has not only stepped out of its way to legalize slavery, but which has also stepped between the master and the slave to make the slave capable of giving testimony in courts of justice, and to make the master liable to capital punishment for the murder even of his own slave. It is moreover difficult to understand, and perhaps it would be difficult for the Madras governor in council to explain, how justice and police can operate gradually or be administered in a spirit favorable to personal liberty, without that direct interference on the part of government with which they are contrasted. Assuming however the non-interference principle of the Madras government, it is fair to ask whether that government itself has conformed to it. The law doubtless is one thing and the spirit in which it is administered is another. Have justice and police been administered as between master and slave under the Madras government in a spirit favorable to personal liberty? Let Mr. Baber and Mr. Campbell bear testimony, both highly competent witnesses, and possessing an acquaintance with the provinces situated on the opposite coasts of the peninsula, within the Madras presidency; and we are compelled to conclude from their averments that justice and police have been administered in a spirit eminently unfavorable to personal liberty. Look at the innovation introduced, or promoted and extended, by the Madras government, of selling slaves away from their native soil, and separating members of the same family. Look at the system of compulsory slave-labor for the benefit of government, which, at the risk of insurrection and in violation of an express stipulation with the natives, the Madras government openly and shamefully upholds as a necessary evil. Look at the discountenance cast on Mr. Baber's philanthropic exertions, and at the rejection of the ameliorations proposed by him, by Mr. Warden, and by Mr. Campbell. Look at all this, and then think of the effrontery of the same government holding out as a specific for the gradual cure of the evils of slavery, the administration of justice and police in a spirit favorable to personal liberty!

Mr. Colebrooke has objected to the abolition of slavery, to the prevention of enslavement, and to the prohibition of the sale of actual slaves, on the ground of the unobjectionable nature of the means by which free persons are rendered slaves, the infrequency of the practice, and the general good treatment of slaves by their masters. "I conceive," he says, "that there is no occasion for abolishing slavery, or for preventing enslavement, or for prohibiting the sale of actual slaves, within the limits of the British territories in India. Neither the means by which free persons (for the most part children in a tender age) are rendered slaves, nor the frequency of the occurrence in an objectionable form, nor the common treatment of those who are already slaves by their masters, is such as to call for the interposition of legislative authority in a strong form." In the same spirit, Mr. W. H. Macnaghten says:—"The sales of children which do take place (setting aside the fact of their illegality) are devoid of all the disgusting features which characterize the slave-trade: they are not occasioned by the *auri sacra fames*, but by absolute physical hunger and starvation; and the morality must be rigid indeed which would condemn as criminal the act of a parent parting with a child under circumstances which render the sacrifice indispensable to the preservation of both." On this view of the subject I must refer you to the sixth of these letters, in which the nature of the means by which free persons have been and are made slaves, and the extent to which these means are employed, are examined with a wider induction of particulars than appear to have come under the consideration of these respectable writers. You will judge, and the public of England will judge, whether the capture of prisoners in war, the probable source of the largest amount of agrestic slavery in India; whether the sale of free children by their parents, sometimes from the strength of natural affection in the midst of famine and distress, sometimes from the want of natural affection for the purposes of prostitution, probably the next largest source of slavery, particularly domestic slavery, in India; whether the sale of freemen by themselves; the sale of criminals, outcastes, concubines, and their offspring; the kidnapping of children; and the importation of slaves—whether these, which have been the chief, perhaps the sole means of creating the slave-population of India, can be generally regarded with moral approbation. With regard to the extent to which these means are now employed, let it be admitted—what plain and numerous facts disprove—that they have entirely ceased to be employed, does it follow that an inherited bondage, originating in these or similar causes, is the less an injustice to the individual, and an evil to society, because it is inherited? Is slavery the less a curse because the earliest perceptions of the senses, the earliest dawnings of the intellect, the earliest breathings of the affections, have been framed into the mould of a base and debasing servitude, and the human being, body, soul, and spirit, has been absolutely and completely mechanized into an automaton, exhibiting some of the phenomena of vitality, but possessing no thought, or will, or feeling of its own except at the caprice and dictation of another? Some such judgment appears to have been formed by Mr. Colebrooke when he mentions as an extenuating circumstance that the free persons who are made slaves in India are for the most part children of a tender age. To my mind the very language employed implies not a mitigation, but an aggravation, of the evil. It is in the tender age of childhood—it is in the very budding of life—that the root and spring of all life's happiness and goodness is destroyed.

The general good treatment of slaves by their masters is a distinct ground of objection to the abolition of slavery taken by Mr. Colebrooke, and enforced at greater length: "I trust not to be considered an advocate for slavery," he says, "nor indifferent to the miseries incident to the most degraded condition in human society, when I observe that in this country slaves are in general treated with gentleness and indulgence. The slave is a favorite and confidential servant rather than an abject drudge; and is as often held superior to the hireling in his master's estimation and his own, as placed beneath him in the scale of employment and of comforts. The mildness and equanimity of the Indian's temper, (or his apathy and slowness, if this better describe the general disposition of the people,) contribute to ensure good treatment to the slave. I should however only demonstrate unacquaintance with the human character if I affirmed this to prevail universally, without any exception. I cannot doubt that bad temper and dispositions sometimes constitute a harsh, severe, and even cruel master; nor have I been without occasions of being convinced that such characters are to be found among the owners of slaves." The court of Nizamut Adawlut, in opposition to Mr. Leycester's proposal that slavery should be abolished, urge the same consideration, viz., that in India "the state of slavery is not so injurious to the objects of it as in other countries where it is still maintained." Speaking of Muhammadan slavery in India, Mr. W. H. Macnaghten states that "in India (generally speaking) between a slave and a free servant there is no distinction but in the name and in the superior indulgences enjoyed by the former: he is exempt from the common cares of providing for himself and family; his master has an obvious interest in treating him with lenity, and the easy performance of the ordinary household duties is all that is exacted in return." Speaking of Hindu slavery, the same writer adds:—"Whatever objections may be theoretically advanced to its existence, the condition of the slave himself differs in not much more than in name from that of a hired servant."—"I have no reason to believe that the system of slavery as it exists among the Hindus is productive of much individual misery, however baneful its effects may be to society at large. The courts of justice are accessible to slaves as well as to freemen, and a British magistrate would never permit the plea of proprietary right to be urged in defence of oppression. If then but few grievances are complained of, it is fair to infer that few exist."

In these quotations there are two points to be considered, the alleged fact and the inference from the fact. With regard to the alleged fact of the general good treatment of slaves in India, I have not the least doubt that Mr. Colebrooke, Mr. Macnaghten, and the court of Nizamut Adawlut stated it in perfect good faith, and with a full conviction of its truth, but it is to be regretted that they should have given the sanction of their authority to allegations professing to describe the treatment of slaves throughout the whole of India, but in reality descriptive of the treatment of slaves only under the Bengal presidency, and even there it is to be feared descriptive of that treatment with very large exceptions, such as Mr. Colebrooke has partially admitted. Mr. Colebrooke's argument is expressly directed against the abolition of slavery "within the limits of the British territories in India;" Mr. Macnaghten and the court of Nizamut Adawlut speak of India and of Hindu and Muhammadan slavery universally; and Mr. Macnaghten even implies by one of his remarks that he considered domestic slavery as the only description of slavery known in India. This is explained by the circumstance that Mr. Colebrooke, Mr. Macnaghten, and the judges of the Nizamut Adawlut were all permanently connected with the Bengal presidency; that none of them, it is believed, had any opportunity of becoming acquainted by personal observation with agrestic slavery as it exists in the provinces of the Madras presidency; that this deficiency of personal observation does not appear to have been compensated by reading or other sources of information; and that they were thence led to infer that slavery existed in no other form throughout India than as they saw it in Bengal, or knew it from the records of cases tried in their courts. What is the fact? To determine that, we must distinguish between agrestic and domestic slavery, and in speaking of the latter we must distinguish between male and female domestic slaves. To judge of the treatment of agrestic slaves, read the statements made from personal observation and knowledge by Mr. Baber, Mr. Campbell, Mr. Græme, and Dr. Francis Buchanan, already quoted in Letter VII., and then pronounce whether the two hundred thousand in Malabar, Canara, and Arcot, and the "many thousands" more in Tanjore, are treated by their masters with gentleness and indulgence, are exempt from the common cares of providing for themselves and their families, are protected by British magistrates and courts of justice, and differ in name only from hired servants. I think it not improbable that an investigation into the condition of the alleged eighty thousand slaves in the Bengal district of Silhet, would prove that many of them are agrestic slaves, and that the treatment they receive is not widely dissimilar from that of those in the Madras presidency. With respect to female domestic slaves, read the statements of Mr. Campbell and Mr. Baber, and then also pronounce whether, kept as they are almost universally for sensual purposes, immured in the harems of Muhammadans, secluded from access to the society of free persons and from all appeal to courts of justice, often treated with caprice, frequently punished with much cruelty, and sometimes murdered with impunity, their condition and treatment are such as has been described by the Bengal authorities I have quoted. There are facts which tend to show that female domestic slaves are treated as ill in the Bengal as in the Madras presidency, and I am not acquainted with any reasons, ignorant as all Europeans are of the internal economy of native families, particularly those of wealth and consideration, that render their better treatment probable. With regard to male domestic slaves, let it be borne in mind that many of them—certainly however a minority—are eunuchs: that fact alone speaks intelligibly as to *their* treatment. It is to the remaining number of male domestic slaves and to them only that the picture of gentle and indulgent treatment that has been drawn can be deemed to apply, and even to them with the exceptions acknowledged by Mr. Colebrooke, produced by occasional examples of harsh, severe, and even cruel masters.

Admit the alleged fact that the gentle, indulgent, and considerate treatment of slaves throughout India is all but universal. What is the legitimate inference from the fact?

Mr. Colebrooke considers that slavery even in its mildest form is "the most degraded condition in human society," to which peculiar miseries are incident, and trusts not to be considered an advocate for it. The court of Nizamut Adawlut "fully participate the sentiments expressed by Mr. Leycester in abhorrence of hereditary slavery, and earnestly wish it could be discontinued." Mr. Macnaghten deems it unquestionable that "the evils of slavery are manifold," and holds that "its effects" are "baneful" "to society at large," although not productive in his judgment of much individual misery. Now, putting altogether out of view its effects on the individual, whatever they may be, and looking at the subject only with an eye to the interests of government and society, it cannot be denied that the extinction of an institution which, even in its least repulsive and least hurtful form, is so abhorrent in its character, so degrading in its tendency, and so baneful in its consequences, is eminently desirable. Assuming this as admitted, let any one endeavor to conceive any possible combination of circumstances in which slavery could be abolished with greater facility and with less danger than that in which, according to Messrs. Colebrooke, Macnaghten, &c., it has been reduced to a mere name, a nullity, as far as such an effect can be produced by the kindness of the master and the loyalty of the slave, without destroying the acknowledged inherent vice of the institution. No possible, no conceivable contingency can be deemed more favorable to such a result than precisely that which these writers have described as the actual state of slavery in India—a state admitting of an almost imperceptible transition to the rights and privileges of personal and industrial freedom.

Either then slavery in India is the halcyon state which it has been described to be, or it is not. If it is, then let us lose not a moment; let us avail ourselves of the fortunate occasion; let us abolish slavery without delay, while the master is so favorably disposed towards the slave, while the slave has so loyal an attachment to the master, while the fetters have been allowed almost to fall off by the one and are scarcely felt by the other, and while every circumstance promises an easy passage from a state of servitude to a state of liberty. This is just the time and the occasion which a wise statesman would desire, and which he would signalize by a prompt and decisive act of liberal policy. But if the case is otherwise,—if slavery in India is not the mild and gentle, the innocent, harmless, and benevolent thing which it has been represented—if in a very large majority of instances it presents a picture of nakedness and starvation; of perpetual, compulsory, and unrequited labor; of stocks, floggings, chains, and murders; of slaves sold to strangers and torn away from their birthplace, families separated, and all the bonds of natural affection snapped asunder to meet the demands of a foreign, a cruel, and an avaricious government; of temptations held out to kidnappers to steal children, and to hardhearted parents to sell their own offspring in order to supply the demands of private debauchery and of public prostitution—if these are the chief features of slavery in India—if these are the crimes whose cry ascends to Heaven to witness against us,—in this case also let us lose not a moment; let us relieve ourselves, our nation, and as far as depends upon us our race, from the oppressive burthen of such dire, such black, such flagrant iniquities; and if the English people have hitherto in ignorance tolerated such abominations, practised or permitted in their name, let them do so no longer, but with a voice of indignation, that shall strike shame and dismay into the hearts of its money-seeking rulers, demand that slavery in British India be instantly and forever abolished.

There are other arguments against the general and immediate abolition of slavery in India, which are expressed in language so vague and indefinite that they will be best understood by quoting the words of those who have employed them, without attempting to convey them in my own. I find them first suggested by Mr. Richardson in his letter of March 23, 1808:—"Aware of the great importance and convinced of the caution with which innovations should be attempted, or the ancient laws, customs, or prejudices of a people infringed, I presume not even to sketch out the mode or to fix the period of general emancipation; and perhaps the sudden manumission of those now actually in a state of bondage, though abstractly just, might be politically unwise." The court of Nizamut Adawlut, in reply to Mr. Leycester, allege that slavery in India "has from time immemorial been sanctioned by the laws and usages of the country." Mr. Macnaghten says:—"That the evils of slavery are manifold, is unquestionable. That its total and immediate suppression might be followed by mischievous consequences, can admit but of as little question."—Again: "It must be owned that the recognition of legal slavery in any form must tend to perpetuate its existence; but at the same time long-established usages should be respected, especially where society has not attained such a state of civilization as to admit of a clear perception of the general benefits intended to result from an invasion of individual rights; and so long as the legislature in its wisdom and from a respect for ancient institutions shall not deem it advisable to interfere with a view to the suppression of the system, it can only be hoped that the gradual diffusion of knowledge, and the consequent spread of enlightened notions, will tend to convince all ranks of the community that rational liberty is the condition most conducive to the happiness and interests of mankind." Mr. Campbell also, or the Madras Board of Revenue who express their sentiments through him, recognise "the injustice of interfering with the private property which masters possess in their slaves, and the danger of too suddenly disturbing the long-established relations in society subsisting between these two orders." Three distinct grounds of objection to the immediate abolition of slavery, or of argument in favor of its gradual abolition and continued recognition and maintenance, are assumed and mixed up in these passages, according as each writer was disposed to depend either on the progress of knowledge; or on the reverence due to long-established usages and institutions and the danger of disturbing them; or on the injustice of interfering with private property; or on all those grounds jointly. Each of these will be separately examined.

It is Mr. Macnaghten who, with the aspiration characteristic of a generous mind and the indolent and indiscriminating judgment uncharacteristic of a distinguished Indian statesman, gravely hopes "that the gradual diffusion of knowledge and the consequent spread of enlightened notions will tend to convince all ranks of the community that rational liberty is the condition most conducive to the happiness and interests of mankind," and who in this hope coolly proposes to postpone for the present the suppression of slavery in India. There are two classes of men in the world, those who trust too little to the diffusion of knowledge and those who hope too much from it. Undoubtedly Mr. Macnaghten belongs to the latter class. Who are to be convinced by the diffusion of knowledge of the advantages of rational liberty? It is not the English rulers of India: it is to be presumed that they are already convinced. It is not the slaves: full work and half-feeding, in addition to many other similar arguments, have long since convinced them too. It is the slave-holders then who are to be convinced; but they also are convinced, in their own sense of the phrase, of the advantages of rational liberty, and with them it consists in the liberty of living, not by their own labor, but by the labor of others. It would be just as reasonable to expect by the diffusion of knowledge to convince slave-holders of the fallacy of this interpretation, and of the advantage *to them* of liberating their slaves, as it would be to expect to convince the British government that India ought to be liberated from British control, because it was unjustly and fraudulently acquired and has been most cruelly misgoverned, and because "rational liberty is the condition most conducive to the happiness and interests of mankind." Mr. Macnaghten knows how vainly such an argument would be addressed to the British government; but he seems to forget that slave-holders are likely to treat the same reasoning with the same contempt. If there were a higher human power than Great Britain to which she should be legally amenable for her misdeeds in India, unquestionably the appeal would be made against her. There is no such power; but although Great Britain cannot be expected to convict herself, yet when she herself is the power to which the appeal is made, and when the cause of master and slave in India is pleaded at the bar of her own tribunal, she may be expected to pronounce an impartial judgment, because it is equally for her honor and for her interest that justice should be done. It is not then on the gradual diffusion of knowledge and the consequent spread of enlightened notions amongst slave-holders in India that any hope is to be reposed, a hope too utopian for practical use; but it is on the diffusion of knowledge and the spread of just views in England that dependence is to be placed. She is the arbitress in this cause, and every thing may be hoped from her justice and humanity if she can be made to understand its real merits.

The next ground is the respect due to ancient institutions and to immemorial laws and usages, the mischievous consequences of a total and immediate suppression of slavery, the political danger of too sudden a disturbance of the long-established relations between master and slave. It is evident from the terms employed that there is much vagueness and indefiniteness in the conception of this argument or objection in the minds of those who advance it. Mr. Campbell speaks of "danger," without letting us understand the nature, or probable extent, or apprehended form of the danger. Mr. Richardson speaks of the evil of innovation generally, and considers that sudden manumission, though abstractly just, might be politically unwise, at the very moment he is proposing a sudden, an important, and a sweeping innovation on the existing law of slavery, which would have largely affected the Muhammadans, the most sensitive, discontented, and turbulent portion of the whole Indian population. Mr. Macnaghten deems it unquestionable that the total and immediate suppression of slavery might be followed by mischievous consequences; and yet these consequences are so little formidable, that he is prepared to encounter them as soon as the legislature shall deem it advisable to interfere with a view to the suppression of the system, although the mere *fiat* of Parliament could not alter or lessen the mischievousness of the consequences. The reverence professed by the Nizamut Adawlut for immemorial laws and usages is merely urged collaterally and subordinately to the primary argument of that learned body, that East India slavery should be maintained because West India slavery still existed, and the main ground being not only in reason, but having become in fact invalid, the subsidiary one is less entitled to attention.

It is difficult, however, to believe that a consideration presenting itself in so many forms to different minds is wholly without foundation. Let us endeavor to form a clearer and more precise idea of the argument than appears to have been possessed by its authors. Any proposed innovation on, or interference with, the ancient and established institutions, laws, and customs of India, may be designed either for the benefit of the people or for the benefit of their foreign rulers, and may produce either injury to the people or injury to their rulers. Elsewhere the good of the people and the good of rulers may be identical or coincident; but under the system of government pursued in India, it is essential to distinguish between objects and results wholly different. Keeping this distinction in view, the following propositions may, I think, be successfully maintained: *that there have been, and that there are now in progress, innovations on the established institutions, laws, and customs of the country, designed for, and tending to, the sole benefit of its foreign rulers, and productive of great danger to the stability of their government; that there has been no innovation truly designed for, and plainly tending to, the sole benefit of the people, productive of any such result; and that the proposed abolition of slavery in India belongs to the latter class of innovations.*

With reference to the former class, it would be necessary to write a history of the internal government of India by the English in order to enumerate and expound the innovations which it includes. It is true that the native religions are tolerated, and the native laws are administered—a conservatism dictated, it is hoped, in part by a just regard for the enlightened principles of religious and civil liberty, and in part, it is believed, by the consciousness of weakness, by the physical impossibility of giving scope to religious intolerance or to English law, and by the absence of all fiscal temptation to introduce either. But what, it may be asked, are the successive conquests of the English in India—the English, a foreign, an unclean, and an unbelieving race—but so many usurpations and innovations on all established institutions, laws, and usages? In the internal politics of the country, have not truth, and justice, and fair-dealing been often trampled on in order to acquire territory or to extend British power and influence? In the internal administration of the government have not native institutions standing in the way of the increase of revenue been systematically superseded, neglected, and despised? Has not the administration of justice been always made subordinate, often subservient, to the collection of revenue? Has not the revenue-system added tax to tax and monopoly to monopoly, unsettling property in the soil, lessening its value, and attacking individual rights? Have not the provinces of the Bengal presidency been for years past in a state verging on rebellion by the attempt to tax lands immemorially held tax-free? Are not the learned institutions of the country drooping and decaying because their resources have been largely appropriated by the government? Has not a late distinguished civil servant of the East India Company (the Honorable Frederick John Shore) publicly declared and left on record, that "whether true or false, there is an undoubted impression among the government servants, both here (in India) and in England, that a man who treats the natives with much civility and attention will be in bad odour with his government?" Surely, surely, a government conducted on such principles and in such a spirit must not be permitted to cloak its hostility to a measure of humanity and justice, such as the proposed abolition of slavery, under the pretext of its respect for ancient institutions and long-established usages.

With regard to the second class of innovations, those truly designed for and plainly tending to the sole benefit of the people, the number of these is not great, but some of them are sufficiently notorious. I will merely mention the subjection of Brahmans along with other classes of the community to capital punishment, an innovation on Hindu law most offensive to Hindu prejudices; the subjection of the murderer of a slave as well as of any other person to capital punishment, even if the murderer be the slave's master, a most offensive innovation both on Hindu and Muhammadan law, making the lives of slaves of equal value with those of their masters; the prohibition by the Marquess

Wellesley's government of the practice of mothers presenting their offspring as sacrifices to the Ganges at Gunga Sagur, the effect of which was that they were devoured by sharks and alligators, a prohibition directly infringing on a popular and cherished superstition; the attempts, hitherto only partially successful, to prevent female infanticide among certain tribes and castes addicted to it; the completely successful prohibition by Lord William Bentinck's government of the burning of Hindu widows with the bodies of their deceased husbands, a cruel superstition, sacrificing the lives of hundreds annually throughout India, and supported by the bigotry, fanaticism, and interest of the whole Brahmanical priesthood; and, finally, the sudden, unprepared, and yet peaceful prohibition of the sale of slaves in the Southern Mahratta country, where it had been immemorially practised. All these were measures truly designed and plainly tending to preserve human life and to encourage natural affection, to maintain equal justice and to protect the good order of society; and whatever temporary dissatisfaction some of them may have occasioned, they led to no disturbance of the peace, and their ultimate effect has been to strengthen the English rule by inspiring the natives with respect and affection for the British government and people.

Now it is certain on the plainest grounds of reason, as well as admitted by the objectors, that the abolition of slavery would belong to the latter class of innovations, and that its sole design and effect would be the good of society. There would be no direct accruing advantage to government in the form of revenue to excite doubt or suspicion of its motives. It would be a disinterested interference on the part of government as the common protector, to shield the weak from the strong, the poor from the rich, and to give to the slave the lawful possession, hitherto unjustly withheld, of his own body, and the fruits of his own labor.

Such a measure would array in its support the whole moral force of the community, which would drown the grumblings of the slave-holders if they should attempt to make themselves heard. Even if, on the worst and most improbable supposition, not a single slave-owner could be made friendly to the change, still their number is less than that of the slaves, and government consequently, by the proposed measure, would make more friends than enemies. But why suppose this extreme case? According to the objectors, the majority of the slave-owners, at least in the Bengal provinces, are very favorably disposed to their slaves, and it is to be hoped might be made friendly to their emancipation; while under the Madras presidency the difficulty which many slave-owners often experience to find labor and subsistence for their slaves would equally facilitate an arrangement with them. Upon the whole, I arrive with unhesitating confidence at the conclusion, that the dread of innovation on existing institutions and of danger to the British government is a bugbear, and that the measure would be attended with equal benefit and safety. It is only necessary that a wise, humane, and powerful government—powerful to will and to do justice to all—should speak the word, and slavery would no longer exist.

The only remaining ground of objection taken against the abolition of slavery in India is the alleged invasion of individual rights and the injustice of interfering with the private property which masters possess in their slaves. This places the question on the footing of right and justice, and viewed in this light there is no question of morality or of law that admits of an easier solution. In any disputed question of property, there are, at least, two parties; and in the present instance those parties are the master and the slave. The property in dispute is the body and labor of the slave. In these, the master claims an exclusive proprietary right; while the slave asserts that his body and the fruits of his labor are his own. In a civilized country, in a civilized age, under a civilized government, the mere statement of the case is decisive in favor of the slave's claim. It is impossible that any man can possess any property by a more intimate and perfect right than that by which every man possesses the property in his own person; and the property in the profits of his lawful labor follows as a necessary consequence, all acts of capture and violence, buying and selling, being vitiated and rendered null and void by the previously existing, permanent, and indefeasible right of the man to himself, a right which, like many other rights, may be long in abeyance, but which can never be lost, and may be always resumed when the fear of violence or the pressure of actual force is removed.

But it will be said that the question does not lie between the master and the slave, but between the master and the government which has legalized slavery and legalized the master's property in the slave. To this it may be replied, that human law is merely an expression of the will of individual men, and that no man or number of men can change wrong into right. The right, therefore, of the slave to himself is unaffected by the act of any government. But a government cannot be expected to admit its own solemn act to be wrong without good reason assigned, which may or may not convince, and therefore let it be further remarked, and repeated, if necessary, a thousand times, that even according to the existing law of slavery in British India, on the high authority of Mr. Macnaghten, "THOUSANDS *are at this moment living in a state of hopeless and contented, though* UNAUTHORIZED *bondage.*" Let it be further observed that slavery in India has not been legalized by a formal enactment of the British Parliament, nor even of the British Indian government, but by a mere interpretation, and, as I firmly believe and maintain, by a gross and palpable misinterpretation, of a rule of law which, it is admitted by the expounders, makes not the slightest mention of, or allusion to, slavery. If this alleged misinterpretation of the law should be established by competent authority, then the whole question of slavery in India is settled, and in no instance does the master possess a legal any more than a rightful property in the slave.

Finally, let it be assumed that the law of slavery in India is what it is generally supposed to be, and that the legal property of the master in the slave is undisputed and indisputable. Then let the government and people of England consider the small number of slaves compared with the whole population, at the most probably one million in a hundred millions; let them remember the low prices of slaves in India as already specified; let them reflect on the eighteen or twenty millions sterling annually wrung from the people of India and lavished on unnecessary wars and armaments, or on wasteful civil establishments, at home and abroad, by which an official aristocracy are enabled to trample on the necks of the subject people; and then let them determine whether a small portion of this revenue might not be more justly, more humanely, and more honorably employed in purchasing from their masters the freedom of a million of British subjects held in legal bondage. Nor let it be forgotten that the decree has already gone forth from the Parliament of Great Britain, that means shall be taken "forthwith" to mitigate the state of slavery, to ameliorate the condition of slaves, to extinguish slavery itself throughout British India, "so soon as such extinction shall be practicable and safe," and to prepare and transmit drafts of laws and regulations for these purposes; but that up to the present time, that is, after a lapse of seven years, or a full third of the period for which the government of India has been delegated to the East India Company, notwithstanding the urgency of the injunction addressed to them from the highest authority, slavery has not been extinguished; the condition of slaves has not been ameliorated; the state of slavery has not been mitigated; drafts of laws and regulations for these purposes have not been prepared and transmitted; nothing whatever has been done or attempted by the East India Company or by their local government to render the accomplishment of the will of Parliament more practicable or more safe than it was or was deemed in 1833; and from criminal inattention to a high and sacred trust, everything remains in the state in which it then was. Shall these things be and not excite shame, indignation, reprehension, reform? It is for the people, the Parliament, and the government of England to determine.

I am, Sir,
with high consideration,
your obedient Servant,
W. ADAM.

Cambridge, New England,
February 29, 1840.

APPENDIX.

No. I.

MR. H. T. COLEBROOKE'S OPINIONS ON SLAVERY IN INDIA.

MR. H. T. COLEBROOKE's opinions on any subject connected with India are deserving of great consideration, and in the preceding letters his opinions regarding slavery in that country have been repeatedly referred to. Justice to so important a subject and so high an authority requires that his views should, as far as possible, be presented in a connected form, and the following extracts are accordingly subjoined. The first is from a treatise usually, and no doubt justly, attributed to Mr. Colebrooke, entitled, Remarks on the Husbandry and Internal Commerce of Bengal, originally written in 1794, corrected and published in Calcutta 1803–4, and republished for the author, London, 1806. All the remaining extracts are taken from an official paper, stated by Mr. Harington (Analysis of the Laws and Regulations, Vol. III. p. 743) to have been written by Mr. Colebrooke in the year 1812, but, Mr. Harington believed, not entered on the public records. All that I know of the official paper is by the detached extracts which Mr. Harington has given from it in the Sixth Part, Section V., of the above-cited work, and it does not appear whether those extracts include the whole of it, or whether any material portion of it has been omitted. I am not aware of any other expression of opinion by Mr. Colebrooke on this subject.

(*From Remarks on the Husbandry and Internal Commerce of Bengal*, London, 1806, p. 129.)

" Slavery, indeed, is not unknown in Bengal. Throughout some districts, the labors of husbandry are executed chiefly by bond-servants. In certain provinces, the ploughmen are mostly slaves of the peasants for whom they labor; but treated by their masters more like hereditary servants or like mancipated hinds than like purchased slaves, they labor with cheerful diligence and unforced zeal.

" In some places, also, the landholders have a claim to the servitude of thousands among the inhabitants of their estates. This claim, which is seldom enforced, and which in many instances is become wholly obsolete, is founded on some traditional rights, acquired many generations ago, in a state of society different from the present; and slaves of this description do, in fact, enjoy every privilege of a freeman, except the name; or at the worst, they must be considered as villains attached to the glebe, rather than as bondmen laboring for the sole benefit of their owners. Indeed, throughout India, the relation of master and slave appears to impose the duty of protection and cherishment on the master as much as that of fidelity and obedience on the slave, and their mutual conduct is consistent with the sense of such an obligation; since it is marked with gentleness and indulgence on the one side, and with zeal and loyalty on the other.

" Though we admit the fact that slaves may be found in Bengal among the laborers in husbandry, yet in most provinces none but freemen are occupied in the business of agriculture."

(*From the official paper of* 1812.)

"The Hindu law fully recognises slavery. It specifies in much detail the various modes by which a person becomes the slave of another; and which are reducible to the following heads, viz.: capture in war; voluntary submission to slavery for diverse causes, (as a pecuniary consideration, maintenance during a famine, &c.;) involuntary, for the discharge of debt, or by way of punishment of specific offences; birth as offspring of a female slave; gift, sale, or other transfer by a former owner; and sale or gift of their offspring by parents. It treats the slave as the absolute property of his master, familiarly speaking of this species of property in association with cattle, under the contemptuous designation of 'bipeds and quadrupeds.' It makes no provision for the protection of the slave from the cruelty and ill-treatment of an unfeeling master; nor defines the master's power over the person of his slave; neither prescribing distinct limits to that power, nor declaring it to extend to life or limb. It allows to the slave no right of property even in his own acquisitions, unless by the indulgence of his master. It affords no opening to his redemption and emancipation, (especially if he be a slave by birth or purchase,) unless by the voluntary manumission of him by his master; or in the special case of his saving his master's life, when he may demand his freedom and the portion of a son; or in that of a female slave bearing issue to her master, when both she and her offspring are entitled to freedom, if he have not legitimate issue; or in the particular instances of persons enslaved for temporary causes, (as debt, amercement, cohabitation with a slave, and maintenance in consideration of servitude,) on the cessation of the grounds of slavery by the discharge of the debt or mulct, discontinuance of the cohabitation, or relinquishment of the maintenance.

"The Muhammadan law equally acknowledges slavery, originating however in fewer sources; namely: capture of infidels in war; birth as issue of a female slave; to which some authorities (who are chiefly followed) have added sale of their offspring by parents in a dearth or famine. The property is so absolute and complete that it is assigned as a reason for subjecting an owner to no worldly punishment or penalty for the murder of his slave; he has of course entire power over his person, being restrained by no provisions of the law adapted to protect the slave from ill-treatment. Manumission cannot be exacted from the owner, unless in the case where, for some cause, the slave is already emancipated in part; in which case he is entitled to redeem himself by emancipatory labor equivalent to the remaining portion of his value. In all other instances, emancipation depends wholly on the will of the owner. But manumission of slaves is strongly recommended as a pious act, and the law leans much against the slavery of Muhammadans. A female slave bearing issue to her master does not acquire freedom; but gains other privileges, of which the chief is that of not being liable to be sold to another person. Her issue is free, and ranks with other illegitimate but acknowledged offspring of her master."

"We find domestic slavery very general among both Hindus and Musalmans. More trusty than hired servants, slaves almost exclusively are employed in the interior of the house, for attendance on the members of the family, and in all the most confidential services. Every opulent person, every one raised above the condition of the simplest mediocrity, is provided with household slaves; and from this class chiefly are taken the concubines of Musalmans and Hindus; in regard to whom it is to be remembered that concubinage is not among people of these religions an immoral state, but a relation which both law and custom recognise without reprehension; and its prevalence is liable only to the same objection as polygamy, with which it has a near and almost necessary connexion. In the lower provinces under this presidency the employment of slaves in the labors of husbandry is nearly, if not entirely, unknown. In the upper provinces, beginning from Western Behar and Benares, the petty landholders who are themselves cultivators are aided in their husbandry by their slaves, whom they very commonly employ as herdsmen and ploughmen; and landholders of a higher order have in a few instances the pretensions of masters over a part of their tenants long settled on their estates, and reputed to be descended from persons who were acknowledged slaves of their ancestors. Their claims to the services of these hereditary serfs are nearly obsolete, and scarcely attended with any practical consequences. The serfs pay rent and other dues for the lands which they till and the pastures on which they graze their herds, and are not distinguished from the rest of the peasantry, unless by a questionable restriction of the right of removing at choice. But those employed in husbandry by the inferior class of landholders are strictly slaves; and their condition differs from that of household slaves only as the one is occupied in out-door work and the other in business of the interior of the house. The employment of slaves in handicraft is more rare, but not entirely unknown. It would be difficult to form a computation of the number of slaves throughout the country, or of the proportion to the free population. Any steps towards the preparation of an estimate which should approach to accuracy would involve inquiries which must excite alarm, and could not but be attended with circumstances offensive to the people. But taking a more general view, it may be stated that slaves are neither so few as to be of no consideration, nor so numerous as to constitute a notable proportion of the mass of population. The number, which certainly is not relatively great, has been kept up, or, to apply language of commerce to this subject, the demand for slaves has been supplied,—1st, by their marriages among themselves, or with free persons; 2d, by the sale of free children into slavery within the country; 3d, by importation from abroad, whether by sea or land, previous to the late prohibition of that traffic. Neither the disposition of the people nor their accustomed mode of treating their slaves tends to impede the rearing of children by any discouragement to marriages. I of course except the instances of concubines and prostitutes. In other cases, a sense of propriety leads very usually to provide a match for the household slave; and the offspring following the condition of the mother, and the child of a female domestic slave being considered to be attached to the family by a stronger tie than the simple relation of slave to a master, no requisite indulgence is wanting to enable the mother to devote due care to the rearing of her progeny. It is not necessary to suppose the number of children born and reared to be deficient, for the sake of accounting for the call for a supply from other sources, of foreign importation and home sale of free children. Opulent persons, in whose families more slaves may be born than they are desirous of retaining in their employ, do not sell, but emancipate, those whose services they do not require; and persons of reduced circumstances, no longer needing nor able to employ so many domestic slaves as before, are not less unwilling to dispose of slaves by sale, which is a highly discreditable act, but give them their freedom without a price, however acceptable the value might be to them in their actual state of indigence. The manumission of slaves, being deemed an act of piety and an expiation of diverse offences, frequently takes place from religious motives, without either of the inducements before described; and slaves are often redeemed by purchase either expressly for that purpose, or from a less laudable impulse, as attachment to a courtesan, or some other cause. The number of slaves continually diminishing, a demand constantly exists for the purchase of them, which is supplied chiefly by the sale of children by their parents in seasons of scarcity and famine or in circumstances of individual or peculiar distress. The low price at which these sales are effected is an argument that no very urgent demand commonly exists. Neither is there any brisk traffic of slaves, which would be proof of an extensive demand and ample supply. During a famine or a dearth, parents have been known to sell their children for prices so very inconsiderable and so little more than nominal, that they may in frequent instances have credit for a better motive than that of momentarily relieving their own necessities, namely, the saving of their children's lives by interesting in their preservation persons able to provide nourishment for them. The same feeling is often the motive for selling children when particular circumstances of distress instead of a general dearth disable the parents from supporting them. There is no reason to believe that they are ever sold from mere avarice and want of natural affection in the parent. The known character of the people and proved disposition in all the domestic relations must exempt them from the suspicion of such conduct. But the pressure of want alone compels the sale, whether the immediate impulse be consideration for the child, or desire of personal relief. So long, therefore, as no established fund or regulated system for the relief of the indigent exists, it does not seem practicable to prevent or restrain the disposal of children by their parents, which is lawful by their own laws. There are two classes of purchasers, however, by whom larger prices are given than intimated in the general view here taken. The one comprises various religious orders, the members of which purchase children to bring them up and initiate them in the religious order to which they themselves belong. Being restricted in their selection of subjects to the higher castes of Hindus, they do not readily find persons of the requisite caste willing to part with their children; and being in general opulent from the union of the commercial with the religious profession, they are able to tempt the cupidity of parents by a large pecuniary consideration, and often by a provision for life. The greatness of the reward has been supposed to lead to kidnapping in some instances of this nature, though not frequently, since the purchaser requires to be ascertained of the parentage of the child. The other description of purchasers alluded to consists of the owners of sets of dancing women, who buy female children and instruct them for public exhibition. As they generally become courtesans when they grow up, it might seem to be incumbent on a government attentive to the morals of the people over whom it rules to prevent this practice by prohibitory laws. I apprehend, however, that it would not be easy to frame rules which would not be open to easy evasion. Instead of sale as of a slave, it is already common to make an engagement for a long term of years. It would be an obvious expedient to shorten the term: it might be going too far to presume the intention of prostitution, and to prohibit all instruction for purposes of exhibition of dances, which the people are very partial to, and which are a regular part of their religious festivals and celebrations.

" The remaining source of the supply of slaves was (until lately prohibited by law) importation both by sea and by land. The importation by sea consisted of a very few African slaves brought by Arab ships to the port of Calcutta. Having been led to make some inquiries into this traffic previous to its abolition, I had reason to be satisfied that the whole number of slaves imported was very inconsiderable;

not exceeding annually a hundred of both sexes. I found cause at the same time to be convinced that the means by which slaves are procured on the Eastern Coast of Africa for the Arab dealers who supply Arabia and Persia, and who used to bring the small number mentioned to this port," (Calcutta,) "are not less abominable and nefarious than those practised on the West Coast of Africa, consisting for the most part in the forcible seizure of the slaves, either in predatory war undertaken for the purpose, or by open robbery, often attended with the murder of the parents. The importation by land was principally from the territories of Nepaul, whence a regular traffic in slaves appears to have been carried on; and occasionally from the western and middle parts of India, whenever a local scarcity of provisions gave a temporary impulse to a trade which was otherwise in general languid. Although the subject was brought under the notice of this" (the Bengal) "government by representations from the local authorities in the Nepaul provinces, it is understood that the traffic owed its existence to the oppressive administration of those very authorities, which drove the wretched inhabitants of those provinces to the sad resource of selling their children or themselves into slavery, when all other means of meeting the insatiable exactions of their Nepaulese rulers were exhausted. It was however stated that, under cover of a trade which originated in this cause, kidnapping was practised. And at all events, it was highly expedient to prohibit the importation altogether, whether it gave occasion to the commission of this offence, or only served to crown the last act of extortion of Nepaulese governors from their unhappy subjects.

"I have not spoken of the exportation of slaves from the British territories, as there is not any cause to believe that such a trade at present exists. Many years ago a clandestine export by sea to the French Islands was detected, and being immediately prohibited by proclamation, and the first subsequent instance which was discovered being prosecuted to punishment, it was entirely suppressed, and no surmise of its revival has since been entertained. Slaves may have been carried out of the country by land in attendance on their masters, or under other peculiar circumstances; and possibly for sale when a scarcity has existed within the territories. But the instances must have been few and rare, and little apprehension can be entertained of the recurrence of it as a traffic. At all events, should such apprehensions be felt, or should the importation of slaves by land not be entirely stopped by the regulation and penalties already enacted, it will be easy to enforce the prohibition by severe penalties, which need not however be carried to the length of those which the late act of Parliament" (51st George III. chap. 23) "has provided to enforce the abolition of the traffic by sea. Adverting to the known object and design of that enactment, we have considered its provisions to be limited to the trade by sea; and I trust such will be the construction which will be put on it by magistrates and courts of justice, should any question on it be raised, and the case brought before them. I cannot, however, but think that the terms of the act are very general, and rigidly construed may bear a different interpretation. It declares the removal of any person (and dealing with him as a slave) from one country to another to be felony, punishable by transportation; and does not apply to the East Indies the exception which it allows in the West for the removal of a person already a slave from one part of the West Indies to another. Now this exception is not less needed in these seas than in those of the western hemisphere. For, not to speak at present of the removal of slaves from one province to another on the continent, the case must continually recur of a British subject, or inhabitant of the British territories, a native probably of these countries, embarking at one port for another on the Indian continent, or proceeding from one island to another in the

Eastern Archipelago, attended by a domestic slave. As the law now stands, there can be no doubt that in every such instance the individual unwillingly subjects himself to the enormous penalty of felony, under an act passed in a distant country, without any preliminary discussion as it respects this; without any previous intimation that slavery or the traffic of slaves was to be here abolished; and without even an intention on the part of the legislature to impose any penalty or punishment, much less so severe a one, for the act now specified."

"I conceive that there is no occasion for abolishing slavery, or for preventing enslavement, or for prohibiting the sale of actual slaves within the limits of the British territories in India. Neither the means by which free persons (for the most part children in a tender age) are rendered slaves, nor the frequency of the occurrence in an objectionable form, nor the common treatment of those who are already slaves by their masters, is such as to call for the interposition of legislative authority in a strong form. I trust not to be considered an advocate for slavery, nor indifferent to the miseries incident to the most degraded condition in human society, when I observe that in this country slaves are in general treated with gentleness and indulgence. The slave is a favorite and confidential servant, rather than an abject drudge; and is as often held superior to the hireling in his master's estimation and his own, as placed beneath him in the scale of employment and of comforts. The mildness and equanimity of the Indian's temper (or his apathy and slowness, if this better describe the general disposition of the people) contribute to ensure good treatment to the slave. I should however only demonstrate unacquaintance with human character if I affirmed this to prevail universally, without any exception. I cannot doubt that bad temper and dispositions sometimes constitute a harsh, severe, and even cruel master. Nor have I been without occasions of being

22

convinced that such characters are to be found among the owners of slaves. But although the Hindu and Muhammadan laws have not provided for the protection of the slave from the barbarity of an inhuman master, the regulations passed by British authority have done so, by expressly annulling the exemption from *kisas*, or retaliation for murder, in the case of a slave slain by his master. Since the period (nearly fourteen years ago) when that regulation was enacted, slaves have not been considered as out of the protection of the law, either in case of murder or of barbarous usage; and instances have occurred of recourse to the officers of police for redress against the cruelty of a master in cases falling short of that extremity. And it might perhaps be expedient, upon a future occasion of enacting rules bearing relation to the subject of slavery, to provide specifically for the interposition of the magistrate in an ascertained case of barbarous treatment of a slave, and adjudge his emancipation, with further penalties against his owner if the case be heinous."

No. II.

DR. FRANCIS BUCHANAN ON SLAVERY IN THE SOUTH OF INDIA.

In the Letters, the account given of slavery in the South of India is taken from the statements that have appeared in the names of Mr. Baber. Mr. Campbell, Col. Welsh, Capt. Bevan, and the Rev. Mr. Fenn, written in 1832, and published the same year by a parliamentary committee. Limiting myself to the most recent authorities, whose descriptions may be assumed to represent most accurately the actual state of slavery, I have made little use of Dr. F. Buchanan's work which was published in 1807, and which records the results of observations and inquiries made in 1800 and 1801. It is proper however to show that the most important facts connected with the state of slavery in the South of India were presented in an official form to the East India Company by one of their own servants nearly forty years ago, and the following extracts from Dr. Buchanan's Travels in Mysore, Canara, and Malabar are therefore subjoined.

THE LOWER CARNATIC, *or Carnatic below the mountains, that is, the British territory situated to the west and south of Madras.*—"The greater part of the Brahmans in the lower Carnatic follow secular professions. They almost entirely fill the different offices in the collection of the revenue and administration of justice; and they are exclusively employed as Hircaras, that is, guides or messengers, and as the keepers of inns or choultries. Much of the land is rented by them; but, like the Jews, they seldom put their hands to actual labor, and on no account will they hold the plough. Their farms they chiefly cultivate by slaves of the inferior castes called Sudra and Panchum Bundum. The Panchum Bundum are by far the most hardy and laborious people of the country, but the greater part of them are slaves. So sensible of their value was Hyder (Ali) that in his incursions it was these chiefly whom he endeavored to carry away. He settled them in many districts as farmers, and would not suffer them to be called by their proper name, which is considered opprobrious, but ordered that they should be called cultivators. The Panchum Bundum consist of four tribes, the Pariar, the Baluan, the Shecliar, and the Toti. The Shecliars dress hides; and from among the Toti is chosen a particular class of village officers. There are a few Musalman farmers who possess slaves; but the most numerous class is composed of the different tribes of the Sudra caste. Some of these possess slaves, but many of them cultivate their farms with their own hands."—Vol. I. p. 19.

SOUTH MALABAR.—"Some poor men, chiefly of the Shanar caste, cultivate with their own hands the lands which they hold as farmers (Cudians), but Brahmans never labor, and the Nairs or Moplays very rarely. By far the greater part of the labor in the field is performed by slaves or Churmar. These are the absolute property of their Devarus or lords, and may be employed in any work that their masters please. They are not attached to the soil, but may be sold or transferred in any manner that the master thinks fit, only a husband and wife cannot be sold separately; but children may be separated from their parents, and brothers from their sisters. The slaves are of different castes, such as Parriar, Vullam, Canacun, Erilay, &c.; and the differences in the customs by which the marriages of these castes are regulated occasion a considerable variation in the right of the master to the children of his slaves, according to the caste to which they belong. The master is considered as bound to give the slave a certain allowance of provisions; a man or woman while capable of labor receives two *edangallies* of rice in the husk weekly, or two-sevenths of the allowance that I consider as reasonable for persons of all ages included. Children and old persons past labor get one-half only of this pittance; and no allowance whatever is made for infants. This would be totally inadequate to support them; but the slaves on each estate get one twenty-first part of the gross produce of the rice, in order to encourage them to care and industry. A male slave annually gets seven cubits of cloth and a woman fourteen cubits. They erect for themselves small temporary huts that are little better than large baskets. These are placed in the rice-fields while the crop is on the ground, and near the stacks while it is thrashing.

"There are three modes of transferring the usufruct of slaves. The first is by *jenmum*, or sale, where the full value of the slave is given, and the property is entirely transferred to a new master, who is in some measure bound by his interest to attend to the welfare of his slave. A young man with his wife will sell for from two hundred and fifty to three hundred fanams, or from 6*l.* 4*s.* 1½*d.* to 7*l.* 8*s.* 11½*d.* Two or three young children will add one hundred fanams, or 2*l.* 9*s.* 7¾*d.*, to the value of the family. Four or five children, two of whom are beginning to work, will make the family worth from five hundred to six hundred fanams, or from 12*l.* 8*s.* 3*d.* to 14*l.* 17*s.* 11*d.* The second manner of transferring the labor of slaves is by *canum* or mortgage. The proprietor receives a loan of money, generally two-thirds of the value of the slaves; he also receives annually a small quantity of rice to show that his property in the slaves still exists; and he may re-assume this property whenever he pleases to repay the money borrowed, for which in the mean while he pays no interest. In case of any of the slaves dying, he is held bound to supply another of equal value. The lender maintains the slaves, and has their labor for the interest of his money and for their support. The third manner of employing slaves is by letting them for *patum* or rent. In this case, for a certain annual sum, the master gives them to another man, and the borrower commands their labor and provides them with their maintenance. The annual hire is eight fanams (3*s.* 11½*d.*) for a man, and half as much for a woman. These two tenures are utterly abominable, for the person who exacts the labor and furnishes the subsistence of the slave is directly interested to increase the former and diminish the latter as much as possible. In fact, the slaves are very severely treated; and their diminutive stature and squalid appearance show evidently a want of adequate nourishment. There can be no comparison between their condition and that of the slaves in the West India islands, except that in Malabar there are a sufficient number of females who are allowed to marry any person of the same caste with themselves, and whose labor is always exacted by their husband's master, the master of the girl having no authority over her so long as she lives with another man's slave."—Vol. II. p. 370.

"In small huts contiguous to their houses, the *Puttar Brahmans* commonly keep four or five cows, and the farmers have generally one or two. When a man's stock of cows is larger, they are kept with the laboring cattle, in a house built at some distance from the abode of freemen, in the place where the slaves are permitted to dwell when the crop is not on the ground; for these poor creatures are considered as too impure to be permitted to approach the house of their *Devaru* or lord."—Vol. II. p. 380.

"*Ani-Malaya*, or Elephant-Hill, is so called from the great number of elephants and hills in its neighborhood. It is a town which contains about four hundred houses."—"Here is a person called *Malaya-pudy* or *hill-village-man*. He rents the exclusive privilege of collecting drugs in the hills south from *Ani-Malaya*. These are collected for him by a hill-people called Cadar, of whom, among the hills two days' journey hence, there is a village of thirteen houses. The renter has there a small house, to which he occasionally goes to receive the drugs that the Cadar have collected, and brings them home on oxen. The men only work for him, and each daily receives in advance four *puddies* of rice, worth half a Vir'-Raya fanam, or about 3*d*. At the end of the year the accounts are settled, every article having a fixed value, and the whole that each person has delivered having been estimated at this rate, he receives the balance if any be due. In Tippoo's government the renter paid annually thirty Canter'-Raya pagodas, or 6*l*. 4*s*. 1¼*d*. His rent has this year (1800) been raised to one hundred and fifty pagodas, or 31*l*. 0*s*. 8¼*d*.; but then he is allowed to take all the ivory that is found where elephants have died, and which formerly belonged to the government."—"At *Ani-Malaya* are three persons called tamarind-renters, who pay a trifling rent for the exclusive privilege of collecting the tamarinds, honey, wax, *Nonaputta*," (a kind of *morinda* used as a dye,) " that are found in the woods which lie near the town. The people employed by them are called *Malasir*, and are also the wood-cutters of the country."

" The forests here are divided into Puddies, each of which has its boundary ascertained, and contains one or more families of a rude tribe called *Malasir*. Both the Puddy and its inhabitants are considered as the property of some landlord, who farms out the labor of these poor people, with all that they collect, to some trader (*Chitty* or *Manadi*), who treats the Malasirs much in the same way as the *Malayapudy* of *Ani-Malaya* does the rude tribes under his authority, and receives from them nearly the same articles. In fact, this is a most iniquitous mode of taxing the Malasir, and the produce of it is a mere trifle. The most productive Puddy in the whole district pays only four rupees a year. A capitation-tax on the *Malasir* might raise a greater income to the proprietors of the woods, and be much less oppressive. Having sent for some of these poor Malasirs, they informed me that they live in small villages of five or six huts, situated in the skirts of the woods on the hills of Daraporam, Ani-Malaya, and Pali-ghat. They speak a mixture of the Tamul and Malayala languages. They are a better looking people than the slaves, but are ill-clothed, nasty, and ill-fed. They collect drugs for the traders to whom they are let; and receive from him a subsistence when they can procure for him anything of value. He has the exclusive right of purchasing all that they have for sale, and of supplying them with salt and other necessaries. A great part of their food consists of wild yams, (*Dioscoreas*,) which they dig when they have nothing to give to the trader for rice. They cultivate some small spots in the woods after the *Cotu-Cadu* fashion (hoeing), both on their own account and on that of the neighboring farmers, who receive the produce and give the Malasirs hire. The articles cultivated in this manner are *Rali* (*Cynosurus corocanus*), *Avaray* (*Dolichos lablab*), and *Tonda* (*Ricinus Palma Christi*). They are also hired to cut timber and firewood. In this province they pay nothing to the government."—Vol. II. pp. 331, 334, 337, 383.

With reference to the last extracts, it seems necessary to point out that, although the Malasirs are distinguished nominally from slaves, yet they are expressly stated to be considered and treated as property like the forests they inhabit; that they and the Cadars have not the disposal of their own labor, nor permission to buy and sell of and to whom they please; and that their labor is without their own consent farmed to persons who in one instance pay for it a rent to government, and in the other to a private landlord.

North Malabar.—" The daily allowance here established for slaves is of rough rice,

		Cubical Inches.		*Bushels.*
To able-bodied men,	6 Nallis heaped, =	$148\frac{1}{4}$	which is yearly	$25\frac{1}{4}$
To able-bodied women,	6 ditto streaked, =	$103\frac{1}{4}$	ditto	$17\frac{1}{4}$
To old persons and chil.,	3 ditto heaped, =	$74\frac{1}{4}$	ditto	$12\frac{6}{10}$

The average, allowing one child and one old person to every two men and two women in the prime of age, will be $18\frac{4}{10}$ bushels, of which one-half is husks. When the scarcity that usually happens every year prevails, they get part of their allowance in yams (*Dioscoreas*), jacks (*Artocarpus*), or plantains (*Musa*). When harvest is over they receive each, according to their activity, a present of three or four porays of rough rice, or from one to $1\frac{4}{10}$ bushel, which will make the annual average about $9\frac{1}{2}$ bushels of rice; their masters give them also some salt, oil, and pepper, and they are allowed to keep fowls. Each person has annually three pieces of cloth. The slaves say, what indeed cannot be doubted, that they are much better used by their own masters than when they are let out on mortgage (canum) or hire (patum). In some parts of the province, *Churmun* is a term applied to slaves in general, whatever their caste may be; but it is in some other parts confined to a peculiar caste who are also called *Polian*, or in the plural *Poliar*. Even among these wretched creatures the pride of caste has full influence; and if a *Churmun* or *Polian* be touched by a slave of the *Parian* tribe, he is defiled, and must wash his head and pray."—"The *Parian*, or in the plural *Pariar*, belong to a tribe of Malayala all of whom are slaves. In all the countries where the Tamul language prevails"—that is, in the districts of South Arcot, Salem, Coimbetore, Kumbhakonam, Tanjore, Trichinopoly, Madura, Dindigul, Tinnivelly, and great part of Mysore, in all which it is spoken by more than five millions of people—"a tribe of the same name is common; but the customs of the two castes are by no means the same. In Malabar there are three kinds of this tribe: the *Parian* properly so called, the *Perum Parian*, and the *Mutruva Parian*."—Vol. II. pp. 491, 493.

"In Curumbara Nada there are some great farmers who have ten ploughs, twenty oxen, twenty male and female slaves, ten male and female *Tiar*" (a free caste) "servants, and twenty-five milch cows. The number of such in the whole district does not exceed ten or twelve, and by far the greater number have only one or two ploughs. Almost all the farmers (*cudians*) have slaves; they are a very few only that are reduced to the necessity of laboring with their own hands. Male slaves sell at from twenty to sixty old *Vir'-Raya fanams*, or from 9*s*. 6½*d*. to 28*s*. 8*d*.: women sell at only one-half of this low price. The difference of caste makes no variation in the value, although the children of different castes are not divided in the same manner. A male slave lets at four *fanams* a year, and a woman at half as much; the person who hires them providing for their maintenance. In the parts of this district that are situated towards the frontier of Wynâd live a rude tribe called *Panian*. They dwell in small villages, each consisting of four or five huts, which are called *Madum*. They are not called *Churmun* or slaves, but are in fact such, and belong to *Tamburans* or lords, who give them daily subsistence and exact daily labor precisely in the same manner and of the same kind as is done with slaves. Disputes that happen to arise among them are settled by their masters, who must also furnish money to procure wives for their *Panians*. A wife and the marriage expenses amount to twenty-five fanams."—"Another caste of *Malayala* condemned to slavery is called in the singular *Catal* or *Curumbal*, and in the plural *Catalun* or *Curumbalun*. They reckon themselves higher than the *Churmun*, *Poliar*, or *Parian*."—Vol. II. pp. 495—497.

SOUTH CANARA.—"The cultivation is chiefly carried on by *Culialu* or hired servants; but there are also some *Muladalu*, bought men or slaves. A hired man gets daily two hanies of clean rice, or annually 21¾ bushels, together with 1½ rupee's worth of cloth, a pagoda in cash, and a house. A hired woman gets 1½ rupee for cloth and three-quarters of the man's allowance of grain. In planting season the women hired by the day get two hanies of rice, or 128¼ cubical inches. These wages are very high, and may enable the hired servants to keep a family in the greatest abundance."—"At the end of the year the hired servant may change his service, if he be free from debt; but that is seldom the case. When he gets deeply involved his master may sell his sister's children to discharge the amount, and his services may be transferred to any other man who chooses to take hire and pay his debts to his master. In fact, he differs little from a slave, only his allowance is larger, but then the master is not obliged to provide for him in sickness or in old age.

"A male slave is allowed daily 1½ hany of rice, or three-fourths of the allowance for a hired servant; a woman receives one hany. The man gets 1½ rupee's worth of cloth and two rupees in cash; the woman is allowed only the cloth. They receive also a trifling allowance of oil, salt, and other seasonings. A small allowance is given to children and old people. When a slave wishes to marry, he receives five pagodas (two guineas) to defray the expense. The wife works with the husband's master. On the husband's death, if the wife was a slave, all the children belong to her mother's master; but if she was formerly free, she and all her children belong to her husband's master. A good slave sells for about ten pagodas, or about four guineas If he has a wife who was formerly free and two or three children, the value is doubled. The slave may be hired out; and the renter both exacts his labor and finds him in subsistence. Slaves are also mortgaged; but the mortgager is not obliged to supply the place of a slave that dies; and in case of accidents, the debt becomes extinguished, which is an excellent regulation. Freemen of low caste, if they are in debt or trouble, sometimes sell their sister's children who are their heirs. They have no authority over their own children who belong to their maternal uncles."—Vol. III. pp. 35—37.

Central Canara.—"Having assembled some of the Corar or Corawar, who under their chief Hubashica are said to have once been masters of *Tulava*, I found that they are now all slaves, and have lost every tradition of their former power. Their language differs considerably from that of any other tribe in the peninsula. When their masters choose to employ them, they get one meal of victuals, and the men have daily one hany of rice, and the women three-quarters of a hany. This is a very good allowance, but when the master has no use for their labor, they must support themselves as well as they can. This they endeavor to do by making *coir* or rope from cocoa-nut husks, various kinds of baskets from *ratans* and climbing plants, and mud walls. They pick up the scraps and offals of other people's meals, and skin dead oxen and dress the hides. They build their huts near towns and villages. Their dress is very simple, and consists in general of a girdle in which they stick a bunch of grass before and another behind. Some of the men have a fragment of cloth round their waist; but very few of the women ever procure this covering. They are not however without many ornaments of beads and the like; and even when possessed of some wealth do not alter their rude dress. Some few of them are permitted to rent lands as *gaynigaras*. In spite of this wretched life, they are a good-looking people, and therefore probably are abundantly fed." —"When a man dies, his wives, with all their children, return to the huts of their respective mothers and brothers, and belong to their masters."—"They follow all the oxen and buffaloes of the village, as so much of the live stock, when these are driven in procession at a great festival which the farmers annually celebrate."—Vol. III. pp. 100, 101.

"In the northern part of Tulava are two castes called *Bacadaru* and *Batadaru*, both of whom are slaves; both speak no other language than that of *Karnata*, and both follow exactly the same customs. Each disputes for a pre-eminence of rank, and they will not eat nor intermarry with one another, except in certain cases of adultery, when, a ceremony of purification having been undergone, a (male) slave of the one caste may marry a female of the other. Although they do not use leaves to cover their nudities, they seem to be poorer and worse looking than the *Corar*, whom I lately described. Their masters give annually to each slave, male or female, one piece of cloth worth a rupee, together with a knife. Each family has a house and ten hanies' sowing of rice-land, or about a quarter of an acre. At marriages they get one mudy of rice, ($\frac{3}{10}$ bushel,) worth about 2*s*., and half a pagoda, or 4*s*. in money. When their master has no occasion for their work, they get no wages, but hire themselves out as laborers in the best manner they can; for they have not the resource of basket-making, nor of the other little arts which the Corar practise. The master is bound however to prevent the aged or infirm from perishing of want. When they work for their master, a man gets daily 1½ hany of rice to carry home, with ½ a hany ready dressed, in all 2 hanies, or rather more than one-sixteenth of a bushel; a woman gets 1¼ hany of rice to carry home, and ½ hany ready dressed; and a boy gets 1 hany of rice."—Vol. III. p. 106.

NORTH CANARA.—"In the farms of the Brahmans, most of the labor is performed by slaves. These people get daily 1½ hany of rice; a woman receives 1 hany. Each gets yearly 2½ rupees' worth of cloth, and they are allowed time to build a hut for themselves in the cocoa-nut garden. They have no other allowance, and out of this pittance must support their infants and aged people. The woman's share is nearly 15 bushels a year, worth rather less than 14¼ rupees; to this if we add her allowance for clothes, she gets 16¾ rupees a year, equal to 1*l.* 16*s.* 8½*d.* The man's allowance is 22½ bushels, or 23¾ rupees, or 2*l.* 3*s.* 0½*d.* A male free servant, hired by the day, gets 2 hanies of rice. Both work from seven in the morning till five in the evening; but at noon they are allowed half an hour to eat some victuals that are dressed in the family as part of their allowance; and every caste can eat the food which a Brahman has prepared."—Vol. III. p. 140.

SOONDA or *Sudhapura, above the Ghauts, but included in Canara.*—"In this country a few slaves are kept; but most of the labor, even in the grounds of the Brahmans, is performed by the proprietors, or by hired servants."—"A male slave gets daily 2 pucka seers of rough rice, with annually one blanket, one handkerchief,"—more properly *head*kerchief, being intended to cover the head,—"a piece of cotton cloth, and some oil, tamarinds, and capsicum. He gets no money except at marriages; but these cost 16 pagodas, or 6*l.* 8*s.* 11½*d.*, for the woman must be purchased. She and all her children, of course, become the property of her husband's master. The woman slave gets daily 1¾ seer of rough rice, a blanket, and annually a piece of cotton cloth and a jacket. Children and old people get some ready-dressed victuals at the house of the master, and are also allowed some clothing. The men work from sunrise till sunset, and at noon are allowed one *Hindu* hour, or about twenty-four minutes, for dinner. The women are allowed till about eight o'clock in the morning to prepare the dinner, which they then carry to the fields, and continue to work there with the men until sunset."—Vol. III. p. 226.

"A farmer who has five ploughs is esteemed a rich man. With these he must keep six men and six women, and ten laboring cattle; and at seed-time and harvest he must hire additional laborers. Farmers who are not Brahmans, unless their farms be large, work the whole with their own families; but rich men must hire servants or keep slaves; and to hold their plough, Brahmans must always have people of the low castes. This is a kind of work that even a *Haiga Brahman* will not perform.

	£	s.	d.
A man slave gets daily 2 seers of rough rice, or yearly about 26 bushels, worth	£1	2s.	0½d.
A handkerchief, a blanket, and piece of cloth, worth 2 rupees,	0	4	0¼
A pagoda in money,	0	8	0¾
Six candacas of rough rice at harvest,	0	14	6
	2	8	7½
The women get one piece of cloth annually, and a meal of ready-dressed victuals on the days that they work, which may amount annually to	0	8	1

Hired men get four seers of rough rice a day, worth less than three halfpence."—Vol. III. p. 243.

Principality of IKERI *in Mysore.*—"Most of the cultivation is carried on by the families of the cultivators. There are very few hired servants; but a good many slaves, by whom on the farms of the Brahmans all the ploughing is performed. A slave gets annually 1½ rupee for a blanket; 3 rupees' worth of cotton cloth; ¼ rupee for a handkerchief; 6 candacas of rough rice, worth 4 rupees, to procure salt, tamarinds, &c.; and daily 1½ colaga of rough rice, or annually 27½ candacas (or almost 49 bushels), worth 1*l.* 16*s.* 11¾*d.*; add the annual allowances, 17*s.* 7¼*d.*, the total expense of maintaining a male slave one year is 2*l.* 14*s.* 7¼*d.* A woman slave gets as follows: 365 colagas, one daily, and 3 candacas at harvest; in all 21¼ candacas, or 36¼ bushels, worth 14$\frac{3}{16}$ rupees; 2 rupees' worth of cloth, and ¼ rupee for a jacket; in all nearly 16½ rupees, or 1*l.* 13*s.* 2*d.* The marriage of a slave costs 10 pagodas, or about four guineas. The wife belongs to the husband's master. A master cannot hinder his slave-girl from marrying the slave of another man, nor does he get any price for her. The widow and children, after a slave's death, continue with his master. If a slave has no children by his first wife he is allowed to take another."—Vol. III. p. 280.

Notices of the NUMBER OF SLAVES *in Malabar and Canara, scattered through Dr. Buchanan's work.* The gentlemen whose names are mentioned below were the magistrates and collectors of revenue in the different districts of those provinces at the time embraced by Dr. Buchanan's Travels.

			Locality.	*Slaves.*		
Mr. Warden's	Districts	in	South Malabar,	16,574	Vol. II.	p. 362
Mr. Wye's	"	"	Cent. Malabar,	16,201		p. 442
Mr. Baber's	"	"	"	4,765		p. 485
Mr. Coward's	"	"	N. Malabar,	8,592		p. 508
Mr. Strachy's	"	"	"	161		p. 526
Mr. Wilson's	"	"	"	100		p. 543
Mr. Hodgson's	"	"	"	4,670		p. 562

	Locality.	Slaves.		
Mr. Ravenshaw's	Districts in South Canara,	7,924	Vol. III. p.	2
"	" " "	47,358	p.	7
Mr. Read's	" " N. Canara,	1,099	p.	195
"	" " "	445	p.	246

It is not improbable that the smaller number of slaves, 7,924, stated to be in Mr. Ravenshaw's districts in South Canara, is included in the larger number stated to be found in the same districts. The larger number is taken from a table, respecting which Dr. Buchanan states that "reliance may be placed on its accuracy with respect to numbers."

No. III.

MR. D. LISTON ON SLAVERY IN GORAKHPUR.

Mr. Liston's information respecting slavery in the district of Gorakhpur in Oude has been quoted in part; but it seems desirable to give in full the paper in which it is communicated to the editor of the Journal of the Asiatic Society of Bengal, Vol. VI., p. 950, in the number of that publication for November, 1837.

"*Translation of a Servitude-Bond granted by a cultivator over his family, and of a Deed of Sale of two slaves. By* D. Liston, *Esq., Gorakhpur.*

"Some months ago I was requested by Captain Lawrence, under whose charge the survey of the eastern division of the district is placed, to furnish answers to statistical inquiries regarding *Sidowa Jobena*, a parguna of *Gorakhpur*, bounding on *Sarun*. I in turn thought of applying for aid in the compilation of the replies to a friend who has been settled as an indigo-planter* for several years in *Sidowa*, and who proved to be possessed of a competent acquaintance with the habits and usages of the natives in his neighborhood.

* "Mr. J. Finch, of Bubnowli."

"One of the queries put was, 'How do Zemindars pay people who water and cultivate lands for them?' The reply was to this effect: 'They employ bond-servants, who are paid at half a cooly's rate, and are at the same time liable to fine in case of absenting themselves from their superior's work.' Further inquiry procured me the accompanying bonds or deeds, and as they appear curious and valuable from throwing light on the condition of the agricultural population of this portion of India, I have translated them, and now forward them to your address. If you regard them in the same light as I have done, perhaps you may think it worth while to publish them in the Journal; if you do not think them of sufficient importance for this purpose, pray dispose of them as you may think proper.

"The deeds you will observe are blank, but still such as are daily executed and in full force. They were written out by a common village *Putwari*, and are in the rustic dialect or *Patois* of the section of the province where he resides. The spelling you will also see is not ordered according to any very uniform system.

"SERVITUDE-BOND.

"*Translation.*

"DEED—ABHEEMAN KOOROOMEE and his children's plough-bond for fifty-one rupees, written, signed, rupees fifty-one, 51.

"[Place for the master's name.*]

"WRITING—ABHEEMAN KOOROOMEE, inhabitant of *Futapoor*, perguna Sidowa Jobena Elaka Sooba Oudes Zillah *Gorakpur*, having received a loan of fifty-one (51) rupees from† (the above-mentioned individual,) I have

* "MR. FINCH's name is set down in the original, which, it is hardly necessary to repeat, is fictitious."

† Blank in original.

granted a bond agreeing to pay interest for the said rupees at eight anas per month; for these same rupees I of my own will and accord execute (this) deed of *Hurwuhubundhee*" (*i. e.*, absolute bondage) "(to have force) over my whole family for the driving of a plough, and for remaining always at hand to execute every kind of labor that may occur. If I remain absent a day from my plough or work, then shall I be held responsible to the extent of a rutee weight of gold for each day's absence. If I go any where in the manner of flight, then let my whole family be seized. If any other person give (me) a greater sum, he must pay at once principal and interest of this loan. That man may then take my family. If he do not give the money, then may my family be seized without dispute; any other interfering will be in vain indeed. This is written that the first engagement may remain in force.

"Written 29th Falgoon, year 1244, forty-four, at *Emelia*."

"DEED OF SALE OF TWO SLAVES.

"*Explanation and Translation.*

"DHODHO MAHTO *Kumkur*, of his own will and accord, sells AJUNSIA and RUPIA, having executed and delivered a deed of sale of slaves signed or a *mofurkutee loonkutee*.

"[I do not find the five or six first lines very intelligible, but what follows presents no great difficulty.]

"The deed commences with the invocation usual in Sanscrit documents of *Sosti Sri;* the two first lines are taken up nearly with the enumeration of the titles of VIKRAMAJIT and of SALIVAHUN's power. In the fourth line the forty-third year of some king is indicated. ALUMGIR is then mentioned, and the thirty-second year of *Nawáb* MIRZA AMANI BEG spoken of. Then follows the year of the rule of the Honorable English Company, viz., the thirty-third, Mr. CURRIE being administrator, (local). The locality *Gorakhpur*, south of which runs the *Ganges*, and to the north the *Gunduk*. The country *Bharuthkum*, sirkar *Gorakpur*, sooba *Aoadh*, *Akternuggur*, perguna *Sedooa Jobena*, talooka *Bansgaon*, tuppah *Thadeebaree*. The twenty-fifth year (of the rule) of Babu ESRI KUMAR SAH (talookdar), the twenty-second year (since the establishment of the English perguna). Sekh JUMALUDIN being foujdar and tehsildar at the tehsildaree of *Peronna*.

"In the village of Buderuha a sale of slaves was effected. Purchaser, UDHO SINGH; amount, 43 furakabad rupees. Seller, by name DHODHO MAHTO *Kumkur*,* of his own will and accord, he sells BULBHADER's wife † and son, two adults. The woman's name AJUNSIA, the lad's name RUPIA, (this) slavery-bond being executed and delivered. The woman's age 22,‡ complexion fairish. RUPIA's age 28, complexion dark, eyes dark. Of these people DHODHO MAHTO Kumkur has completed the sale; wherever they go, thence they may be brought back, as slaves they are sold to perform every kind of work; wherever they may flee, thence they may be seized and brought back without objection or complaint or murmur, without obstacle may they be brought from under the king's or prince's throne; whoever receives these servants, he may (legally) be adjured—the Hindu by the sacred cow;—the Musalman by HUSEN, by the Sekh, Seyd, Mogul, Peytan, Sumbut, year 1894, month Jet, dark half 13th day, Sunday, year 1244, place *Buderuha*, two ghurees of the day being spent, this was written and signed."

* "The *Kumkurs* are Kuhars or bearers."

† "A slave-holder may sell a whole family or what part of it may suit his convenience."

‡ "In the original the word is thirty, the ciphers twenty-two as here."

" [We have not thought it necessary to insert a lithograph of the deeds themselves, which are in the ordinary *Kayasthi* or *Kaiti* form of Nagari.—Ed.]"

No. IV.

CASE OF THE SHIP ADRAMYTTE.

I think it desirable to place upon record the principal document in my possession relating to the case of the ship Adramytte. Although it contains a repetition of the details already given, yet the whole case will probably be better understood by a perusal of the paper in full. The case is one which, it appears to me, demands explanation from the Bengal government as to the grounds on which they abandoned the prosecution of legal measures against parties accused of the importation of slaves, to the establishment of which charge the strongest testimony was within reach.

Affidavit of William Adam.

William Adam, of the Circular Road, in the town of Calcutta, gentleman, maketh oath and saith, that on the evening of the thirty-first of October last, Mr. Constantine Pandazie, a Greek merchant resident in Calcutta, with whom he had been for some time previously acquainted, called on him at his house in the Circular Road, and informed him that he had reason to believe that the Arab ship Adramytte, Nacoda Ruhim Seyud, which had recently arrived in the port of Calcutta, had brought for sale three slave-girls, one Greek and two Africans, belonging to one Hajee Durvesh, a passenger on board the said ship, and requested the advice and assistance of this deponent in the endeavors of him, the said Constantine Pandazie, to procure their liberation. That he, the said Constantine Pandazie, then and there farther stated that he derived his information above stated from a person who had been on board of the said ship, and had been assured by two of the Lascars belonging to the said ship that there had been three slave-girls brought on in the said vessel to Calcutta, one of whom was a Christian, but that they had been taken on shore at Calcutta by night a few days after the arrival of the said ship, and which said two Lascars had promised to come on shore and give evidence, if required, to that effect. That he, the said Constantine Pandazie, then and there further stated that the said Hajee Durvesh had been known to make frequent voyages to Calcutta, but that he had never brought, as far as the said Mr. Constantine Pandazie's information and observation extended, any legal merchandise, but, although professing to be a merchant, had on all occasions apparently come without any cargo, consignment, or shipment of any kind. That this deponent had frequent communications with the said Mr. Constantine Pandazie between the first and fifth instant, the result of which was that it was found impossible to get the said two Lascars on shore. That on the evening, however, of the last-mentioned day, the said Mr. Constantine Pandazie called at the house of this deponent and informed him that a Malay woman, who had for many years associated with the Greeks in Calcutta, and could speak the modern Greek, and was acquainted with the said Hajee Durvesh, had in the absence of the said Hajee Durvesh called at the house in which he kept his said slaves, and had seen one of the said African girls, and had conversed with the said Greek girl, who stated that she had been bought as a slave by the said Hajee Durvesh, and was kept by him in a state of slavery and restraint, and entreated that means might be employed to set her at liberty. That on the morning of the sixth instant this deponent went to the house of the said Mr. Constantine Pandazie, who had engaged to procure the attendance of the said Malay woman in order that this deponent might write down on paper a plain statement of the facts with which she had become acquainted, preparatory to their being thrown into the form of an affidavit or deposition by an attorney at law who had consented to give his services for that purpose, to the truth of which affidavit it was intended that she should have sworn before a magistrate with a view to ulterior criminal proceedings against the said Hajee Durvesh. That on arriving, however, at Mr. Constantine Pandazie's house, this deponent was informed by him that the said Hajee Durvesh, having become acquainted with the designs of this deponent and of the said Mr. Constantine Pandazie, and with the nature of the evidence they had obtained against him, had come voluntarily forward and offered to surrender the said Greek girl to the Greeks at the house of Mr. Lucas, a Greek gentleman long resident in Calcutta. That they accordingly proceeded to Mr. Lucas's house, where they found that the said Hajee Durvesh, with two other Turks, had already brought the said Greek girl. That when she had satisfied herself that she was surrounded by friends and countrymen, she gave at intervals a brief history of herself, and said that her name was Paraskeve, that she was a native of Crete, and that her mother had died by the plague; that at the commencement of the Greek Revolution, her father, with herself, her sister, her brother, and many other Greeks, had fled from the plains to the mountains to avoid the fury of the Turks; that her father, rashly returning to the plains, had been slain, and herself, her sister, and her brother taken prisoners; that they were taken by an Algerine Turk to Alexandria, and there sold as slaves, with the exception of the brother, who was forced to become a Musalman; and that after various changes she had been at last brought to

Judda, where she was sold to the said Hajee Durvesh, who immediately put her on board the Adramytte, which shortly after sailed for and arrived at Calcutta as aforesaid. That through the medium of an interpreter this deponent spoke to the said Hajee Durvesh, and the two other Turks which accompanied him as aforesaid, of the illegality and danger of the trade in which they were apparently all implicated, and particularly to the said Hajee Durvesh, whose engagement in it was so evident; but in answer to the inquiries of this deponent, the said Hajee Durvesh denied that he had the two African girls who, this deponent suspected, were in his possession, although when the Greek girl was interrogated thereto she affirmed that he had brought them also with him to Calcutta. That this deponent was accordingly desirous of employing her evidence to prove the fact, but was disappointed to find that his Greek friends, having obtained the liberation of the said Greek girl in manner aforesaid, were unwilling to proceed any further as to obtaining the liberation of the said two African slaves; that after several ineffectual endeavors to remove the scruples and groundless apprehensions of the Greek friends of this deponent, he, this deponent, found by a note, under date eighth instant, from the said Mr. Constantine Pandazie, that this deponent must give up all hope of their further co-operation. That the two following days this deponent was employed in consulting his friends as to the course which, under such circumstances, he was called upon to pursue, and in conformity with their advice, as well as his own convictions, he, this deponent, resolved to lay the whole affair before government, and leave them to adopt such measures as might appear to them proper, rendering such aid as his acquaintance with the circumstances of the case might enable him to afford. That this deponent accordingly wrote to Mr. Secretary Lushington, on the eleventh instant, regarding the subject, and was answered by Mr. Acting-

Secretary Molony, who favored this deponent with an audience on the same day, when this deponent made him acquainted with the principal features of the case. That on the twelfth instant he received a letter from the said Mr. Molony, informing him that he, the said Mr. Molony, had submitted the matter to government, and that they had directed him to put it into the hands of R. C. Barwell, Esq., chief magistrate of Calcutta, for the adoption of such steps as might appear to him fit and proper, and requesting this deponent to wait on that gentleman for examination. That this deponent accordingly called on the fourteenth and seventeenth instant at the police office, and after a long examination on the last of these days was requested to prepare and bring a statement of all the circumstances known to this deponent in the form of an affidavit, to which he should be sworn. That in compliance with such request the preceding particulars have been thrown together into their present form.

(Signed) W. ADAM.

Sworn this 24th day of November,
1826, before me,
(Signed) R. C. Barwell,
Chief Magistrate of Calcutta.

No. V.

ABOLITION OF SLAVERY IN CEYLON.

The government of Ceylon not being administered by the East India Company, but by the ministers of the Crown, it did not come within the object of the Letters to advert to the successful abolition of slavery in that island in 1816. But the example should not be overlooked, both for the sake of the lesson which it teaches, and as a means of showing due honor to the distinguished philanthropist, Sir Alexander Johnston, by whose exertions the measure was effected, and to the benevolent slave-proprietors who unanimously co-operated with him.

Sir Alexander Johnston appears to have left England the first time for Ceylon in 1802, and in 1806 he became Chief Justice, First Member of the High Court of Appeal, and President of His Majesty's Council. From the time of his arrival in Ceylon, he felt it to be his duty to adopt such a line of policy in his official capacity as might prepare the way for the extinction of slavery in the island, which appears to have existed there only in the domestic form; and with this view, in 1806, he proposed to the principal proprietors of slaves a measure, the details of which are not given, and the adoption of which it was deemed at that time advisable to postpone. In 1809, he returned to England, and in 1811 to Ceylon, and having brought out with him the act of 1811, declaring the trading in slaves to be felony, and a commission authorizing himself and certain other commissioners to try all offences against that act with a grand and petty jury, he caused the act to be publicly promulged upon the island; and a case of importance having occurred in 1813, all the prisoners, one of them a man well known throughout Arabia and India, were tried and convicted before him, which called the attention of the people to the nature of the offence, and prevented the commission of any more offences of that description. In consequence of the proceedings at this trial, the remarks which he made upon the subject at all the criminal sessions to the persons who were on the roll of jurymen, and finally a letter which he wrote in 1816 to the Dutch gentlemen whose names were on the list of special jurymen for the province of Colombo, much interest was excited, and a meeting of the special Dutch jurors was assembled by general consent and held at Colombo on Monday, the 15th July, 1816, at which certain resolutions were framed and adopted, declaring in substance that all children born of their slaves after the 12th of Aug., 1816, should be considered as born free. This example was immediately followed by the jurymen of the different castes of natives at Colombo, who passed resolutions declaring their unanimous acquiescence in the measure adopted by the Dutch special jurymen; and shortly after by all the proprietors of domestic slaves on the island. It was also provided that the children born free after the 12th of Aug., 1816, should be maintained by the masters of their parents, if females, until the age of twelve, if males, until the age of fourteen, it being supposed that after they attained that age they would be able to support themselves.

The Dutch special jurymen of Colombo consisted of about 130 of the most respectable Dutch gentlemen of the place; and in this number were contained almost all the Dutch who were large proprietors of slaves. Besides these gentlemen, there were jurymen of all the different castes among the natives, such as vellales, fishermen, men of the Mahabadde or cinnamon department, Chitters, and Muhammadans; and all the proprietors of slaves in Ceylon were on the list of jurymen. The total number of slave-proprietors was 763; the number of slaves was between 9,000 and 10,000; and the population of the then British territories on the island was about 600,000. Domestic slavery had been in existence for a period of 300 years.

These details have been collected from Sir Alexander Johnston's Evidence before a Select Committee of the House of Commons in 1832, with accompanying documents; and they show, amongst other things, that the act of 1811, making the slave-trade felony, was not in Ceylon either unduly limited in its application, or allowed to remain a dead letter, as in the Bengal and Madras territories of the East India Company, but that, under a commission from the Crown, it was rigorously and effectually enforced. We see also how powerful official influence was in Ceylon, when employed on the side of justice and humanity. Europeans and natives—the pride of the one class, the prejudices of the other, the pecuniary advantage of both—all gave way. Other examples are not wanting to show how powerful for evil is that same influence, how benumbing and deadening, when arrayed, as it too frequently is in India, against useful and benevolent designs. To this the fruitless, because unsupported, exertions of Mr. Richardson in the Bengal, and of Mr. Baber in the Madras presidency, to ameliorate the law of slavery and the condition of slaves, bear witness.

Sir Alexander Johnston states in his Evidence that since his return to England he has been engaged as chairman of the Committee of Correspondence of the Royal Asiatic Society, with the assistance of Mr. Baber, the late judge on the Malabar Coast, in collecting such information relative to the state of slavery in the peninsula of India as may enable the British government to adopt, on the continent of India, the same policy as that which has been successful in Ceylon. The Committee of Correspondence of the Asiatic Society have already collected some very useful information, he adds, from various quarters, particularly from the papers published by order of the House of Commons in 1826, and they soon expect to obtain much more from different parts of India. This was stated in 1832, and if the information thus collected has been published, I have never happened to hear of it. If it has not been published, why has it not? Has the Royal Asiatic Society, since 1832, passed under any influence unfavorable to the prosecution and publication of such inquiries?